CW00747305

The Way It Was

A History Of The Early Days Of The Margaret River Wine Industry

Peter Forrestal
Ray Jordan

EasyRead Large

Copyright Page from the Original Book

First published in Australia in 2017
by Margaret River Press
PO Box 47
Witchcliffe WA 6286

www.margaretriverpress.com
email: info@margaretriverpress.com

Copyright © Peter Forrestal and Ray Jordan 2017
Copyright © photographs to individual photographers
The moral rights of the authors have been asserted.

This book is copyright. Apart from any fair dealing for the purpose
of private study, research, criticism or review, as permitted under the
Copyright Act, no part may be reproduced by any process without
written permission. Enquiries should be made to the publisher.

Cataloguing-in-Publication entry data is available from the
National Library of Australia

ISBN 978-0-64802753-9
Printed in Australia by Scott Print, Perth, Western Australia

Published by Margaret River Press

FSC
www.fsc.org
MIX
Paper from
responsible sources
FSC® C113956

The paper in this book is FSC certified. FSC promotes
environmentally responsible, socially beneficial and
economically viable management of the world's forests.

TABLE OF CONTENTS

For Elaine, and all the years
Peter Forrestal

To Jennifer, Dan and Jack. We have
had our challenges but remain a family
built on courage and character.
Ray Jordan

I do know that you can't always win; that failure is an orphan, but success has a thousand fathers; and that you can't please everybody. There is no pleasure like climbing a ladder against a 2,000 gallon, icy-cold stainless-steel tank of riesling at six o'clock on a cold May morning, with nobody else around for miles, sticking your head under the lid and taking a deep breath. That almost makes everything worthwhile.

Tom Cullity

Introduction

A Time and Place

When Perth cardiologist Dr Tom Cullity planted his first vines in 1967 on a small plot of land off the road that now bears his name, he did so with a simple aim: to make the best possible wine. Cullity could not understand why it had not been done before or why someone had not shown any interest in doing it. Nor could he have envisaged that when he planted that tiny plot of cabernet sauvignon, malbec, riesling and shiraz on what would become Vasse Felix, it would be the catalyst to create one of the world's great wine regions.

In just five decades, Margaret River was transformed from a poor rural backwater—known to few other than surfers, hippies and struggling farmers—into a premier wine region that merges the characters of quaint and grand wineries, individual regional architecture, innovative food and distinctive wines, with the magnificent natural beauty of this south-west corner of Australia. It is a region of contrasts. Where two great oceans pound onto the rugged coast of granite and limestone; where low shrubs near towering cliffs gradually merge into the rolling hills, dense bush and richer productive soils further inland; and where traditional rambling agriculture is still pursued alongside neat and precisely tended vineyards.

Vines and wines have been part of the area from the times of the earliest settlers in the 1830s, yet it wasn't until more than 120 years later that anyone would suggest its suitability for world-class viticulture. Agronomist Dr John Gladstones, working at the University of Western Australia in the mid-1960s, combined scientific rigour with his personal knowledge of what would become known as Margaret River to write two seminal papers which suggested that the region could produce exceptional wines.

This all started in the 1960s, a time of momentous global social and cultural change, and while perhaps not on the same scale as that music festival on Bethel Common or that giant leap out onto the Sea of Tranquility, it was significant for the local wine industry. This was a time when Australians were starting to move away from the traditions of nearly 200 years of British influence, exploring new cuisines and moving from drinking largely fortified wines to lighter table wines. It was fortunate that a mix of dynamic and creative people emerged: intellectual, motivated individuals who were inquisitive, resourceful and driven. That the collective skills and contributions of these people came together in just a few short years is one of those serendipitous events of history.

The outcome was the birth of Margaret River and a new era for the West Australian wine industry. It is a fascinating and complex tale.

But it is also a story that over the years has been distorted, largely due to the paucity of factual documented information. It has resulted in perpetuated myth through various pieces of reporting and commentary in books, magazines and newspapers. Nothing deliberate or calculated, but simply an outcome. As wine writers, with a combined output of more than seventy years—much of it writing about the evolution of Margaret River and its wines and people, from its early years to its current position of pre-eminence—we believed this compelling story needed to be told, or it risked being lost. When we set out to write this book more than ten years ago, we had no idea of its complexity or what we would find. Over the years of writing about wine we have tasted thousands of wines from Margaret River and discussed them with the people who made them. But that is only one part of the story. We were both surprised and captivated as we dug into the archives and fading memories, a process which gradually gathered momentum until we were satisfied that in the fiftieth year of Margaret River as a wine producing region, we could tell the story of Margaret River 'the way it was'. We found struggles that nearly resulted in failure; argument and conflict that put learned men at one another's throats on one day and brothers in arms the next; twists of fate and good fortune; and gradually a triumph that spoke much about the spirit of those who forged their way.

Our research revealed how a remarkable group of people from disparate backgrounds were drawn together with a common purpose: to rejuvenate the West Australian wine industry by taking it in a bold new direction. Some were well known and have been recognised for their significant contributions. People like Dr John Gladstones and visiting US academic and researcher Professor Harold Olmo, who brought scientific discipline and observation. The doctors, Tom Cullity at Vasse Felix, Bill Pannell at Moss Wood, and Kevin Cullen at Cullen, who sacrificed time and money outside their busy practices in pursuit of a dream. The women, such as Veronica Cullity, whose family life suffered because of the regular weekend absence of her cardiologist/vigneron husband; and Sandra Pannell, Di Cullen and Anne Gregg, who shared the long hours toiling in the vineyard and cellar and who, in many cases, took on the hard work of establishing their winery. The financially savvy but equally brave to roll the dice, such as the Hohnens at Cape Mentelle and the Horgans at Leeuwin Estate. And the industry people—Bill Jamieson and Dorham Mann from the Department of Agriculture, who went above and beyond their roles to help the early pioneers.

Then there were others whose contributions have been lost or ignored in the hype of all that has happened since those first vines of Tom Cullity were planted at Vasse Felix in 1967. There was the significant contribution of Charles Court, who as minister for industrial development saw an opportunity for the State and wielded his considerable political muscle to carve a path to make it happen. His insistence created an urgency within government and bureaucracy. And there was Les Slade, a name possibly long since forgotten and probably overshadowed by his later achievements as a high-ranking bureaucrat and diplomat, but whose report gave Court the evidence to get things started. And there was Houghton winemaker Jack Mann. In the early 1960s, Mann was a revered figure in the West Australian and Australian wine industries. He brought wisdom and vision that was ahead of its time and, in recognising the danger signs within the industry, saw where the future lay.

There was a time when we had hoped that the book would be called A Thousand Fathers. This was inspired by a proverb which Tom Cullity quoted on more than one occasion: 'Failure is an orphan, but success has a thousand fathers.' Although we realised that, as a title, it might be read in a way that overlooked the significant contribution of women, we were attracted to it because it emphasised just how many people were involved in establishing the industry. What transformed the region was the fortuitous combination of so many men and women all eager to tackle something new and exciting.

The pioneers of the late 1960s and early 1970s faced a Margaret River quite unlike today's wine region, with its modern amenities and infrastructure. Many of the roads were unsealed, or in the case of the main coastal road (Caves Road) impassable for lengthy periods because of flooding. Basic equipment was unavailable, there were few places to stay and even fewer places at which to eat. This was a depressed region and it looked and felt like it.

A great deal has been made of the involvement of so many doctors-turned-vignerons in Margaret River. In some ways, this appears to us to carry the subtext that this is the case because they were wealthy. Nothing could be further from the truth. Tom Cullity, whose family was wealthy because of its timber business, needed to be frugal during the early years establishing Vasse Felix. Bill Pannell was a newly qualified doctor when he started Moss Wood and money was scarce the entire time he and his family were at Margaret River. The Cullens had invested heavily in coastal land during the 1960s and until the 1980s were continually struggling financially. The Hohnens became involved in the wine industry after John Hohnen started Margaret River Land Holdings. Its survival was precarious and aided, in no small measure, by Mark Hohnen's ability to sell off land owned by the company. Although the

Horgans were well off, they agreed to become involved in the wine industry because of the promise of a Seattle-based joint venture funding its establishment costs. This didn't work out and so the Horgans threw themselves wholeheartedly into winemaking.

There are two themes central to this book. One is the ingenuity of all these pioneers as they coped with the lack of infrastructure and the dearth of funds. The other is just how hard it all was to establish viticulture, winemaking and a regional industry. The personal toll was substantial: burnout affected many.

That they succeeded is testament to their courage and determination. They put just about everything on the line to prove that quality wine could be made in Margaret River. The authors salute these people and hope that this book about their struggles and ultimate triumph is worthy recognition of their efforts and gives you, the reader, a better understanding and appreciation of *The Way It Was.*

Chapter 1

Beginnings

Early Vineyards

Almost from the outset, land around the Swan and Helena Rivers was identified as the most suitable for viticulture due to their excellent soils and proximity to the marketplace of the growing colony.

One major land grant led to the establishment of Houghton, which has been part of the Western Australian winescape for more than 160 years and its winemakers some of the best Australia has produced.

Throughout the nineteenth century, vines flourished in various locations outside the Swan Valley, at Vasse, Australind, New Norcia, Geraldton, Bunbury, Frankland River and Albany. In most cases, these would have been grown to produce table grapes as few of the English settlers had experience of winemaking. Plantings tended to be small as the inadequacy of transport meant that the market was restricted to family and friends. One exception to this was around Vasse where a demand was created by the significant number of American whalers who made annual trips to the West Australian coast during most of the nineteenth century.

The dramatic increase in the population in the 1880s and 90s caused by the Gold Rushes and the consequent building of railways led to a quadrupling of the production of wine in the 1890s. Much of this expansion occurred in the Perth Hills and other parts of the Darling Ranges at places such as Glen Forrest, Armadale, Darlington, Bakers Hill and Toodyay. As the railways moved south at this time, vineyards and orchards were planted along the line from York to Albany, notably at Boyanup, Katanning and Mount Barker.

Margaret River and Vasse

Vineyards were established at Vasse from the earliest days of settlement in the 1830s. There were vines on the Bussell property *Cattle Chosen,* and when, in 1845, Charles Bussell established his own place, *Sandilands,* nearby, one of his priorities was establishing a small (0.1 hectare) vineyard.

Elijah Dawson's Vasse homestead circa 1852.
Photo courtesy Doug Feutrill

In his autobiography, Kevin Cullen quotes his wife Di's research as indicating that *our district's first wines were produced from a three-acre vineyard by the Dawson family in Busselton.* The key to the commercial success of the Dawsons' enterprise was the market provided by the whalers, who plied their trade in the area. Elijah Dawson (a veteran of Waterloo) was one of the original settlers at Augusta and, later, at Vasse. In 1844, he bought 240 hectares on the West Brook in Vasse where he prospered. Shortly after moving there, he planted 1.2 hectares of vines and sold the wine he made to Keyser's timber venture in nearby Wilgarup and to the visiting American whalers. He built a thatched cottage with a below-ground wine cellar in 1844 and his brick homestead, *Westbrook,* from 1848 to 1852. This contained 'The Barter Room', which was set up on his veranda specifically for his trade with the American whalers.

The grape varieties planted included the Spanish black malaga, identified from the surviving vines more than a hundred years later, after the property had been purchased by the Feutrill family. Doug Feutrill grew up in the Swan Valley, went to school with John Gladstones, and knew viticulture. His father worked for the Department of Agriculture, and was a wine judge and a regular at the poker table with Jack Mann on Friday nights.

The Duces at Boyanup

Duce's vineyard and winery at Boyanup played a significant role in the history of wine in Western Australia.

Operated by John Duce from 1902 to 1923 and his son Basil until 1956, it was the first major commercial vineyard in the South West, at one stage producing 90,000 litres per year. With the railways as its cornerstone, it operated with a state-of-the-art winery and cellar, modern equipment and a strategic state-wide distribution network for sales. The Duces also unwittingly influenced developments in Margaret River in the 1960s. Tom Cullity was so impressed by a shiraz from their vineyard that he commented, 'it offered practical support to me that the effort to make quality wine in the cooler regions of the South West would be worthwhile.'

John Duce believed that the *South West would be peculiarly fitted for producing clarets and Burgundies* and suggested that *capital results have been achieved* by several Italian wine growers around Waterloo (about 20 kilometres away in the hinterland of Bunbury and close to Burekup, which would later be the site of Tom Cullity's first vineyard). Duce's winery flourished until the 1950s, when production declined. Harold Olmo explained that an eelworm infestation was responsible.

An aerial view of Duce's winery at Boyanup.
Photo courtesy Duce family

Ephraim Clarke

Ephraim Mayo Clarke was another of the early vignerons and winemakers. Old-timers for many a day called his small vineyard *Clarke's Folly* but they all sounded his praises when he demonstrated that what had previously been regarded as arid land was ideal for grape growing. Clarke's wines were sold under the Punchbowl label through the Clarke general store in Bunbury.

There are also links between the Clarkes and other important West Australian winemaking families. Jock Duce, of Boyanup, married Ephraim Clarke's granddaughter, Freda, while Ephraim's daughter, Elvie, was the maternal grandmother of Margaret River pioneer, Kevin Cullen.

The Spanish Settlers

Between 1906 and 1909 seven Spanish families (Casas, Delafcus, Espinos, Mas, Pifferers, Rauls and Torrent) came to Western Australia from a small village in Catalonia, about 130 kilometres north of Barcelona. They settled in a cluster around Yoongarillup, about thirteen kilometres from Busselton, in what became known as the Spanish Settlement.

The Mas, Torrent and Espinos families planted grapes and made wines for the group's consumption and for sale to the locals—for about eleven pence a bottle. Wine was very much part of everyday life for these Spanish settlers. Joseph Torrent says, 'pure (fermented) grape juice was always on the table.

No one drank to excess.' The Mediterranean diet was the norm: morning toast was rubbed with garlic and olive oil; grapes were cut off the vines, dried and eaten like sultanas. In his memoir, Alejandro Torrent commented that it was only the first generation of Spanish settlers that kept the winemaking tradition alive; after them, winemaking stopped and the vineyards ceased to be productive. Joseph Torrent tells the story of young George Espinos going to school for the first time. The students were sitting around eating their lunches when George pulled a bottle out of his bag and prepared to drink from it.

'What have you got there, George?' said Miss Diamond.

'Wine, miss.'

'What are you going to do with it?'

'Drink it, miss.'

'You can't do that here!'

'Do it at home, miss.'

Naturally enough the group of friends drank the bottle on the way home.

Giacomo Meleri (1884–1968)

In 1910, Giacomo Meleri emigrated to Western Australia from mountainous Sondrio in Lombardy (about 140 kilometres from Milan) where the vines were grown on hillside terraces. He married Dorothy Smith in Perth in 1915 and bought a 225-hectare farm at Yallingup in 1917. By 1920, he had planted a 0.8 (expanded to 4) hectare vineyard with fragola, doradillo and other varieties. The vineyard was on Commonage Road about two kilometres from the corner with Wildwood Road, close to, but on the opposite side of the road from the current cellar door of Deep Woods. Although the production of wine was just one part of the farm's activities, Giacomo took it seriously. He handcrafted barrels from local she-oak for maturing his reds and built a cellar about two metres deep with a ladder at the entrance.

The life of those who were involved in the Group Settlement Scheme of the 1920s was unrelentingly hard. In his

'Tribute to the Group Settlers', Philip Blond described how some of those from Wilyabrup's Group 20 attempted to liven up their celebrations of Christmas 1923.

A group of about eight men set off for Meleri's at 11.00am, intending to return by about 3.00pm. They were hot and tired by the time they arrived. Giacomo Meleri offered free drinks to quench their thirst before selling them bottles to take home. The sugar bags carrying the bottles seemed to get heavier as they trudged home and so frequent stops were necessary to take a sip to help regain their flagging strength. One of the group arrived at the Christmas party about 11.00pm and asked that horses and a dray be sent to collect the others who were *unable to make further voluntary progress.* The high-spirited travellers were dumped at their humpies an hour or so later: not all were invited in. Giacomo Meleri found the local dances were the best venue for his wine sales. His Red Dynamite sold for a shilling a bottle, or two shillings for a flagon (called 'flagoons').

The Credaros

No one has been growing grapes and making wine continuously in Margaret River longer than the Credaros. Cesar Cesar Credaro settled in the Carbunup area in 1922. He worked for Giacomo Meleri, who allowed him to take cuttings from which he planted a quarter of an acre of fragola for family use. The small plot at the Credaro home has survived and tiny quantities are still made as a delicious light-bodied, fruity red, available from the cellar door. Credaro is now a major winery in the region.

Sam Moleri: The Man Who Never Was

Tom Cullity mentions Sam Moleri, who 'grew grapes, made wine and sold it door-to-door in Margaret River in the 1930s. He is said to have lived about five kilometres north of Vasse Felix'. Moleri has been mentioned subsequently in many articles, reports and books about Margaret River.

After much searching for this elusive winemaker, we have come to believe that Tom Cullity was mistaken, possibly confusing him with Giacomo Meleri (called 'Jimmy' by some) who lived nineteen kilometres north of Vasse Felix. We think it unlikely that anyone sold wine door-to-door in Margaret River in the 1930s. It is our view that Sam Moleri is the man who never was.

'Clear the plates, we're closing'—Wining and Dining in Perth

For a little more than a century, eating out in Perth had been a largely forgettable experience. The food was pedestrian and most people ate at home where the meals were based almost exclusively on traditional Anglo-Saxon stodge. In his eighties, Vasse Felix founder Tom Cullity recounted his vivid and unflattering memories of eating out in Perth in the years after the end of World War II. Never one to mince words, he described it as a 'culinary desert'.

Australian historian Manning Clark in the dining room of Perth's Palace Hotel. Photo courtesy The West Australian

From the 1950s until the 1970s, there were few suburban restaurants in Perth. When West Australians went out to dinner, it was usually to the dining rooms of suburban or city hotels. There were three famous hotels in Perth in the 1950s and 1960s—the Esplanade, the Palace and The Adelphi, which later became the Parmelia Hilton. The Esplanade and the Palace were the grandest by Perth standards. The Palace on the corner of William Street and St Georges Terrace, was a favoured haunt of hard-drinking local newspaper rogues. It was there that they regularly put on displays of limp-falling, which required, on cue, members of the limp-fallers to fall to the ground. Limp-falling spread from St Georges Terrace to London.

The Esplanade, on the corner of William Street and Mounts Bay Road, as well as being Perth's most beautiful hotel, had an important claim to fame. It was there that Herbert Sachse claimed to have created the Pavlova in honour of Russian ballerina Anna Pavlova. Cullity remembered going to both the Palace and the Esplanade 'because they were the only two places you could get a feed after six o'clock in the evening in Perth.

'Even before the Second World War, I remember being with my father and although I only went about two or three times, I can clearly recall that you would never see any wine on the table. The rules and regulations covering when you could eat and drink were absurd. I recall the waitress who came up to us in the Palace and took the plates away while I was still eating my pudding. She said that dinner had finished and that was it. It was about 7.30pm.'

Cullity also lamented the limited menus of the time. 'There was a place in Barrack Street ... where you could get a feed, but it was the same sort of stuff, either roast mutton, or beef, or pork with potatoes and soup. Never any wine.'

Cullity recalled another encounter at a hotel in Bunbury, about 160 kilometres south of Perth. 'I ordered a white wine and there were things swimming around in it. I said to the waitress, "Look, I'm sorry there are things swimming around in this could you bring us another bottle".' According to Cullity, her response probably summed up the attitude towards wine at the time: 'And who do you think you are, a bloody connoisseur?'

In the main, roast chicken and roast beef with lots of gravy were the standard fare before the late 1950s when the Continental European influence started to see garlic being used. Of course, steak and eggs were popular, prompting the irreverent wine and food critic Richard Beckett (under his nom de plume Sam Orr) in the anti-establishment weekly *Nation Review* in the 1970s to remark that *as long as you can still get steak and eggs, the poofters will never take over the world.*

If wine was served it had usually been in the refrigerator for days or weeks, and it mattered not if it were red or white. However, in many ways, this was the dawning of a new era for a largely Anglo-Saxon population who approached new food and tastes with trepidation. By the early 1960s, the people of Perth were discovering that a plate of steak and eggs or a roast didn't have to be the norm. This food renaissance had a lot to do with air travel to Europe becoming more accessible and affordable, and Australians travelling more and travelling younger. Such exposure to new cultures, new ways of eating and, of course, wines, created an awareness of something more substantial than what had been hitherto served up on their plates or in their glasses.

It took many years for Perth to break away from its culture of unappetising food, although an alternative to traditional dining habits existed in the slightly Bohemian environs of Northbridge on the northern edge of the CBD of Perth, and in the port city of Fremantle, where there were strong Italian and Greek influences. Restaurants such as the Capri and the Roma in Fremantle became immensely popular, while Northbridge, which became known as Little Italy, was a lively environment of colourful characters, pioneering restaurateurs, and lively conversation. Names such as the Sorrento, the Romany, Marto's, Mama Madera, Ristorante Italiano and La Tosca became synonymous with the area, serving largely Anglo-Saxon versions of traditional Italian cuisine.

You might get the minestrone and bread free and, with the main course, you could get a cup of what was referred to as coffee but was, in fact, a creative way to get around the restrictive licensing laws. Things were also changing on the homefront. At the end of World War II there was another influx of migrants, which brought new ideas and approaches, along with new ingredients and flavours. This willingness to experiment and discover new taste experiences transformed Australian cooking and dining

The Wines They are a-Changing

Until the 1960s, Australians were simply not wine drinkers. However, that was changing as a result of the introduction of a style we take for granted now but which was, in the 1950s, revolutionary, refreshingly different and thoroughly appealing. It was the introduction of perle wines. In 1953, the long-established firm of Gramp & Sons, in South Australia, started using cold and pressure-controlled fermentation to make a light sparkling style similar to those being made in Austria and Germany. In November 1956, Gramps introduced Barossa Pearl, a naturally sweet sparkling wine that appealed particularly to women and had a massive impact on the Australian wine market. Barossa

Pearl was as much a part of wedding feasts as awkward best man speeches and chicken Maryland. This new style helped move young drinkers toward table wines rather than fortifieds, which were already on the wane.

A bottle of Orlando Barossa Pearl of the 1960s

A few years later, in the early 1970s, a similar phenomenon occurred with the introduction of slightly sweet white wines that were often erroneously referred to and labelled as moselle. Perle wines and moselle styles were the catalyst for more experimentation with table wines of greater sophistication. Then along came the Bag in the Box. The wine cask was an invention of Australian Tom Angove and it meant that anyone could have a glass of wine on tap for their evening meal without having to open a bottle.

Importantly, this was also the era when food magazines and associated wine and food journalism started to make an impact. It had started with Len Evans in 1962; then *Epicurean* and *Australian Gourmet,* the forerunner for today's *Australian Gourmet Traveller,* were launched in 1966. Food shows began to appear on television and, most famously, Graham Kerr brought his *Galloping Gourmet* TV program to screens across the country.

In the late 1960s came another important impetus to Australia's food and wine culture—the BYO (bring your own) licence. The BYO restaurant revolution started in Victoria and was gradually adopted in other states, including Western Australia. Being able to take your own liquor to restaurants made dining out a lot more affordable. The BYO licence led to the development of a solid core of reasonable restaurants that delivered value and quality, and reached a new middle-class demographic. It was also the catalyst for people to start taking an interest in wine.

Finally, Tom Cullity had reason to smile, just as his wines were starting to see the light of day.

I Drink, Therefore I Am Australian

By today's more liberal standards, West Australian liquor licensing laws were, until the 1970s, stifling. Regulating how people could drink and how wine could be sold were hardly encouraging for producers, retailers and the more enlightened consumers, who saw the virtues of having wine with their meals at home or in some of the emerging restaurants.

In its editorial of 30 October 1950, Perth's afternoon newspaper, *Daily*

News, declared: *there are two major obstacles to the rapid expansion of the Australian wine industry: (1) The stupidity of the law relating to drinking of alcoholic liquor; (2) the excessive charges for wine in hotel dining rooms.* The editorial highlighted the difference in the laws in each state and described how *travellers from civilised countries are amazed to find their bottles and glass whisked away from the dinner table at 8 o'clock.*

It was against this backdrop that the first tentative steps of the modern wine industry in Western Australia were taken and, in the light of such draconian liquor laws, it makes the actions of the wine pioneers all the more courageous. It was a highly risky venture with no guarantee of success and no clear idea of what to do with the grapes or the wine if they could be successfully produced.

In the 1950s and 1960s, table wine was a tiny part of the traditional Australian way of life and, in the main, Australians drank in pubs, largely because of tradition and because the law prevented wine being consumed in restaurants outside the dining rooms of Australian hotels. From the earliest days, the pub, whether it be in a small country or outback town, in the suburbs or in the heart of the capital, was fundamental to Australian society. They were the latter-day parish pump where men, and it was almost exclusively men for well over a century, congregated in a daily ritual to communicate over a few schooners or middies of beer with unparalleled freedom. It was not until the 1970s that women were permitted into the public bar for a drink. Beer was the drink of choice and woe betide anyone who asked for anything else. Spirits, perhaps, but wine was frowned upon. There were two restrictions on the retail sale of liquor: it could only be sold in stores which had groceries available; and those stores were only given a Gallon Licence. This meant that wine could not be bought by the single bottle.

Migrants Making a Difference

Western Australia's population growth was based on migration. Migrants from the United Kingdom were still the majority, but people from other nations—Yugoslavia, Italy, Greece, Spain and China—began to influence Australian culture. The xenophobic Anglo-Saxon – dominant population treated these people with suspicion—they either worked too hard or drank wine. However, the drinking habits of European migrants in particular began to influence Australian society for the better. These were more about sharing wine at home with family and friends as an integral part of life.

In 1969, journalist Duncan Graham wrote about the difficult choices faced by anyone wanting to find somewhere to have a decent glass of wine. He wrote that *you could risk the sudden hush of a crowded bar and the barmaid's question: "A glass of what?" or creep furtively into a wine saloon where you could drink but not eat.*

In November 1967, amendments were made to the licensing act permitting wine saloons to serve food without a full restaurant licence. How coincidental was it that this was the same year Cullity began planting his Margaret River vineyard?

Eventually Western Australia's licensing laws were rewritten and they could not have come at a more opportune time. Grapes had been planted just three years earlier in Margaret River and Mount Barker and were just a few years from revealing their potential.

With new liberalised laws governing what, where and how people drank and ate, the ground was prepared for the emergence of a new era for Australian wine. For the new wine regions in the South West and Great Southern, they could not be arriving at a more fortuitous time.

Chapter 2

Change in the Wind

Early in the second half of the twentieth century, the West Australian wine industry was at a crossroads and the path it chose would determine its future. Would it continue to stumble along and, in all likelihood, become irrelevant, or would it find new life and a future as part of a changing Australian winescape? Fortunately, there were people who saw the danger signs and, importantly, the need to change and move in a new direction. They were not entirely sure in which direction, either geographically or philosophically, but they knew that to remain static was courting disaster.

Change would not be an instantaneous big bang, rather a confluence of events, people and necessity, with an element of natural evolution creating the irresistible force for change. It was influential people in the industry becoming aware of fundamental problems, especially in the biggest wine-producing area of the Swan Valley. It was deep thinkers and intelligent people with inquiring minds. It was old-fashioned pioneering spirit and initiative. It was a logical process of societal and cultural evolution enabling legislative shift. There were the evidence-based documents of agronomist Dr John Gladstones which pointed to the South West, and Margaret River particularly, as suitable for producing table wines. And fortunately, there were people—doctors mainly—who understood the science but, almost as importantly, wanted to test their creativity.

And finally, there were the drivers and the motivators—a fortuitous combination of politicians, bureaucrats and professionals with curiosity and stubborn belief in exploring new ideas that challenged contemporary convention. These were people who were not afraid to question the status quo, take risks and work hard without any guarantee of success.

No one had the complete picture, just pieces of the puzzle. But the fact that it all came together in just a few years in the 1960s created the energy and impetus to make it happen. Perhaps it was also fortunate that all of this occurred in a decade of momentous global social, economic and technological change that came together in a cultural statement at Woodstock and a technological achievement on the surface of the Moon.

It was a culmination of many things that would ultimately lead to the modern Australian wine era and the beginning of the most exciting period in the West Australian wine industry.

The 1960s was a time of growing interest and changes in wine styles, the likes of which were unknown in Western Australia. Elegant, refined table wines closer to the styles of Europe were being made in a small but increasing number of other Australian wine regions. It was the early stages of what would be an unrelenting move away from fortified wine drinking, which had dominated Australian wine preferences for more than a century.

In Western Australia, most wine production was fortified, a style obviously well suited to the warmer climate of the Swan Valley. However, the Swan Valley, which was still the major wine region of the State, had its limitations. Most of the land suitable for wine production had been planted and there was little room to move. As well, the warm-to-hot early ripening season was not conducive to the varieties and styles that preferred longer, cooler ripening times.

In the south of the State, areas of orchard and other crops were being grubbed for more profitable sheep farming, and vines in the Swan Valley were being removed as the poorer soils and bad drainage were impacting on both table wine grapes and currants, hitherto an important product for the valley. Compounding this were the poor returns for dried currants in the late 1950s, which made it tough for growers in the Swan Valley and threatened the viability of the region.

Change may have been in the wind but the big question was where would it blow. It was something of a catch-22. It was all well and good to be thinking of table wine production, but without demand why would people bother with an unprofitable pursuit. It was hardly an encouraging environment in which to develop a sophisticated wine industry.

In the 1950s, seventy-five per cent of the State's grape plantings were concentrated in the small area of the Swan Valley and about ninety-six per cent were within eighty kilometres of Perth. The remaining vines were in tiny vineyards dotted in disparate locations from Geraldton to Albany. Most of the wine grown outside the Valley, and in fact much within it, was sold locally.

Soils suited for viticulture in the Swan Valley were something of a curate's egg, with patches that were very good, but a lot of what could be considered marginal at best. Unfortunately, a lot of vineyards were planted on these marginal soils so that even if consumer tastes had changed for better quality table wines, winemakers would not have had quality fruit to produce it. It was inevitable that if there was to be a major expansion in the grape-growing industry it would have to take place outside of the Swan Valley. The question was where, although, even at this stage, there were reasonably strong pointers to areas in the south of the State.

Mann for the Times

Among those who realised things had to change was Houghton winemaker Jack Mann, the leading figure in the State's wine industry. Mann, especially, was questioning how long the current dominance of fortified wines could be maintained. He was also aware of the negative consequences of excessive fortified wine consumption. In fact, while Mann championed wine as a socially acceptable beverage, he was an early advocate of wine drunk in moderation and he often drank his with water or ice. The State was fortunate to have a person like Mann, revered as a winemaker yet someone who also possessed foresight not limited by current dogma and who saw wine as an important part of a cultured society.

Jack Mann, the visionary elder statesmen of the WA wine industry. Photo courtesy Roger Garwood

He also understood the potential of the south of the State for wine grape production, having already made wine from fruit sourced at the Duce's property at Boyanup (see Chapter 1). He also almost certainly had a significant influence on the work of Professor Harold Olmo.

Mann was a contemporary of Hunter Valley winemaker Maurice O'Shea, and the two of them used to exchange wines regularly. O'Shea, despite never having visited Western Australia, had already expressed to Mann a belief, based on soil and climate information, that Albany, on the south coast, 400 kilometres from Perth, would most likely be suitable for premium wine production. In fact, according to Mann, O'Shea had mentioned several times that if the opportunity had arisen, he would have planted vines in this southern region. Both men were well ahead of their time and are still recognised as two of Australia's most important and influential winemakers.

Jack's son Dorham, who would later contribute to the development of both the Great Southern and Margaret River, recalled in an interview in 2000 the profound comments of his father Jack.

Jack enthused about table wines and said wine would never dominate in Western Australia until people started to appreciate drinking good table wines. Dorham said: 'And he often would say that as a standard wine ... we should drink lots more table wine with the ... old-time European custom ... of an equal volume of water. But to do that you have to have full-flavoured table wines. He used to get stuck into cold fermentation. He used to call that cold castration of grape juice. His principal philosophy was always to process ripe fruit—beautifully ripe fruit—for the particular wine style that you were making. Because you always got the most flavour from well-grown ripe fruit, and more softness in the style.'

For Old Jack, cabernet sauvignon was supreme and he was often quoted as saying it was 'the only grape that would be tolerated in Heaven'. The West Australian wine industry was fortunate that it had the right Mann in the right place at the right time.

The Olmo Impact

One of the most influential decisions that would shape the future of the wine industry came from a related body but one not directly involved in the wine industry. At the time, dried fruit viticulture in Western Australia was a bigger industry than growing grapes for wine, but it had major problems that needed to be addressed.

The Vine Fruits Research Trust was established in 1949 with funds from industry levies. Its purpose was to fund research to identify and solve these problems. During a visit to California in 1952, the Trust's chairman, Walter Ashton, invited Harold Olmo, Professor of Viticulture at the University of California Davis, to come to Western Australia to investigate the grape problems in the Swan Valley and to suggest possibilities for viticulture in this State.

The Fulbright research scholarship that enabled Professor Harold Olmo to spend nine months in Western Australia, from early February to late October 1955, was, albeit indirectly, a major catalyst for the establishment of the Margaret River wine region. It was Olmo's breadth of knowledge, his ability to translate that into practice, his intellectual rigour, and his quiet charisma that gave his final report an impact far beyond its subject matter.

Problems in the Swan Valley

Olmo reported that there were few good viticultural soils in the Swan Valley and, interestingly enough, the best of them were planted by the region's pioneers. More than 400 hectares had been planted on unsuitable sites—in shallow soils with underlying clay that prevented downward drainage, which led to root drowning in the growing season. Olmo pointed out that there was no ready solution other than abandoning these plantings and resettling vignerons on better land.

Olmo highlighted other problems and made it clear that the Swan Valley had a limited future. Table grapes and dried fruit would be better grown in the sandy coastal plain, underlaid by limestone, from Wanneroo to Yanchep; and in the deep, loamy sands of Gingin and to its east almost as far as Bindoon. He saw a significant need for technical advice and described most of the small winemaking operations as 'poor indeed'. He recommended the appointment of an extension oenologist (preferably a graduate of Roseworthy College, at the time Australia's only educational institution which offered training in viticulture and winemaking) and the construction of a small modern winery and research laboratory in the Valley.

Olmo's Legacy

Olmo asserted that the greatest economic benefit of viticulture to the State would be in the production of light, dry table wines. He asserted that the industry in Western Australia would have difficulty competing in the export market, especially with wines from the irrigated areas of the east, unless it sourced new and improved grape varieties such as cabernet sauvignon, malbec, and merlot. He also recommended the use of varietal rather than generic names (such as claret, chablis, burgundy).

Olmo noted that, in examining temperature and specifically heat degree days, much of the South West was *equivalent or better than other areas to be found in the present[day] quality wine districts of Australia or California.* His most far-reaching recommendation, was that the south coastal area along the Frankland River be considered for production of high-quality light table wines. In support, he noted its 750 to 900 millimetre rainfall range was mainly in winter, with not much in the growing season. Consequently, it would produce a vigorous productive vine on the better alluvial soils (deep, loamy, well-drained). The cool summer climate would enable the grapes to ripen slowly and so achieve optimum quality.

There is a story that Harold Olmo bypassed Margaret River. He had been at Mount Barker with a group (including State Viticulturist Bill Jamieson) and they were running late for dinner in Busselton with CSIRO's Eric Bettenay, who had spent many years mapping the soils of Western Australia. As they drove by Margaret River, Olmo exclaimed, 'Look! Is there country of interest through there?' 'Nothing there,' he was told.

John Gladstones commented that Olmo excluded the higher rainfall country which would have taken in Margaret River, Pemberton and Manjimup. 'He thought that the wetter areas would be too damp, and diseases would be too much of a problem. But he had pointed out the cooler areas down south which he thought, from analogy with the California experience, looked promising for table wines.'

Professor Harold Olmo with State Viticulturist Bill Jamieson at the Perth Show in 1955. Photo courtesy The West Australian

Jack's son, Dorham, recalled Olmo being a regular visitor to the Houghton vineyards. Said Dorham: 'He was out at our place with his family just about every second weekend. Dad and he spent a lot of time together and I believe he was well and truly indoctrinated by my father with the prospects of cool climate table wines being produced in the Mount Barker region.'

Dorham recalls he and his siblings spending countless weekends playing with Olmo's children—Jeanne-Marie, Paul and Daniel—at the Mann family home in the Swan Valley during the visit. Moss Wood founder Bill Pannell sat alongside Paul Olmo at St Louis School in Claremont. Jack Mann and Bill Jamieson grew close to Olmo, and their own belief in the future of viticulture in the State's cooler regions was galvanised during the time they spent with the American. Furthermore, Jamieson's work was aided immeasurably by his association with Olmo. Jamieson imported cuttings of chardonnay, sauvignon blanc, semillon, cabernet franc, pinot noir, and zinfandel from the University of California, Davis. This ensured that high-quality grape varieties were available to local vignerons as they expanded into the cooler regions where they would flourish.

John Gladstones made it clear that Olmo's work provided an important background to his own thinking. Their offices at the University of Western Australia were opposite each other.

Gladstones later visited him to see his vine breeding program at Davis. When Gladstones came to musing about Margaret River's potential for viticulture, Olmo and his work was a clear influence.

In 1978, Harold Olmo was honoured by his peers at the 20th International Horticultural Congress in Sydney. He was presented with a scroll of honour and a dozen bottles of West Australian wine by the Australian Wine Board in recognition of his work in the State. His collection of wine included a 1975 Vasse Felix cabernet blend and 1976 cabernets from Cape Mentelle and Moss Wood.

While certain recommendations of Olmo's report, *A Survey of the Grape Industry in Western Australia,* in relation to vineyards in the Swan Valley were adopted, his identification of the south of the State as suitable for modern cool climate viticulture and premium grape production was largely ignored at that time, certainly by those in government with the capacity to act on it.

That there had been such a long delay in responding to Olmo's recommendation was not entirely due to bureaucratic inertia. The State's Agriculture Minister, Crawford Nalder, was an ardent teetotaller and reportedly not disposed to seeing his department promoting alcohol. In addition to the lack of initiative through Nalder's office, others close to the department believed that there was also a lack of interest at senior departmental levels to Olmo's report, despite regular approaches from Bill Jamieson.

One close source said: 'Jamieson was always knocking on the door of Superintendent of Horticulture (Harley) Powell, who was an apple man, and his 2IC was Frank Melville, an orchardist type, and they were well and truly not interested in wine. Anything you would put to Harley Powell he would automatically go the other way.'

Of course, the reality of 1950s–60s bureaucracy meant that Jamieson was unlikely to risk the ire of his immediate boss, Powell, by going direct to department head George Baron-Hay, despite the fact he may have found a more receptive hearing. But Jack Mann was not about to let such stubborn views get in the way. It was evident that if there were to be any hope of reinvigorating the wine industry and adopting aspects of the Olmo Report, a course had to be navigated around departmental bureaucracy, and Nalder himself.

To those who understood the parlous state of the wine industry there was just one person with the opportunity and economic savvy to appreciate the problem and the political muscle to drive it—Charles Court, the Industrial Development Minister. Court was a man on the rise. He would be the next premier of the State, and everyone knew it. To suggest that Nalder and Powell were deliberately obstructionist might be unfair, but government inaction on several of Olmo's findings was a source of significant frustration for many in the industry. The fact was that Olmo's report lay doggo, gathering dust, until the early 1960s when Court's interest was piqued.

It may well have been clever lobbying by Jack Mann that drew Charles Court's attention to expanding the State's wine industry south. In the early 1960s, Houghton regularly hosted a Christmas gathering for senior figures in the Department of Agriculture. Mann was on good terms with department director George Baron-Hay, who was subsequently chosen to head the Grape Industry Committee after he had retired. Tom Dunne, who succeeded Baron-Hay as director, was also a regular guest at those Christmas soirees. Dorham Mann believes Jack, with his passion for the cool climes of Mount Barker, regaled these people with his thoughts on the potential for the Great Southern and cool-climate viticulture, with the express aim of getting this message to Court. It was clear that as Minister for Industrial Development, Court carried a far bigger stick than Nalder.

Timing is everything. Court was a tireless and dynamic promoter of any industry that would benefit the State. He could see a fundamental shift in the south of the State away from traditional land use such as orchards, which were struggling. Consequently he was keen to diversify the agricultural sector to generate new jobs.

Industrial Development Minister Charles Court—timeless promoter of the West Australian wine industry before all others. Photo courtesy The West Australian

The importance of Court's interest in the wine industry cannot be overstated. His reach and influence was wide and deep, and his constant urging and demands for action were fundamental to what was about to transpire. Court was a proud West Australian and he was prepared to take on anyone, including Prime Minister Sir Robert Menzies, in the interests of his beloved State. When Menzies reminded him of the government's embargo on iron ore exports and how it might impact on the ability for Western Australia to deal with Japan, Court's response perfectly illustrated his undaunted single-mindedness and refusal to be intimidated—by anyone:

'Sit back and watch,' he is reported to have said to the Prime Minister.

Court's energy and drive were instrumental in igniting the chain of events which would have far-reaching consequences and change the West Australian wine industry forever.

Stirring the Pot

Further fuel to the debate on the future of the grape industry was provided by Les Slade, who was then Sales Promotion Officer with the Department of Industrial Development. Those who were close to the department and who knew Charles Court well, believed that Slade worked energetically at Court's behest and was effectively Court's mouthpiece in some bureaucratic circles.

On 27 April 1962, Slade released a report on the grape industry in Western Australia that appeared to have been commissioned by Court, who had been successfully lobbied by a group which included Jack Mann. However, he needed something more concrete to get the wheels turning. Slade's report did more than simply frame and document the current position of the industry. It created the basis for further investigation which would contribute to the creation of a viable commercial industry. It was also significant in adding to the groundswell of interest in wine that was building at that time.

The report was controversial, causing more than a little friction within bureaucratic circles as there was a suggestion that Slade had gone outside his departmental remit by dabbling into things that were more agricultural based. It was exactly what Court wanted him to do. In the course of his research, Slade had discussions with many at government and departmental level and with leading wineries. His report built awareness and started people thinking about the wine industry. It was a significant document. It was the catalyst for the formation of the Grape Industry Committee with the dab hand of Charles Court pulling the strings, even though grape growing and winemaking wasn't his bailiwick. The fact that Court got the committee up and running by early 1963 was testament to his power and influence within government, when things normally proceeded at funereal pace within bureaucracy.

Various exchanges of departmental memos and minutes appear to confirm what was common knowledge at the time—that Nalder was not particularly enamoured with promoting or, indeed, diverting his departmental officers towards the wine industry. His views were probably largely conveyed verbally to his senior bureaucrats and drip-fed down the line. Although Slade's report also dealt with the table grape and currant industries, Nalder believed that the true picture was not as dire as Slade and others in the grape industry suggested.

Crawford Nalder—Minister for Agriculture and stumbling block for those who saw the potential of a vital wine industry. Photo courtesy The West Australian

In fact, on 25 September 1963, *The West Australian* newspaper reported Nalder in the Legislative Assembly saying: *The WA grape industry was in no danger though there had been a decline in grape production over the past few years,* which he attributed to a variety of reasons including uncertainty of some overseas markets. The article included reference to the Slade Report and noted that a committee had been formed to study it and submit recommendations.

This questioning of the report, which also supported the Olmo suggestion of investigating grape growing for wine in the south of the State, was making it more difficult to generate any momentum. But Court was not to be put off by such a suggestion and Slade was equally steadfast in responding to internal murmurings and criticism. Slade, in a note to his departmental chief, C.R. Gibson, of 26 March 1963, reinforced the industry expectations created by the report. He restated his own terms of reference in its compilation, clarifying that key Agriculture Department officers had been interviewed and consulted and that subsequent comment on an initial draft was sought from government minister and Member for Toodyay Jim Craig and State Viticulturist Bill Jamieson.

Slade said: *I should send this draft first to the Hon J.F. Craig, MLA, for Toodyay, and then to the Viticulturist, Mr W.R. Jamieson, in order that they would both be satisfied that the report did not in any way usurp the function of another department. In fact, I made it clear on Page 1 of my report that: 'In compiling this report I have endeavoured to deal only with the marketing economics and techniques...*

In that note to Gibson, which was sent after the Grape Industry Committee had held two meetings, Slade also noted that:

Messrs, Mann, Roe and Taylor (three key members of the Grape Industry Committee) *are most enthusiastic about the Committee and all feel that this is the first time that a positive approach has been made by any government or government department to assist an industry that is so much in need of assistance.*

Growers, both large and small in the Swan Valley, and local winemakers are watching with great interest the functions of [this] *Committee and I believe that they would feel very let down and disheartened unless the Department of Agriculture can be persuaded to co-operate to the fullest and permit the Committee to carry out its functions in accordance with your Hon Minister's directive of 7/2/63.*

I would suggest that the Hon Minister for Industrial Development be shown the minute dated 26/2/63 from the Superintendent of Horticulture, the minute dated 28/2/63 from the Director of Agriculture and the final minute of 1/3/63 from the Hon Minister for Agriculture.

The Nalder note of 1/3/63 referred to by Slade was a brief three-paragraph statement defending his position and stating that his department was on top of things, with the resources to complete the job. It suggested the other two notes were slightly defensive and in line with the demarcation between departments, which Slade appeared to be referring to as the basis for his note to Court.

The Slade Report

Slade's report dealt with the marketing, economics and techniques rather than grape growing processes. The entire report covered all aspects of grape production, but there was considerable focus on the wine industry. His conclusion was stark and foreboding. The State's grape industry was in serious jeopardy and a significant income to the State and hundreds of associated jobs were at risk.

Slade made specific mention of the key aspect of the Olmo Report which stated that: ... *grapes for quality table wines were best produced in cooler regions where higher development of colour and flavour, high acidity and only moderate sugar content could be achieved.*

Les Slade, an able ally of Charles Court and author of the report which did much to shape the beginning of the new wine industry. Photo courtesy The West Australian

When Slade's report was compiled there were just thirty-seven wine producers in the State, processing more than ten tonnes of grapes for the 1960 vintage. Of these, there were three major producers—Houghton and Valencia (both owned by the Emu Wine Co Pty Ltd, Adelaide and London), and Sandalford. Of the remainder, about half bottled under a registered label and sold mainly to hotels in the Midland vicinity or at roadside stands. At that stage, most of the wine produced was fortified.

Slade noted that for the period 1959 to 1960 *there has been an unprecedented demand for cheap 'dumped' SA wines and sales of WA wines have declined ... The price therefore for wine grapes must inevitably fall and this, together with the decrease in the sale of local wines, is having serious repercussions within the WA viticulture industry. Not only are local wineries and their employees affected but the livelihood of hundreds of vignerons and their families.*

Under the subheading of 'Merchandising of Wines Generally', Slade noted that local winemakers, even in 1960 and in common with Eastern States winemakers, were promoting the sale and drinking of quality wines. Efforts were being made to encourage the public to choose the correct wines to drink with certain foods and under certain conditions. He also noted two other mitigating factors for local producers. He described the standard of West Australian wine saloons as 'appalling' and *instead of encouraging the public to drink wine seems to have the faculty of attracting the wrong type of people.* The prices being charged by hotels was another factor discouraging the drinking of quality wines. Especially, he said, *the prices charged at the table in the lounge are mostly so far in excess of being reasonable that only people with high incomes or expense accounts are able to drink wines in hotels.*

Evidence of the damage being done to the image of Australian wines was relayed to Slade by MLA Jim Craig after a trip to the United Kingdom where he had discovered that bulk Australian wine was being blended with inferior Continental wines, giving Australian wines an unfortunate reputation. The Emu Company was mostly at fault on this score. Unsurprisingly, when Emu sold to the Hardy Wine Company in the 1970s it was greeted enthusiastically by wine purists. But that was more than a decade away and in the interim the practice was continuing to do the Australian and West Australian wine industry considerable harm.

Interestingly, a decade earlier, in 1950, in a debate on the Supply Bill in federal parliament, West Australian senator Don Willesee said that about 500 different brands (he may have been referring to different wines rather than brands) of Australian wines and brandies, unknown in Australia, were being marketed in Britain. He said that about 200 people were exporting to London any sort of concoction that could be sold. An editorial in the *Daily News* in 1950 supported this observation noting that:

Australian visitors to Britain will agree with Senator Willesee that any good dry wines in this country are unknown in England and what is sold in hotels and restaurants as Australian wine is prejudicing our prospects of establishing a market in the United Kingdom.

Having seen the draft of Slade's report, Craig, both as a government minister and a local member under pressure in an electorate that included the Swan Valley, immediately saw some leverage and corroboration of his own views. He started to push Court to move on the flagging grape industry. Craig, in notes to Court, mentioned other regions of the State which indicated he was aware of the Olmo Report and had almost certainly been lobbied by leading figures in the grape and wine industry urging some action on it. Craig obviously had a good relationship with Court and even addressed a later note to the impeccably formal minister and future premier with the salutation 'Dear Chas'. Whether it was because of this relationship or simply because he didn't feel he was going to get anywhere with Nalder, he wrote once again to Court on 4 September 1962:

Whilst making representation to you on behalf of the winemaking and grape industry, you will recall I mentioned the high opinion held by experts as to the potential of the Mt Barker area in regard to this industry.

Recently, in a discussion with Mr Jack Mann, Manager of Houghton, the matter was again raised and Mr Mann stated that his view was that this district could be developed into the most suitable vineyard land in Australia.

The first paragraph of Court's response of 11 September 1962 indicates he had already prompted action within his department:

...I am arranging for the Industries Advisory Committee to have a copy of your minute without delay as they have this particular subject under consideration at a meeting to be held this week.

No doubt they will confer with the Department of Agriculture and I will let you know when they have made a decision regarding an inspection.

A person with the experience of Mr Jack Mann could be very valuable in advising the Department of Industrial Development as well as the Department of Agriculture.

The wheels were well and truly in motion and Court had all the evidence he needed to put pressure on Nalder.

Chapter 3

A New Direction

With the Slade Report in play, the future of the State's wine industry was well and truly on Court's radar. It gave him a strong base from which to get things moving and light a fire under the previously inert Department of Agriculture and its minister.

At the same time, the Industries Advisory Committee held discussions with the former Director of Agriculture George Baron-Hay, to gather his views on the Slade Report. Baron-Hay had retired in 1960, but was a highly respected figure in bureaucratic circles, and the lobbying by Jack Mann and a few others was about to pay dividends.

In that meeting between the committee and Baron-Hay, the Craig memo to Court of 4 September was referred to and, most likely, Court's interest in the matter discussed. Baron-Hay indicated that the Mount Barker area had been *under consideration for some time as probably the best suited for the growing of grapes to produce quality table wine.* Given that the Olmo Report had been effectively stymied, it is highly likely the degree of 'consideration' was probably cursory from a departmental perspective, but there is little doubt those Christmas soirees at Houghton and Jack Mann's gentle nudging would have made him, at the very least, aware of the possibilities of Mount Barker.

In a minute to Court the Industrial Development CEO, C.R. Gibson, concluded:

...the Advisory Committee recommended that a committee be formed to enquire into the various problems of the grape industry, with the prospect of establishing it in the area already suggested—this is just west of Mount Barker.

Gibson recommended that this be discussed with Agriculture Minister Nalder to gather his views and support as well as his consent for State Viticulturist Bill Jamieson to act on the committee.

Once again Court stepped in with a note to Nalder on 19 September 1962 in which he attached a copy of the 4 September minute from Craig and stated that:

As you know the Government has been interested in the possibilities of an expansion of the winemaking and grape industry and the position now arises as to where we should look for the most logical developments.

I have had the matter considered by my Industries Advisory Committee.... Both our departments are involved and I was wondering how you would feel about the establishment of a committee comprising Mr J. Mann, of Houghton Wines, Mr D.F. Roe, of Sandalford, Mr L.W. Slade, Representing the Department of Industrial Development, and a Nominee of your own department.

Court had taken up the recommendation that Baron-Hay should chair the committee.

Even after Court's memo of 19 September, Nalder, in a note of 10 October 1962, expressed some reservation about the formation of a grape committee, noting that suggestions

...for the development of an industry at Mt Barker is based on the climatic conditions prevailing in that district and nothing is in reality known concerning the growth of suitable grape varieties for the type of wine which can be obtained therefrom.

Enthusiasm did not seem to be Nalder's strong suit. His following comments showed a cautious position at best:

This does not mean that I am opposed to the formation of a committee to investigate the position but merely indicates the difficulty in arriving at a definite conclusion.

Nalder finally wrote that he

...was agreeable to the formation of such a committee ... but that it include two officers of the Department of Agriculture, namely the Superintendent of Horticulture, Mr H.R. Powell, and the Viticulturist, Mr W.R. Jamieson.

Jamieson's appointment would prove to be an important one. His technical knowledge and understanding of broader industry issues would provide valuable insight in the committee's deliberations. Jamieson was a most important, influential and often underrated contributor to the early years of the wine industry in Western Australia and his commitment and drive would be fundamentally important to its future. In the end, Powell withdrew from the committee citing workload.

Nalder had previously asked both Jamieson and Powell to comment on the note from Court before responding himself. Jamieson wrote to Nalder, through Powell, on 4 October 1962. This was an important document that would form the basis of the committee's deliberations and investigations in the coming months, providing an accurate summary of the key prevailing factors impacting on the wine industry at the time. It shows remarkable perception and foresight. Jamieson wrote:

There is a demand within Australia for fine table wines of a type comparable with the Chateau wines of Bordeaux, the Cote D'or, the Rhône and famous vintages of the Rhine and Moselle Valley. This demand is limited but is still unsatisfied ... Geographically, the Mount Barker – Frankland River area appears to answer the climatic requirements ... Because of its distance from the more densely populated areas of Australia, the Mount Barker area can only be considered as a wine grape producing district if fine wines (high class prestige wines) are produced...

The significance of the Slade Report was highlighted further when it reached the public through the media. This had a twofold impact of fuelling sensitivities within government and bureaucratic circles, but also of stimulating awareness of the possibilities of expanding the wine industry into other rural regions of the State.

On Thursday, 18 October 1962, the *Farmers' Weekly* carried an extensive analysis of the Slade Report under the heading *WA Grape Industry is in Jeopardy*. This was about a month after Court had urged the formation of the Grape Industry Committee and before Nalder's response had reached him. The article clearly caused some departmental embarrassment and resulted in an exchange of internal memos. This was obviously a sensitive topic and the government had not wanted information with such negative connotations to be released prematurely particularly because, at that stage, there was no solution or plan of action.

Six days after the *Farmers' Weekly* article was published, Slade wrote to Director of Agriculture Tom Dunne on 24 October 1962, clearly concerned about the leaked information and any suggestion that it may have come from him as the author of the report. He wrote:

I checked with the Farmers Union of WA as to the origin of the article and they declined to divulge the source of their information. The only copies of the report which have been distributed at this stage are to members of the advisory committee, the Honorable J.F. Craig, MLA, Mr. G. Baron-Hay and Mr. W. Jamieson, government viticulturist ... I would appreciate it if you could bring this to the notice of the Honorable Minister and assure him that the release of the material for the attached article was not made by me.

A handwritten note on the bottom of this document reads:

Noted. Thanks. Tell Mr Slade not to worry over the Press report. Mr Craig and I have traced its origin and he is taking appropriate action.

The signature on the bottom of this note is that of Charles Court, dated 25 October 1962. Court eventually advised Nalder on 15 January 1963, with just a hint of frustration, that

I have asked the Department of Industrial Development to take the necessary action to the get the Committee functioning as quickly as possible so that we can have the benefit of their report.

Court formally appointed the Grape Industry Committee on 24 January 1963 confirming the committee members would be George Baron-Hay, chairman, H.R. Powell, Superintendent of Horticulture at the Department of Agriculture, Bill Jamieson (viticulturist), Jack Mann (winemaker), D.F. Roe (winemaker with Sandalford Wines); 1962 Grape Industry Report author Les Slade as secretary, and W.M. Taylor, representing the local grape growing union. Industrial Development CEO C.R. Gibson scheduled the first meeting for

15 February 1963 and recommended three broad terms of reference:

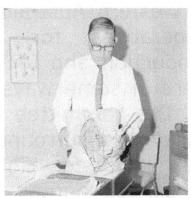

Chairman of the Grape Industry Committee George Baron-Hay (left); H.R. Powell (right), Superintendent of Horticulture at the Department of Agriculture. Photos courtesy The West Australian

a. *The prospects and scope for expanding the grape growing industry of Western Australia;*
b. *The suitability of areas for expansion outside the existing Swan Valley; and*
c. *The factors influencing new development and action which may be taken to ensure success.*

In its final report presented to Court in May 1964, the committee noted that the successful expansion of the wine industry had to consider the increase of wine production in other parts of

Australia and the growing efforts to expand the sale of Eastern States wines in Western Australia. It meant that the imperatives for those in primary production and for those in wine retail were in some ways opposed.

The committee confirmed the Swan Valley and surrounding areas were not well suited for high quality light table wines. It agreed that there was a growing appreciation of lighter tables wines, and that quality table wines were best produced in cooler areas where high development of colour and flavour, high acidity and only moderate sugar content could be obtained.

The committee also noted there was little doubt that several of the older established wineries in the Eastern States were carefully watching Western Australia as not only a growing market for wines, but as a suitable area in which to extend production at some future date. However, the committee felt that an established company would need incentives to establish a trial and plant a big commercial vineyard. Also, the quickest and only sure method to establish wine production in a new district was for the initial field investigations to be carried out under close government supervision.

It believed one experimental area of six acres (2.5 hectares) within the Forest Hill locality would be adequate to prove the suitability of the areas west of Mount Barker. However, any expansion of vineyards for wine production should be restricted to the growing of varieties of grapes likely to produce distinctive high-quality table wines.

On 21 May 1964, Court sent a copy of the Grape Industry Committee's report to Nalder seeking his comments. On 25 June 1964, Nalder, more than a month after Court had sent him the report, wrote to the Director of Agriculture: *Would you let me have your comments on the relevant sections of this report please?*

On 25 January 1965, Court once again wrote to Nalder:

You will recall a committee reported on the above (under heading Grape Growing Industry) and its prospects for expansion. A copy was sent to you on the 21st of May 1964. I am of the opinion a report could be adopted and implemented but as the initial work is primarily work for your department and its offices, it would normally be initiated by you if you concur ... If the Department of Industrial Development can assist with the small amount of funds required at the start, I am sure we could work out something mutually satisfactory.

Another letter was sent from Court's office on 16 March 1965 seeking Nalder's response. Finally, six months later, Court got some good news. A note dated 20 September 1965 from the Minister for Agriculture's office stated that the trial planting was about to begin. In a minute dated 30 September 1965 to the Acting Minister for Agriculture, Court wrote:

Do not hesitate to let me know if there is any way in which either myself or the Department of Industrial Development can assist. I have great interest in this project.

On the same date, Court sent a note to the Director of Industries Promotion. It appears to be a clear message to his own department that they needed to keep a close watch on the urgency with which the Department of Agriculture was treating the matter:

Would you please have the Department of Agriculture minute studied by appropriate officers within the department ... My main purpose in asking you to study the Agriculture Department's comments is, firstly, to keep you informed and, secondly, to ascertain whether there are any matters which require follow up by me or the Department of Industrial Development to ensure that we are gaining the maximum benefit and result from the committee's work.

On 20 October 1965, J.W. Watts, the Director of Industries Promotion, sent a reassuring note to Court:

The Department of Agriculture has accepted the recommendations of the Grape Industry Committee and arrangements have already been put in hand to experiment along the lines suggested.

Finally, things were starting to happen.

Let the Game Begin

In the spring of 1966, all eyes with even a skerrick of viticultural perspective turned towards a tiny plot of land twenty kilometres west of the town of Mount Barker in Western Australia's Great Southern. After numerous reports, a high-powered committee, endless discussions, intensive lobbying, and the judicious use of a very big stick in the shape of Charles Court, the viability of grape growing and winemaking in Western Australia was about to be put to the test.

Planting on Forest Hill had originally been scheduled to start in 1965, however delays pushed the project into 1966. The task of making the vineyard a reality was assigned to State Viticulturist Bill Jamieson and his assistant Dorham Mann. Jamieson and Mann, together with Agriculture Department horticulturist Ray Rodda and leading farm hand Brian Connor, planted the experimental vineyard in late spring of 1966, after deep-ripping and cross-ripping by bulldozer for tree stump removal the previous April. Just one hectare each of cabernet sauvignon and riesling, taken from Houghton cuttings in the Swan Valley, were planted. The cabernet sauvignon cuttings were from clonally selected vines of the 1930 planting at Houghton.

Unfortunately, the gods didn't smile on the trial, with some of the worst weather imaginable contributing to a very poor and somewhat dispiriting result. A combination of one of the wettest springs on record, the soil not having settled properly after the ripping and the lateness of planting resulted in a poor strike of the cuttings, which necessitated them being replanted in 1967.

In February 1967, Bill Jamieson wrote a brief report on the progress of the trial:

State Viticulturist Bill Jamieson who helped the pioneers of both Margaret River and the Great Southern. Photo courtesy Department of Agriculture

The planting of vine cuttings at Mount Barker on August 1966 has been unsuccessful due to the unseasonable spring rains during the September, October, November and December ... That the heavy winter and spring rainfall was responsible for the poor strike of cuttings is borne out by the fact that cuttings have had the same treatment but planted in the Margaret River – Busselton area and the cuttings surplus to the requirements at Mount Barker brought back and planted at the Swan

Research Station have grown successfully...

Success at Last

The vineyard was replanted in 1967 and the young vineyard gradually established itself. Five years later it produced its first significant crop and on 26 April 1972, Stirling MLA Matt Stephens officially picked the first bunch of grapes from that vineyard. The 1972 cabernet sauvignon was then processed at Houghton by Jack Mann and the riesling at Sandalford under the direction of son Dorham, who was then still with the Department of Agriculture. Mann the Younger, who had become winemaker at Sandalford, made all the wines from the experimental vineyard's next three vintages (to 1975) at Sandalford under the Sandalford Mount Barker label. The 1973 vintages performed encouragingly at the Perth Royal Show with silver awards for both the cabernet sauvignon and riesling, which also went on to win the trophy for the best West Australian table wine.

In recognition of Sir Charles Court's contribution to the establishment of the new West Australian wine industry, in December 1974, Bill Jamieson, on behalf of the principals of Sandalford, delivered a carton of both the 1974 Mount Barker and Frankland River rieslings to Court with the accompanying note: *As a token of the appreciation of your efforts in initiating and fostering the development of the wine grape vineyards in the southern regions of Western Australia.*

And the Word Spreads

While it wasn't exactly under a veil of secrecy that the trial proceeded, the Department of Agriculture was not keen to publicise its activities and progress. However, it was inevitable that word would spread and, by early 1967, news of the experimental planting reached the Press. It was hardly surprising as the small trial plot was the one piece of positive news on an otherwise bleak landscape. On 6 January 1967, the *Albany Advertiser* wrote to Jamieson seeking information about the trial.

Bill Jamieson responded, writing that to report prematurely would be unhelpful, pointing out that mitigating factors contributed to the lack of success with the initial planting. In particular, Jamieson believed that any negative reporting might deter potential interstate interest. At this stage, there was a strong belief from those within the industry that established interstate wine companies could be attracted to set up in the region if the trial was successful. And, of course, activity was starting in Margaret River with those initial plantings and Tom Cullity just months away from getting started.

Jamieson was happy with the report that subsequently appeared in the *Albany Advertiser.* However, he was less enamoured with a follow up article in the *Sunday Times* entitled *Winemaking may become big industry.* Its opening paragraph, Mount Barker may become Australia's chief area for the production of prestige table wines, rivalling in quality the best vintages of Bordeaux and the Rhine [SIC] Valley, took things much further than Jamieson would have liked.

Mount Barker may become Australia's chief area for the production of prestige table wines, rivalling in quality the best vintages of Bordeaux and the Rhine [sic] Valley.

A none-too-pleased Jamieson responded on 31 March 1967 in an internal departmental commentary on that *Sunday Times* report under the heading *Mount Barker Table Wine Grape Area.*

Jamieson wrote:

The publicity given to the possibility of establishing Mount Barker as a prestige table wine area is premature and unsuitable at this point in time ... I feel that the matter has been given too much publicity and that the claims have been greatly exaggerated.

By 1969, with the experimental vineyard at Mount Barker two years into its trial and Cullity's vineyard at Margaret River underway, and Bill Pannell's at Moss Wood not far off, it was clear that interest in both regions was growing. However, bureaucratic cautiousness and prejudices remained.

The sensitivities are illustrated to some extent by the following series of written exchanges between Jamieson and Powell. In early 1969, Jamieson was asked by Powell to provide an explanation to a particular paragraph in another article in the *Albany Advertiser* of 17 February 1969, which quoted Jamieson as saying: *We will eventually see a commercial winery at Mt Barker. And there was no reason why a small winemaker could not start up tomorrow.*

On 31 March 1969, Jamieson wrote a minute to Powell addressing these comments, which Powell thought, while factual, were out of context and misleading. Jamieson was forced to produce a 1,000-word response.

Jamieson wrote, in part:

It has become obvious that the great expansion of table wine vineyards throughout Australia is being made now and it is for this reason that I consider winemakers should be encouraged to plant vineyards in the Great Southern and South West areas at this time.

Powell took a different view.

In a note to the Director of Agriculture dated 10 April 1969, Powell wrote:

Official encouragement to plantings by small winemakers could imply some government liability towards loans for developmental costs ... In my view, it would be unwise to give any official encouragement to new plantings until evidence is available that they could be successful.

To some extent this note from Powell explains why much of Jamieson's support of new vignerons such as Cullity and Cullen was done without official sanction.

However, by this time, the emerging interest in the region south of Busselton, which would eventually become known as Margaret River, was starting to resonate. Although the government was still firmly focused on its trial at Mount Barker, Jamieson's note, which made mention of the success of some initial plantings in Margaret River, and correspondence from others, including Dr John Gladstones, was building awareness.

Chapter 4

John Gladstones: The Catalyst

Memories of childhood summer holidays in Augusta were a significant influence on University of Western Australia agronomist Dr John Gladstones when he started to give shape to the 1966 scientific paper which led to the development of the wine industry in Margaret River more than fifty years ago. Gladstones had become interested in wine through visits to Houghton with the family of his friend Ian Pullen, with whom he shared an illegal 'cellar' at St George's, their university college. In particular, he loved 'those unique and vastly fruity malbecs' that Jack Mann made in the 1950s and 1960s which remain among his 'strongest palate memories'. He later got to know Jack Mann well when the Houghton winemaker offered him the use of a hectare of vacant land in 1956–1957 to carry out his postgraduate research into lupins. Subsequently, the winery decided to grow lupins between the vines for green manure and Gladstones took a greater interest in viticulture. Olmo's work was another key influence.

Gladstones began considering possibilities for viticulture in Western Australia other than those suggested by Professor Olmo. While Olmo had discounted the Margaret River and Pemberton regions as being disease prone because of their high annual rainfall, Gladstones challenged this assumption. He knew the country from Busselton to Augusta as he had travelled through it all his life. He also had experimental lupin plots in the 1950s at the Department of Agriculture's Bramley Research Station, just north of the Margaret River township. His work enabled him to verify his theories about climate and to examine the region's soils closely. He knew that both damaging heat spikes and prolonged heat waves were rare in Margaret River. 'The lack of extremes of temperature certainly came into play in my early thinking.'

Another childhood memory of Augusta was of 'the rich distinctive aroma of summer stone fruits from Patmore's orchard at Alexandra Bridge near Karridale. You were almost overwhelmed by the perfumes of the fruit in a way that I had never experienced in Perth.'

Although there was little climatic data, this local knowledge together with his lifelong interest in weather and climate 'added up to a gut feeling that the area could be a very interesting and favourable environment for viticulture'. This led Gladstones to engage in a systematic study of the soils and climates of south-western Australia. He put his results into two scientific papers in 1965 and 1966. The first compared the suitability for viticulture of different regions of Western Australia's South West, while placing these in an Australian and international context. The second (which remains an unpublished though widely distributed mimeograph) focused solely on the Margaret River/Busselton area and recommended suitable localities for viticulture.

In *The Climate and Soils of South-Western Australia in Relation to Vine Growing* (1965), Gladstones explains how the following factors impact on high quality viticulture—growing season temperatures, rainfall, spring frosts, winter temperatures, sunshine and relative humidity, and soils. In a short section on Busselton – Margaret River, Gladstones suggests that the area has 'distinct advantages over all Australian vine districts with comparable temperature summations' because of its high winter rainfall, dry, warm sunny summers, and low risk of frost and hail. Its only significant disadvantage was the relatively high winter rainfall, which meant that vineyard sites needed to be carefully chosen so that the soils were free-draining.

After the first paper was published, he was keen to write a second, offering a detailed examination of the Margaret River area's suitability for viticulture. To supplement his research, Gladstones sought to spend as much time as possible exploring Margaret River and its environs. Pat Gladstones insists that any account of her husband's contribution to the history of the region would be incomplete without the following anecdote.

John Gladstones' early lupin research. Photo courtesy The West Australian

The Gladstones family, including Robert (nearly two) and Helen (three months), spent a few weeks during the Christmas holidays in 1965 at Augusta. John explains: 'I suggested that the family might go on a short run in the car to have a look at some nearby areas that I thought might have possibilities for viticulture. Pat prepared a few essential items that the children might need over a couple of hours and we set out about midmorning. Nine hours later, after 250 miles over rough gravel and dirt roads, we got home just as it was getting dark, with a decidedly hot, cross Mum, two hysterical children and some extremely wet nappies.'

Pat still relishes the opportunity to tell the story, almost with affection, and John reflects, 'I did afterwards try to learn my lesson from this, but balancing an absorbing scientific life against loyalty to family was never easy.' The results of the trip to inspect soils does receive some prominence in the 1966 paper.

This paper, *Soils and Climate of the Margaret River – Busselton Area: Their Suitability for Wine Grape Production,* compares the suitability for viticulture of Margaret River with that of Mount Barker, where all of the Department of Agriculture's focus had been placed. Gladstones explains that good soils for grapes are those with reasonable fertility; gravelly, loamy sand to sandy loam topsoils; and rather heavier, textured subsoils, yet with reasonably good drainage. These are indicated by the presence of red gums, only small amounts of jarrah, and the absence of banksias, she-oaks and any swamp-indicating plants. He felt that there was soil suitable for viticulture in four localities in the Margaret River region: Capel, Vasse, Cowaramup-Bramley and Witchcliffe – Forest Grove. He believed that Capel and Vasse were capable of producing full-bodied table wines similar to, but more reliably produced than, those in the Swan Valley.

After a detailed analysis, Gladstones compared Mount Barker and Margaret River. He believed that there would be little difference between the two in the ability to ripen grapes. However, he felt that ripening would be more gradual and more reliable in Margaret River and would also be less subject to spring frosts, extremes of temperature in summer and to rain or hail during the growing season. The influence of the sea on three sides was the major contributor to these advantages. The only disadvantage that Margaret River had was its higher winter rainfall which meant that care needed to be taken with site selection.

He saw a wine industry centred on Cowaramup or Margaret River for which grapes could be grown to suit all styles of table wines within thirty kilometres north and south of either of those towns, and be serviced by a winery or wineries. The region's moderate temperatures would benefit both the fermentation and the maturation of wines. Much of the land was cleared and well priced because the predominate land use was for the scarcely profitable dairy industry. Alternatively, he felt that farmers would be attracted by the possibility of diversifying into grape growing. He concluded by suggesting that the climate and lifestyle of the region would make it easy to attract and retain labour.

Gladstones recommended the planting of suitable grape varieties in pilot plots in the Vasse and Cowaramup-Bramley areas. He also suggested that the Department of Agriculture's research station at Bramley would be an ideal site. He heard on the government grapevine that his comments regarding Bramley were not welcomed in the corridors of the Department of Agriculture, where territorial divisions were part of the prevailing culture. The research station at Margaret River was focused on animal research and he had been given a plot for his lupin research only because it was animal fodder. Anyway, he was an outsider, and should keep his opinions to himself. The minister's continued opposition to viticulture also acted as a brake on such a possibility.

John Gladstones was to have the last laugh. Vines were planted at the Bramley Research Station in 1976 and, by 2014, Mandoon Estate was making some of Margaret River's finest cabernets from that vineyard.

Spreading the Word

In May 1966, Gladstones sent a letter to Crawford Nalder, the Minister for Agriculture, with copies to the West Australian Premier, David Brand, the Minister for Industrial Development, Charles Court, and Director General of the Department of Agriculture, Dr Tom

Dunne. He recommended that experimental fieldwork be conducted to investigate the possibilities of viticulture because of the potential income that the wine industry could earn the State. He also commented that it might well boost Western Australia's image and reputation overseas. His sole response was a supportive letter from Charles Court saying that the paper had increased his interest in the potential of viticulture for Western Australia and promising that he would take the matter up with his colleagues.

Before he had written the 1966 paper, Gladstones received an invitation from Dr Kevin Cullen to visit his Wilyabrup farm to advise him about growing lupins. The timing was perfect. He advised the Cullens to plant vines rather than lupins and sent them copies of his two papers when they became available. Cullen's enthusiasm for planting vines was further stoked in May 1966 by a weekend of talks with Dr Tom Cullity. Cullen decided to call a public meeting in Busselton to draw attention to Gladstones' paper, publicise the area's potential for viticulture, and galvanise some of the local farmers into action.

Gladstones said: 'The public meeting was quite important, in the context of the dire financial situation down there at the time. Dairying was not paying. They only had the buttermilk factory and that was not a good market. The timber industry had cut out and a lot of people had been in the old group settlements. They went through hell during the Depression and it wasn't a lot better in the 1950s and 1960s. So, there was a ready audience for something that might hold hope for a new industry. The meeting helped get the word around and gather enthusiasm.'

The highlight of the public meeting in July 1966 attended by at least 100 enthusiastic and interested locals was Gladstones' presentation. It had a huge impact on Jindong farmer Bill Minchin, who was the first to plant a vineyard in the Margaret River region following the public meeting. In 1966, with help from Bill Jamieson, he planted 0.2 hectares of riesling and cabernet sauvignon. It yielded about 230 bottles a year for seven vintages, after which the vineyard was destroyed by fire and not replanted.

Gladstones' paper did not spell out which parts of Margaret River had the greatest potential for growing vines, though in a robust exchange with Cullity in June of that year, Gladstones had suggested that Cowaramup would produce better quality wines than Busselton-Vasse with its higher temperatures. He explained that summer temperatures would fall and cloud cover increase in the Forest Grove area, significantly south of Cowaramup. He accepted that, without experience, 'we have nothing better to go on than subjective impressions and opinions'. Consequently, he would be loath to recommend planting south of Margaret River at that time. He explained to Cullity that the evidence suggested the area likely to produce the finest wines was along the coast road (not less than two to four kilometres from the sea) from immediately west of Cowaramup, north as far as Yallingup in the drainage areas of either the Wilyabrup Brook or Big Brook.

In a lecture given to the Wine Barons group in Perth in 1990, Gladstones commented: 'My confident—some thought, rash—advocacy of Margaret River rather alarmed the Department of Agriculture, which at the time was in the throes of establishing experimental vines at Mount Barker.'

There were initial problems at Mount Barker. The cuttings planted at Forest Hill in 1966 failed due to unseasonal spring rainfall. There were 12 inches (305mm) of rainfall—about 3.5 inches (89mm) more than the average—from September to December after a dry winter. The vineyard became waterlogged. Freakishly high temperatures—between 32 and 37°C—and 'dry searing north winds' for five days in mid-November led to most of the cuttings wilting and collapsing. As a result, only about ten per cent of the cuttings took; even those showed very weak growth, and were wiped out by grasshoppers.

In an internal report (2 February 1967) to the Department of Agriculture's Acting Director-General, Harley Powell, Bill Jamieson commented on the poor strike rate of at Forest Hill due to heavy spring rainfall. The cuttings had received the same treatment as those cuttings on Minchin's Jindong property, which had taken successfully. He noted that the rainfall there was close to the thirty-year average yet slightly more than half the rainfall which fell during the growing period at Mount Barker in 1966.

If John Gladstones had been looking for vindication of his paper (especially his view that Margaret River had more reliable rainfall and more equable temperatures than the Great Southern), this memo would have offered strong support.

'I didn't get down to Margaret River a great deal,' said Gladstones, 'but went down in spring of 1966 with Bill Jamieson to give our seal of approval to Tom's site which he was preparing for planting the next year. I returned for the famous party at Vasse Felix to celebrate the gold medal it won for the 1972 Riesling at the Perth Show that year.'

Gladstones did, however, keep a close eye on the progress of the wine industry in Margaret River and has served as a valuable commentator on the region and its wines over the years. His comments on the 1990 vintage illustrates this: 'It was a very good vintage and the styles of cabernet had become better established. Some of the early cabernets had harsh tannins and under-ripe, eucalypt characters. From 1990, the styles seemed much more settled, perhaps as a result of maturing vines, and greater experience and confidence in winemaking. There was more specialisation in grapegrowing and a better understanding of which varieties do best where. The area was attracting more highly skilled winemakers who were happy to take a collegiate approach and help each other when necessary.'

John Gladstones among the vines in Margaret River in more recent times. Photo courtesy The West Australian

The Australian wine industry began to define the legal boundaries of its regions in the 1990s by establishing geographic indications (GIs) to protect those regions. In 1994, Gladstones was asked to propose the boundaries of some of the West Australian regions, including Margaret River. There was only likely to be one controversial issue in this process: the question of whether to include or exclude Jindong from the region.

The brown and reddish alluvial loamy sands on the plains of Jindong are fertile, and have a plentiful supply of water and less severe growing conditions than other parts of the region. Those with a stake in the area argued that, with carefully watering, pruning and canopy management, commercially acceptable yields of high quality fruit were possible from the area. Opponents, such as Cape Mentelle's David Hohnen, who labelled Jindong 'the Entre-Deux-Mers of Margaret River', argued that over-cropping was inevitable. Gladstones explains in *Viticulture and Environment* that, *while the soil and topography are more those of the south-west coastal plain, as is the climate in many respects; ... geographically, it is hard to separate* [Jindong] *from Margaret River and Yallingup.* There were two other factors that influenced him. Firstly, there had been plantings there since the early days. Secondly, he believed that having an area which could produce modestly priced wine would help the region achieve greater market penetration.

His plan was adopted and has been the official boundary of the wine region since 30 October 1996.

In 1999, he was approached by Vanya Cullen and Keith Mugford to write a paper proposing what the Margaret River sub-regions might look like. They organised a major tasting of about eighty year-old cabernets from the 1999 vintage. These were served blind in three tranches—at Wilyabrup, Yallingup and Wallcliffe—and represented the six proposed sub-regions. All went well until after the Wallcliffe tasting, which was held at Leeuwin Estate. Producers from the cooler areas (Wallcliffe and Karridale) claimed they had been set up. The general view was that by comparison with the rich, ripe, plush cabernets of Wilyabrup, those from further south looked under-ripe, skeletal and minty with very firm, extractive tannins. It wasn't long before stellar producers from south of the Margaret River township—notably Leeuwin Estate, Voyager Estate, Xanadu and Devil's Lair—included as much as thirty to forty per cent of Wilyabrup fruit in their flagship blends. The quality of these reds has soared as a result.

Vasse Felix has continued this work of examining the concept of sub-regionality since 2009 by conducting annual tastings along similar lines. Gladstones' boundaries remain the guide. More than fifty local producers are invited to provide barrel samples of year-old cabernet along with comprehensive notes about their site and clone(s) as well as viticulture and winemaking practices. There are usually more than 100 samples which form the basis for what Vasse Felix's Chief Winemaker Virginia Willcock calls 'a unique forum for the continual and collective understanding of this great variety in Margaret River'. The supportive environment enables local winemakers to benchmark their stylistic preferences and develop a shared language around each vintage.

Chapter 5

The Influences on Tom Cullity

Tom Cullity's interest in wine stems from his early days as a medical student in Adelaide. He even ventured to the first Barossa Vintage Festival in 1947 and noted wistfully that visitors weren't allowed to drink any wine. He developed a taste for German riesling during his three years in London in the early 1950s. On his return to Australia, Cullity got serious about his wine. In 1961, he planned a European trip where he arranged visits to stellar producers in the Rheingau and Bordeaux. At the former, he remembers visiting Schloss Johannisberg, which was established as a Benedictine monastery in the eleventh century, with vineyards dating back even further. In the cellars, he tasted the 1959 Schloss Johannisberger (Riesling) Trockenbeerenauslese direct from barrel. 'Every time they took the bung from the barrel, the entire cellar [would] fill with flowers,' Cullity recalled.

'I stayed at this magnificent hotel on the Rhine. Every night, the local winemakers would come dressed to the nines to have dinner there, smoking big fat cigars while drinking fifteen-year-old Trockenbeerenauslese. No trouble at all. I thought, I won't be a wine snob anymore. I remember having lunch there, and we got venison and trout, or what the Germans called trout. They dropped this poor trout into a boiling cauldron of water, still alive. So, we ate it and it was marvellous. I thought, this is living.'

In Bordeaux, Cullity was welcomed at the cellars of Mouton Rothschild where he tasted the outstanding 1959 vintage from barrel. In an interview with Ray Jordan when he was well into his eighties, Tom Cullity recalled his visits: 'It was a hot year, but to have it there, in those cellars, was something else. I was pretty well hooked at that stage and realised that there was a fascinating world that I was keen to know more about.'

Veronica and Tom Cullity outside Notre Dame Cathedral during a trip to France and Germany in 1961. Photo courtesy the Cullity family

Cullity and Jack Mann were good friends 'because we always used to go up from the hospital'. Dorham Mann recalls them being involved in the Chablis Cup—a series of cricket grudge matches between an honest group of Swan Valley lads led by Jack and an effete team of university boffins (which included Tom) skippered by another of Jack's pals, Professor of Microbiology at the University of Western Australia,

Neville Stanley. When Jack Mann died in 1989, Tom finished his moving obituary to Jack remembering him 'creeping up to the wicket at his annual cricket match to deliver underarm spinners that weren't as easy as they looked'. Dorham remembers Tom and Jack often sitting on the veranda at the Mann family home enjoying wines together or, after Vasse Felix was established, doing an analytical tasting in the laundry.

Tom Cullity strongly believed 'Jack Mann, at Houghton winery, was alone (and undaunted) in his idealistic pursuit of the highest possible quality table wine' and in his belief that the best West Australian wines would be made in the cooler south.

Cullity also became a good friend of State Viticulturist Bill Jamieson, who, like Jack Mann, believed that the State's best wines would be made in the southern regions. It was with Jamieson that he tasted a beautiful Hermitage (shiraz) made at Houghton by Jack Mann in the late fifties, sourced from Basil Duce's Bbidecud vineyard near Boyanup. It was a turning point for

Cullity: 'Indeed, the obvious quality of this wine was a practical support to me in deciding that the effort to make quality wine in the cooler regions of the South West was worthwhile.'

Through Jamieson, Cullity visited the first planting at Forest Hill near Mount Barker on Tony and Betty Pearse's property. 'They knew nothing about grapes or wine or anything at that stage, of course. It was a fair way to go and Bill used to go down there when the job permitted him and supervise it.'

Harold Olmo's report was another influence: 'Somehow or another, it became an obsession. I thought that it was obvious that we have to go south if this [University of California] Davis work on temperature is right.'

In 1963, Tom Cullity planted a tiny vineyard (0.1 hectares) of equal amounts of cabernet sauvignon and shiraz on land owned by Cullity Timbers. It was adjacent to his sister Margaret and brother-in-law Frank Wilson's farm, *Tynedale,* on the Collie River Road at Burekup (twelve kilometres north of Bunbury). Frank kept a friendly eye on the vineyard. Also on the Wilson farm was Roderigo Dellavanza, an Italian who worked on the pine plantation and knew how to prune lime trees. As Tom said: 'There was some red dirt there. We made a little vineyard, put a fence around it and prepared the soil. Della was there to look after it and that's what was important ... the Rossis used to come in from Brunswick Junction and they were practically fully employed [on the farm]. 'Tony Rossi, he was a real old boy, old Italian farm type and wine was in his blood. He handled cuttings and he knew all about growing grapes: so, it was an ideal set-up,' Cullity said.

Forty years later, Cullity could still remember that the first wine off the property, made in 1966, tasted 'rather meaty and fleshy'. The grapes were picked at a somewhat under-ripe 10° Baumé because the vines were being plundered by hungry silvereyes. Thirty gallons (136 litres) were fermented in a 44-gallon drum lined with beeswax, with a filter borrowed from Paul Conti at Wanneroo to finish the wine. In 2016, Cullity's nephew Ben Wilson commented, 'Amongst other minor contributions, I lay claim to co-designing the wine press that the Doc used for that vineyard. It utilised a car jack, a cut-off and perforated ten-gallon dairy milk can and a circular plunger made from jarrah. Dad then had it built in Brunswick and Roelands. Jim Crotty, the Brunswick cabinet maker, made the circular plunger and the young guy from the Roelands BP service station modified the dairy can.'

The date of the Burekup planting is important to the chronology of events. However, it has been particularly elusive. Tom Cullity gives a range of dates from 1963 to 1966. He made a statutory declaration in 2003 as a record of what took place and mentions 1964 as the date when the vineyard was planted. Not every detail in that statutory declaration is accurate. Our view is that the Burekup vineyard was planted either in 1963 or 1964 with a strong preference for 1963.

Frank and Margaret Wilson's son Mark was born in 1951 and believes that the vineyard was planted in 1963 or 1964, certainly while he was at primary school. He remembers that 1964 was a particularly wet year and the local bridge was washed away. He believes that it would not have been a great year for planting even a small vineyard, as his father would have been incredibly busy coping with extreme wet and would not have wanted to be distracted. Denis Cullity, chairman of Cullity Timbers, pointed out to us that the vineyard was on property owned by Cullity Timbers, rather than on Frank Wilson's farm as Tom had suggested. Denis also believes that the vineyard was planted in 1963.

In 1965, Giles Hohnen visited Burekup with his father, John, Tom's neighbour from View Street, Peppermint Grove. Giles commented that the vines seemed about two years old at the time. In June 1966, Kevin Cullen wrote to Bill Jamieson about his desire to plant a trial vineyard so that he could compare the wine it produced with the 'Burekup vintage'. This suggests that Tom had already made some wine from that property. Perhaps the most convincing evidence comes from Bill Jamieson, who in a rare interview with Tom Jenkins (for his book *A Vision of Fine Wine*) said: *By 1964, demand for table wines, as distinct from the fortified wines that had mostly come out of the Swan Valley, was taking off.* Tom Jenkins continues: *Bill had already done some work in the south at Tynedale, north of Bunbury, where he advised Dr Tom Cullity about a pilot planting of vines. Dr Cullity was to lead the move to Margaret River.*

Tom's daughter Jude tells the story of a young American fresh out of winemaking college whom Tom happened to meet in St Georges Terrace in the Perth CBD. Tom invited him to lunch, explaining, 'I'd like you to taste my wine and tell me what you think of it.' At the appointed hour, Tom implored the young winemaker, 'Tell me what you honestly think of the wine. Forget about being tactful. I want to know what you really think.' The young man tried the wine and said, 'Frankly, it's awful.' Tom got very upset with him and summarily showed him the door, never to be welcomed again.

'My dad was a bit of a character,' says Jude.

The family made a trip to New South Wales in 1965 so that Tom could go on a fact-finding trip to the Hunter Valley and visit the vineyards at Muswellbrook.

Tom's daughter Veronica tells how during a cricket match, while both were playing for University, Clive Francis said to Garry Cullity, 'I've got a paper by John Gladstones that I think Tom will be interested in.' Francis was a former student of Gladstones and, at the time, a colleague in clover research. He had an interest in vines and often discussed Gladstones' ideas with him. He gave a copy of the 1966 paper to Garry who passed it on to Tom. It was the catalyst that galvanised the ideas that had been swirling in Tom Cullity's head since returning from Europe.

'It seemed that these areas would be more suitable than *Tynedale* and because of Gladstones' ideas and, no doubt, Duce's Hermitage, I decided to investigate the area south of Busselton. Jack Mann and Bill Jamieson were personal friends and both the sort who are unfailingly generous with time, help and encouragement. I think these things are the main reasons why I decided to pursue the matter further.'

Tom Cullity later reflected at length about his decision to go south. The complexities that underlaid his thinking certainly reveal much about him as a person. He was, at heart, a philosopher. In 1990, he explained why he decided to plunge into the unknown to establish a vineyard from a base in Perth without any infrastructure and minimal support. 'Firstly, there is an ancient marriage between wine and Western civilisation and its personal life, tradition, country life, prosperity and achievement, a beautiful traditional environment, hard work, art, solace, and beauty, all of which are deeply felt by many people and communities. Wine is life enhancing and, to some people, the production of great wine is the Holy Grail. It has the same sort of appeal as music.'

Jack Mann in his laboratory at Houghton. Photo courtesty of Houghton Wines

In a 1987 article, Cullity asserts: *The motive for the first planting near Margaret River was not commercial. It was a doubtful proposition without back-up. The only aim was to make the best possible wine. There seemed no reason why this should not be done and it was hard to understand why nobody had done this and why nobody showed any sign of doing it. With every intimation of affection and respect for many friends in the Swan Valley, it seemed obvious that Western Australia should do better.*

There is no question that he appreciated the help he had been given with his first vineyard. He wrote that the experiment at Burekup was enlightening and that without his brother-in-law, Frank Wilson, and the Rossis, Vasse Felix would never have happened. But there was a new challenge. Tom's time at Burekup was at an end. He left the vineyard to the Rossis, hoped that they would look after it, and without a backward glance, took on the next challenge.

In all this talk about the influences that shaped Cullity's wine destiny, it needs to be remembered that the direct stimulus for the planting of Vasse Felix were John Gladstones' 1965 and 1966 papers.

A Burekup Footnote

Frank Wilson has died and Tom's sister Margaret is living in Perth. The farm has been divided off from the pine plantation and sold. The Cullity family still own the pine plantation which includes the vineyard. Plantagenet's Tony Smith made some wine from the vineyard about a decade ago. The 125 vines remain but Tom's nephew Joe says, 'They suffer from benign neglect and are more cottonbush than vines.'

Chapter 6

First Whispers: A Meeting of Minds

The next step in the move towards establishing Margaret River as a viticultural region came following Tom Cullity's decision to abandon his vines at Burekup for cooler climates. In his typically self-deprecating way, Cullity commented: 'I had never been south of Bunbury in my life, had no practical bent, had never changed a car tyre, did not know what a weed was and knew nothing about vines or winemaking.'

In the mid-1960s, Kevin Cullen was a busy GP working from a practice he founded in Busselton. Not your run-of-the-mill GP, mind you! He had spent a decade engaged in higher studies in medicine (both at home and abroad) and conducting ground-breaking research. The activity peaked in 1966 as he put together the infrastructure and launched the Busselton Health Study, which fifty years later still contributes to the community and to medical science.

The previous year, Kevin and Di Cullen contacted John Gladstones to enquire about the possibility of growing sweet lupins as fodder for cattle on their farm. Gladstones explained that their property was more suited to viticulture and, when they were finished, sent them his reports detailing the region's potential for growing grapes.

Cullity contacted Cullen, who was a good friend through medical circles. As Tom Cullity commented, 'The Cullens were a haven, as they delighted in ideas, in change, and in progress. They offered me food and occasional lodging, an extensive knowledge of the whole area and its personalities, encouragement, and somebody helpful to talk to about the idea. Without this I would have floundered.

'I did not know how to proceed but did know that first I must have land. Kevin Cullen told me that I must announce my intentions to "the district", otherwise I would get nowhere. This disquieted me as I did not see what possible good could come of this, particularly as I did not know what the future held...

'Anyhow, Kevin really was a most interesting man. He was a sort of god down there in Busselton ... Kevin always felt, I think, that he got a fairly raw deal from these pretentious people in the cities that came down and thought that they knew every bloody thing, whereas he was a very intelligent man and extremely well-read in his particular way and a very active mind and I think almost hyper-manic.'

Over the weekend of 7 and 8 May 1966, Cullity and Cullen thrashed out Cullity's viticulture plans, which involved finding five one-acre blocks (0.5 hectares) ideal for viticulture in different parts of the region. After buying the blocks, he would pay the farmer to grow grapes under his direction and have them made into wine at a winery which he would build. He said later: 'It was idealistic, poorly conceived logistically, and in an area where it was common to see people with bright ideas flounder.'

The pair agreed to work on a joint project to plant a trial vineyard that year. They were thinking of a seven-year lease of a small block from a supportive and capable farmer who would tend the vines. As well as engaging in detailed planning for this venture, they agreed to continue investigating the establishment of a small vineyard, winery and cellar in Cowaramup.

Having received John Gladstones' second paper in April, Cullen reacted to these discussions with Cullity by calling for a public meeting at the Esplanade Hotel in Busselton to broadcast the area's potential for viticulture and to galvanise some of the local farmers into action. He believed that the timing was appropriate as it would be 'important for people to have a look at their land in August to inspect for the highest winter water tables'.

Chapter 7

The Public Meeting

Esplanade Hotel, Busselton, Thursday, 21 July 1966

John Gladstones was enthusiastic about the public meeting and believed it had a considerable impact in the region. He said: 'There was a lot of interest ... the area was terribly depressed and any prospect of a new industry immediately pricked people's ears ... generally the reaction to all this was way beyond anything I had expected.'

In the 1960s and 1970s the primary industries on which Margaret River depended—mainly beef and dairy cattle—were unprofitable. The Dairy Board, with the aid of $25 million from the federal government, helped phase out small, unprofitable farms. Timber, which had flourished in the final three decades of the nineteenth century, no longer made a significant contribution to the region's economy. There had been some diversification, for example, by those who started pine plantations or who had turned to potato growing. Greater access to cars and better roads led to the formation of the Augusta Margaret River Tourist Bureau in 1956 and signalled, or hinted at, an interest in tourism. At the time, chief among these was the summer influx of holidaymakers from Perth keen to enjoy the area's pristine surfing beaches. However, times were tough, the local economy was stagnant and the outlook bleak. The possibility of a new and profitable primary industry was welcome news to the district.

Kevin Cullen approached the task of organising the meeting with his typical ebullience. Not only did he organise the speakers and the framework of the meeting, he also encouraged individuals to attend. Bill Minchin, the only farmer to plant vines as a direct result of the meeting, attended 'at the behest' of his GP. Cullen's decision to invite John d'Espeissis, a trusted grazier from Cape Naturaliste, to chair the meeting was inspired as it gave the gathering a sense of gravitas. d'Espeissis' father, Jean Marie Adrian (Adrian), had helped establish the State's Bureau of Agriculture and worked as its viticultural and horticultural adviser before taking on significant agricultural roles for the government. His magnum opus, the *Handbook of Horticulture & Viticulture of Western Australia* (1895), was regarded by people such as Tom Cullity, Bill Pannell and David Watson as the definitive text on the subject in the 1960s. Adrian d'Espeissis also helped established the Santa Rosa vineyard (later Valencia) in 1895 and was a pioneer of large-scale viticulture in the Swan Valley. Houghton winemaker Jack Mann once referred to him as the father of the wine industry in Western Australia.

At Cullen's request, Gladstones wrote a letter to the *Busselton Margaret Times* which was published on 14 July 1966, a week before the meeting. In it he set out his belief that the area around Margaret River and north to Yallingup and Vasse had an ideal climate for viticulture. He noted that the high winter rainfall would be a drawback except where there were well drained soils. What was needed were 'practical trials backed by expert advice'.

On the day of the meeting, John Lawson wrote a full-page story in the *Countryman* under the headline *South West is tipped for top-quality wines.* He acknowledged the influence of Professor Harold Olmo and promoted Gladstones' claim that the climate and soils of Capel, Busselton, Cowaramup, Margaret River, Witchcliffe and Forest Grove could do better than Mount Barker, 'where the Department of Agriculture will plant a five-acre (two hectares) experimental vineyard later this year'. He noted that Gladstones believed that first priority should be given to Vasse and Cowaramup, with the Department of Agriculture's research station at Bramley a particularly well-suited site for one of the plantings. While the meeting was attended by at least 100 enthusiastic and interested locals, Gladstones' presentation had its most significant impact on Bill Minchin. He was impressed by 'John's lecture on climate, and [in particular, its] relation to sunlight and temperature. He'd done a comprehensive study of this area and likened it to regions of France where some of the best wines were being produced. He thought there was no reason why this shouldn't become an area to produce wine.'

Cullen invited State Viticulturist Bill Jamieson to attend the meeting to answer questions from the floor. In his internal memo, following the invitation, Jamieson commented that:

Because of varying soil types, it may be difficult to find large enough areas in the one locality to encourage a well-established wine firm to commence operations in this area. It would be well for me to attend the public meeting to point out what is involved ... and give an estimate of the productions costs and returns per acre that could be expected if suitable varieties were planted and a winery was established in this region.

Cullen had invited an adviser from the local Department of Agriculture to offer a hypothetical farm budget including the anticipated return from wine grapes. His inaccurate figures prompted Bill Jamieson to issue a press release in August, which was subsequently reported in *The West Australian,* the *Farmers' Weekly* and the *Countryman.* The statement urged caution, explaining that, while the area's soils appeared promising, the quality of table grapes was unproven. Further, he noted that there was no possibility of a commercial winery being established to process grapes. Jamieson asserted that the information reported at the meeting, which suggested that *20 acres of vines controlled by one man could return an annual profit of $4,000,* was exaggerated. He stated that a figure of about $80 an acre profit (or $1,600 for twenty acres) was more likely. He went on to say that he had made *no suggestion to plant trial plots of grape vines as soon as possible* but advocated further examination of the soils at the end of winter before trial plots were established. While he believed that such trial plots offered the quickest way to assess the area's potential for making light, dry wines, he stressed the difficulty of making and evaluating wines from such trial plots. Jamieson concluded by offering the Department of Agriculture's advice on vine growing in addition to supplying cuttings to anyone wishing to become involved in viticulture.

John Gladstones was disappointed by the tone of the release although it is difficult to determine whether this was because of what Jamieson said or the impact of negative headlines which accompanied each of these articles: *The West Australian* (17 August) *Busselton Warned on Grapes;Farmers' Weekly* (18 August) *Commercial Wine Grapes Unlikely at Busselton* and the *Countryman* (18 August) *South-West wine grape growing 'not practical'.* He sought to correct the impression with a Letter to the Editor in the *Countryman,* which was published on 25 August. While agreeing with Jamieson's suggestion for caution, he stressed *that the climate of the area could be uniquely suited for the production of wine grapes of the highest quality.* He urged the planting of trial plots *which, with expert supervision, could yield very valuable information.*

As a result of the public meeting, the Vasse Viticultural Society was formed with a committee of John d'Espeissis (President), Sue Juniper (Secretary) and Joy Minchin (Treasurer). While it did not achieve a great deal in its short life, it did provide a forum for those interested in becoming involved in viticulture. It was another supportive voice for wine in the community.

On their behalf, Kevin Cullen wrote to the Minister of Agriculture, Stuart Bovell, requesting that *a small experimental planting of a high-quality table wine variety be established in a selected suitable area by the Department of Agriculture* and *that help be given, in the form of vine-cuttings and advice, to those farmers who are prepared to established pilot plots in 1966 and 1967.* The request for an experimental planting was politely ignored but the department, or more accurately, Bill Jamieson (most often in his own time), gave unstintingly of his knowledge to anyone interested in planting vines.

John Gladstones believed that the public meeting was significant in that it raised awareness of his paper and his views on viticulture and a wine industry in a region that was struggling for economic survival. However, he said, 'it only had limited effect on the developments that followed.' Ironically, it was the controversy caused by the Department of Agriculture's press release and the negative headlines that fuelled interest in the possibilities of grape growing.

Chapter 8

Bill Minchin and the First Plantings

Bill Minchin was the first to plant a vineyard in the Margaret River region after John Gladstones' 1966 paper recommended the area as having excellent potential for quality viticulture and the 21 July 1966 public meeting in Busselton reinforced that idea. Minchin spoke to State Viticulturist Bill Jamieson after the meeting telling him he had some of the land Jamieson had described as perfect for growing grapes and the next morning the pair met again at Minchin's Jindong property. They walked around the paddocks digging holes, looking for gravelly dirt with a friable clay subsoil. 'We decided that we would plant it on the very hardest condition. Basically, because if you could produce grapes on that without irrigation, it would be very revealing to what could be done here,' Minchin said. A gentle slope leading down to the Carbunup River towards the back of the block was chosen as the (0.2-hectare) vineyard site, with riesling planted on higher ground than the cabernet sauvignon.

Minchin explained he took on the challenge of planting a vineyard to show what the area could do. Both Bill and his wife, Joy, were fascinated by the experience but it was never intended as a commercial venture. They made up to 230 bottles a year for seven years. 'I gave bottles to different people and relatives but we kept most of it and most of it wasn't drunk. We didn't drink much of it ourselves,' he said in 1996.

Jamieson gave detailed advice at every stage of the planting process. Bill Minchin said: 'It was entirely reliant on Bill Jamieson and Dorham Mann ... they were very keen and were down here frequently. The ground was deep ripped and all the timber removed. As I only had a 35 – horse power tractor, it took quite a bit of effort. In a very short period of time, we had all the big wineries from the Eastern States visiting us to check what was going on and every one of them, when they visited this little plot, were absolutely amazed.'

Because of the scope of the planting, it was not a costly exercise. The vines were planted by Joy Minchin and Robin Harricks, a biochemist and colleague of hers at the Busselton Hospital. Bill Minchin laboured on the block in the time he had spare from milking 100 cows and feeding 100 calves and tending his farm. The cuttings had been donated by Jack Mann and no fertiliser was used. There were few problems with disease or birds. The vines were rabbit-proof fenced and the kangaroos had sufficient food to leave the grapes alone. Possums took all of the first vintage of cabernet grapes and were such a problem that Bill had to get a permit to remove them.

One of the Minchins' cabernets from their Merrifields property. Photo courtesy Minchin family

The first wine from the property, Merrifields, was riesling from the 1969 vintage. Subsequently, until the 1976 vintage, both a riesling and a cabernet sauvignon were produced. The grapes were stripped from the bunch and pressed in an old milk vat which had been waxed. Joy and daughter Kate trampled the grapes. A yeast starter, supplied by Jamieson, kicked off fermentation. Pressing took place in a waxed wooden drawer with holes in the side and bottom. Bill stood on the lid and pressed the juice, which flowed on plastic into containers. It was matured in sealed demijohns and then bottled. The bottles had been purchased from marine dealers in Perth, steam cleaned, and sealed using Tom Cullity's borrowed corking machine. All pretty primitive, yet effective. The first tasting of the Minchin riesling happened by accident. Di Cullen was visiting and was asked by Joy what she would like to drink. When she asked for a sherry, Joy proceeded to open an unlabelled flor sherry which Jack Mann had given Bill. Di's astonishment when she took her first sip led them to realise that Joy had opened the first of the unlabelled riesling bottles.

Bill Jamieson showed Minchin how to prune and returned (in the second year, in the company of Tom Cullity) each year for five more years at pruning time, Minchin recalled later. Cullity was Kate Minchin's heart specialist; she had been born with a hole in the heart. He used to call in regularly once he had bought the Vasse Felix property and always checked Kate over, 'which was exceptionally good of him,' said Bill.

Bill, Joy, Penny, Kate, Pippa and Michael Minchin in 1973. Photo courtesy Minchin family

Fifteen years of hard toil on the farm took their toll on Minchin, as did the recurrence of back pains—the legacy of an injury suffered during his war service. He decided to stop milking cows, which provided the farm with regular cashflow, and switch to beef cattle, where income came from the annual sales. Minchin realised that, if he did this, he would need another source of income. He and farm consultant David Harricks started a successful fencing contracting business, which brought him into contact with the timber treatment company Hicksons. They offered him the job of sales manager and then as State manager, a position he held until 1984. A consequence of his long absences from the farm was that the cattle continually broke into the vineyard and damaged the vines so Minchin pulled out the vines after the 1976 vintage.

In 1977, while the family was in Perth, the house burnt down and the family lost everything, including all their wine stocks. As Ian Minchin says in his family biography: *There is nothing left, only twisted metal and melted glass. Their lives at the farm have been reduced to ash and the children are traumatised by the scene of complete destruction.* At the time, the police informed them of the fire, they were dining with a friend who was general manager of Cullity Timbers. He offered them timber at cost. *Bill chooses the logs to construct the house, cuts them to length himself and machines them to create two flat sides.* [Brother] *Ross undertook the construction, culminating*

*in a house which is very comfortable
...* This remained the Minchin family
home until 1996.

Friends who had been given bottles
of the Minchin wine returned them so
that Bill had a small stock with which
to remember the adventure. He was
also able to share a bottle of the 1975
Cabernet Sauvignon with brother Ross
in 1995. 'It was just out of this world
and the most incredible wine we'd
drunk.'

Postscript

Ironically, there had been a vineyard
on the Minchin property in the 1930s
and 1940s. Max (Marko) Suda planted
'a couple of acres' of vines there. Our
information came from Albert Credaro,
who remembers seeing the vines as he
was coming through Max's place on his
way to and from North Jindong Primary
School in about 1939 ('just after the
War started').

Chapter 9

The Path to Vasse Felix

When he made the decision to go further south and plant vines, Tom Cullity had no idea what form of organisation would suit the venture best: he asked himself should he operate as a sole trader, in a partnership, or collaborate with others. He had no clear view on the matter. Kevin Cullen's enthusiasm and their wide-ranging discussions over the first weekend in May 1966 provided a starting point. He wasted no time in throwing himself into the business of learning more about viticulture and winemaking. He had meetings in quick succession with the Australian Wine Research Institute (AWRI), the West Australian Agriculture Department, and the Institute of Agriculture at the University of Western Australia. While Cullity possessed abundant personal drive, the fact that State Viticulturist

Bill Jamieson warned him that only five per cent of new agricultural ventures succeeded added to his determination.

On May 1966, he flew to Adelaide for a two-hour meeting at the AWRI with its Director, John Fornachon, Senior Research Officer Bryce Rankine and E.W. (Wally) Boehm, Senior Research Officer at the South Australian Department of Agriculture. He was keen to talk about his plans for planting a vineyard in Margaret River. The South Australians were generally supportive of Cullity's plan to encourage local farmers to grow grapes for his winery. They noted, however, that such schemes had succeeded elsewhere when there was a pool of skilled labour and wine knowledge. Tom realised that this would be a key problem in getting established in Margaret River.

They talked about the sourcing of vine cuttings; the best soil types; the need for irrigation; cultivation of the soil; the choice of grape varieties; and pests such as birds and rabbits. The group told Cullity that they did not believe that a trial planting that year would achieve anything worthwhile and that 'a year lost in planning now would be valuable later'. Bryce Rankin showed Tom his small model winery and discussed research into vinification.

Cullity commented later that he remembered visiting John Fornachon just before he died (in 1966). 'I can still see him looking at me in a detached and tolerant sort of way and saying "Goodbye. Come back with some wine in four years and we'll see."

As was his custom, Tom Cullity sent a summary of the meeting to the group at the AWRI and received a detailed letter from Wally Boehm clarifying some of the details they had discussed. Cullity noted the available climatic data on the South West and the criteria for successful viticulture—in d'Espeissis' classic *Handbook of Horticulture & Viticulture* (his edition was 1921)—and decided to work on the notion that Olmo's and Gladstones' indications of a favourable climate were correct; and that well-drained gravelly soil, growing large red gums and only a small amount of jarrah, would offer the best sites for viticulture.

He followed up his reading by contacting John Gladstones, who was generously and practically supportive. Gladstones commented, 'He came and talked to me and we discussed it at considerable depth (I think you can well imagine the kind of depth it would be, knowing Tom), and that was what decided him to seek out a block down there.' In a letter (23 June 1966) to Cullity, Gladstones tackles his queries about the impact of temperature and climate on viticulture in the region and makes a case that the best sites are likely to lie on or east of the coast road (Caves Road) from north of Cowaramup to 'perhaps' Yallingup. He added a page of *Points on looking for vine soil.* In reply to Cullity's invitation to come down one weekend, he pleaded a heavy workload but offered to visit 'when you reach the stage of having some definite spots in mind'. Later in the winter, after Cullity had chosen the site that would become Vasse Felix, he and Bill Jamieson visited together and gave it their seal of approval. Jamieson also indicated that cabernet sauvignon, malbec and riesling cuttings would be the varieties available for planting in the near future. They discussed the handbook on which Dorham Mann was working at the request of Cullity. It would give detailed advice on wine husbandry for West Australian conditions. Perhaps, most importantly, Jamieson and Gladstones reinforced the view of the AWRI group, telling Cullity unequivocally that it would be best to plant cuttings directly in the vineyard, not this year, but the next.

Jamieson also suggested that one two-acre (0.8 hectares) vineyard would be more likely to receive support than several smaller ones. In his letter to Cullen (3 June), Cullity suggested a major change to the plans they had made back in May for one two-acre vineyard rather than five smaller plots.

The Search for a Site

Tom Cullity was adamant that he did not attend the public meeting on 21 July 1966. This is scarcely surprising given that its purpose was to publicise Gladstones' paper and to encourage farmers to consider becoming involved in viticulture. By that stage, Tom was already clearly committed. Additionally, the meeting was held on a Thursday and he would have found it difficult to be there given his work commitments in Perth.

He believed that he attended two gatherings in the winter of 1966. One of these was almost certainly a meeting of the Vasse Viticultural Society. Tom believed that he was attending the meeting to describe his idea of starting a vineyard to interested farmers and others.

Tom Cullity was irritated by all the social talk about getting involved in viticulture—'putting rain gauges on everybody's farm, getting microclimates'—and he was feeling increasingly concerned about his isolation, 'because you're just intruding in a closed community down there'. He explained: 'Because of the Cullens, I met Geoff and Sue Juniper, Bill and Joy Minchin, Henry and Maureen Wright, the Helmsleys, Jim McCutcheon and others who seemed a sort of set, all countrymen and knowing the area, and all benign in attitude to what may have seemed at the time just another of many over-enthusiastic notions by impractical people coming into the country. With the help of my new contacts, I spent the winter (of 1966) digging holes with an auger on various apparently suitable properties. The reason for this was to make sure that the soil was well-drained, the annual rainfall being fifty inches, and the notion being that spring water-logging would be a threat on unsuitable soils. I would have been floundering if it hadn't been for them. I was walking over people's properties and I used to ask if I could dig a hole. Some would say no and some would say, "Can you close the gate after you". I must have looked at twenty or thirty places one way or another. Just south of Busselton's flat, relatively poorly drained basin, in the vague area of Cowaramup (now more often referred to as Wilyabrup), seemed the main place to search for a small area of gravelly loam over clay with predominantly red gum vegetation—this latter indicating good internal drainage. A south-eastern slope as protection against the north-western spring gales would be ideal at flowering time.'

Looking for Vasse Felix

Sometime in the winter of that year (probably during June), for reasons that he chose not to articulate, Cullity decided that he needed to go it alone and become involved in both the growing of the grapes and the making of the wine. He decided that it was time for action. 'What was needed was a firmly-directed individual effort that was reasonably well-informed and carried out, and would take years of application to assess.' The chilly words of the great German pathologist, Rudolf Virchow, seem apposite: 'Speculation is the sterile fruitage of an infertile mind—virtue resides in the hard labour of verification.'

Although Cullity believed that 'Kevin was always for progress and action', he was convinced he was right to go it alone. This decision did not mean an end to the help that Kevin was prepared to offer the Perth-based cardiologist. Cullen mentions in his autobiography:

'In 1966 I'd helped Tom Cullity choose his land for Vasse Felix, by accompanying him as he dug hole after hole on farmers' properties (usually without their permission) until he finally made his choice.'

An ideal eight-acre (3.2 hectares) site—red gum country with well-drained loamy soil—was eventually found on Harmans South Road (now Tom Cullity Drive), not far from the Cullen farm. It was Sussex location 1669. The farmer, Bill Osborn, refused to sell Tom the relatively small parcel of land. It if hadn't been for Cullen's local knowledge and possibly the fact that Osborn worked for him, the deal would not have been struck. The Cullen land was contiguous with Osborn's farm so Kevin brokered a deal to give Osborn sixteen acres (6.4 hectares) of his land on their eastern boundary, alongside Wilyabrup Brook, for the eight-acre (3.2 hectares) vineyard site.

September 1967, Vasse Felix land is cleared, stakes ready for planting with the Osborn house in the background. Courtesy Vasse Felix

Ariane Cullen commented:

'Dad, believing that it would take someone of Tom's ilk to get the industry started, talked Mum into the deal. Tom and Dad were obsessive "medico" types, long-trained in, and driven for life to pursue, the scientific method (and frustrated in equal measure by the vagaries of nature). However, I believe these qualities were necessary for, or at least greatly facilitated, the extraordinary early success of the region.'

Tom Cullity paid $150 an acre for the sixteen acres. In an interview in 2000, he said, 'I had to pay a mint! And it was the astonishing sum of seventy-five bucks [pounds] an acre, fenced and under pasture. Oh, gosh! Seventy-five bucks. And they thought that they were robbing me. And I thought that they were too. Little did I know!'

Cullity was taken aback by Cullen's generosity of spirit, his ability to negotiate with the locals, and to get things done. 'He just organised that [the sale of the land] and rang me up. But that's the sort of thing he did. He'd just take over and do it.' Tom acknowledged his gratitude in the comment (repeated several times in his writings): 'This was vital, and if it had not been for that, I am far from sure that I would have continued.'

Chapter 10

The Juniper Planting: A Diversion

A planting on the Juniper property in September 1966 has generated a great deal of controversy, mainly because of claims made about it. In many ways, it is irrelevant—the planting failed and, according to the best viticultural advice, it was always going to fail. This was also not the first planting of modern times in the region. John Gladstones, however, believes that from a historical viewpoint, it matters. In his as-yet unpublished autobiography, he says, *I doubt that any of us dared to imagine that the seeds then being sown would within 50 years grow into a world-renowned viticultural region. Seen in that context, how it started will always be of historical interest.*

An email (dated 4 Jun 2005) from Sue Juniper, on whose farm the vines were planted, drew the authors' attention to the issue. She complained that an article written by Peter Forrestal perpetuated *a myth that abounds regarding the first plantings between the Capes in the 1960s. The prevailing story is that the Cullens were responsible for a trial planting of vines in 1966 in the Cowaramup area. This is not true and if not corrected the facts will be lost to history.*

In his autobiography, Gladstones revised his earlier account of this planting, explaining that he had written in good faith. His *information came from Di Cullen, sometime after Kevin's death, and she and later their daughter, Vanya, had the clear, and I am sure genuine, impression that Kevin and the Junipers had personally carried out the planting, or at least that the Junipers had done it on Kevin's behalf. In any case, the Cullens took the view in later years that the experimental plot had been a Cullen enterprise with Juniper collaboration, and on that basis claimed in their publicity to have planted (or been involved in the planting of) the first vines of Margaret River's modern viticultural era.*

Collaborating with Kevin Cullen

The Juniper planting had its genesis in discussions between Tom Cullity and Kevin Cullen in early May 1966 (see Chapter 6). Cullity's original plan was to find five suitable plots of land around the region and invite the farmers who owned that land to either sell or lease him an acre or so and plant and maintain a tiny vineyard to supply grapes to a winery he would build. Initially, the two worked collaboratively and proposed a trial planting that year. Cullity kept meticulous notes on the meetings and phone discussions he had with a range of experts during May and June and shared them with Cullen.

Two major differences between them surfaced in June 1966. Bill Jamieson and Dorham Mann advised Cullity to plant one two-acre (0.8 hectares) vineyard rather than several smaller plots. They also agreed with advice given to Cullity by the AWRI that a planting in 1966 would be counterproductive. While Cullity accepted both of these suggestions, Cullen appears to have wanted to continue with the original plan.

In the same letter in which he invited Bill Jamieson to answer questions from the floor at the public meeting, Kevin Cullen put the case for a 1966 planting:

I am most anxious to get planted in September 1966 in the Cowaramup area this year to compare this wine with the Burekup vintage. [Obviously referring to a wine Cullity had made from his Burekup vineyard.]

This small area will probably have to be written off, but if the soil were cultivated now, do you think we could have some cabernet cuttings—put them in under expert instructions? The farmer is very anxious (with me) to do this and he would till this area in the hope that you will judge the soil type as suitable (already inspected by Cullity and myself as very likely to be so)...

Name of the farmer—Juniper.

I realise this is not ideal to cultivate it now, but surely it is worth one small pilot plot.

The incredibly busy lives of the key participants provide an important element in understanding the events leading up to the planting of the Juniper vineyard. From May till July, in addition to his work as a GP, which included being on duty one night in three, Kevin Cullen took on the organisation of the public meeting. He also spent time canvassing support for the event. His major preoccupation that year was working on the Busselton Health Study, specifically, garnering the support of the CSIRO and Perth hospitals, and preparing for the first round of medical examinations of the Busselton population late in 1966.

At the time, Tom Cullity was Senior Visiting Physician in the Department of Cardiology at Royal Perth Hospital and was also lecturing in cardiology at the University of Western Australia. The demanding eight-hour round trip by car to Margaret River, at least every second weekend, added stress to a busy life.

As will become clear, 'the farmer', Geoff Juniper, was nowhere near as enthusiastic about the planting as Kevin Cullen suggests above. In his reply to

Cullen, Bill Jamieson explained that it was already too late in the season to deep-rip the plot, so the trial would be unlikely to succeed. He suggested that, as a minimum, the ground should be broken up before planting by shallow ploughing to a depth of about ten inches (twenty-five centimetres). This was not done. Bill Jamieson used the request for cuttings to seek the approval of his boss, Harley Powell, to support the proposal to establish experimental plots. Powell agreed that Jamieson could provide cuttings and support, as the department would be interested in the results, but there would be no financial commitment.

Geoff Juniper, left, with Tom Cullity wearing his ever-present beret at Vasse Felix in September 1967. Photo courtesy of Vasse Felix

Despite the differences of opinion that emerged in June, Cullity and Cullen spent a considerable amount of time either separately or together during the winter of 1966 checking soil profiles around Wilyabrup, looking for suitable land. Bill Jamieson lent a hand, identifying half a dozen specific lots that he felt met the criteria.

Cowaramup farmer Peter Clews was in his kitchen when he heard sounds outside the window. On investigating, he found his GP, Kevin Cullen, and another person (he is certain it was Gladstones but it was more likely to have been Jamieson) looking intently at a trench he had recently dug. They explained that they were looking at its soil profile to see if it would make good viticultural land. He showed them over the block, which they admired. Jamieson commented on how the gentle slope would make for excellent vineyard territory. A week or so later, Tom Cullity turned up and explained that he was following up on the visit of his colleagues. Clews commented, 'Dr Cullity said that patch was the best block of land he had seen for grape growing.' He did not want to buy the whole block, just three acres (1.2 hectares) of prime vineyard land. Clews wasn't interested in selling, partly because that block was the path along which his cows were accustomed to travel twice daily to be milked. Clews ploughed up part of an adjacent block but Cullity wasn't interested. His proposal involved Clews planting and tending the vines. In return, Tom would pay any expenses. Years later, Clews remained surprised that no mention was made of payment for the labour involved. (Subsequently, that adjacent block was bought by the Steve and Helen Palmer and became the site of Cape Grace, Settlers Ridge and the Palmers' small vineyard project.)

Tom Cullity found another ideal site in the Wilyabrup area on land owned by John Foster. He offered to buy a one-acre (0.4 hectares) vineyard block and finance a vineyard. John Foster chose not to take up his offer although he subsequently became involved in viticulture.

The Planting on Juniper's block

Geoff Juniper was working for the Cullens at the time and the first block to be identified was on his land in Wilyabrup. This block became part of a subdivision in 1969 and was bought by their neighbour, Doug Brockman. The rest of the property was sold to Henry and Maureen Wright and became Wrights vineyard and winery. It was sold in 1998 and is now the successful

Juniper Estate. Maurice Cullity, Tom's uncle, worked for the Department of Agriculture and had told his nephew that the going price for land was $92 an acre. Sue Juniper explained much later:

'Tom comes to us and says, well I'd like that acre right on the road, opposite our front veranda [close to the present-day Vasse Felix] ... and I'll give you $95 for it.' Geoff Juniper added, 'He said, "I'll put $95 in your hot little hand." The Junipers refused Tom's offer but agreed to put in half an acre of riesling and cabernet.

Winter 1966 saw a change in priorities for Cullity and Cullen, though they remained friends. Cullen offered to sell Cullity the block on his farm that in 1971 would become his vineyard. Jamieson urged Tom to buy the land as he believed it would be an ideal vineyard site but Cullity declined. Cullen then showed great generosity of spirit in brokering the deal which enabled Cullity to buy the block that would become Vasse Felix. Once he had purchased the land and the focus was on preparing the Vasse Felix soil for planting in 1967, one suspects he lost interest in the Juniper plot, though Sue Juniper remembers he did pay for a rabbit proof fence to protect the vineyard.

In spring 1966, Tom Cullity and his vineyard worker, Roderigo Dellavanza (Della), forged ahead and planted an acre of cabernet sauvignon and shiraz on Sue and Geoff Juniper's property in Wilyabrup against all expert advice. All involved knew of these comments and can have had no expectation that the planting would succeed.

In 2006, Sue Juniper commented in a letter to Jodie Pannell: *At this time Geoff was working on a farm owned by Kevin and Di Cullen on Caves Road at Wilyabrup. As we remember, there was never any mention from them that they would plant vines. Indeed, the opposite appeared to be the case.*

Having talked to Sue Juniper, Shelley Cullen emailed her siblings (25 Oct 2013) saying 'It seems that Di said that she also didn't want to plant vines on our farm land as she felt she would be left to do the physical work (true!)

and also because it was her prime cattle country and hay block.'

Sue Juniper declared, 'We were doing it for Tom. Tom financed it all.' He also stayed with the Junipers regularly until the shed at Vasse Felix was built in 1968. She remembered with affection: 'He used to come down every second weekend in his Peugeot and he'd bring down a chicken that his wife, Veronica, had cooked and a beautiful bottle of wine.' The Junipers came to love German riesling as a result of his visits.

The cuttings for the Juniper plot came from the Swan Valley Research Station. Cullity brought them down and kept them in a yellow sand pile on Vasse Felix only a few hundred metres from the Juniper's plot, directly across the road. As Geoff Juniper didn't appear interested and Cullity had read books and made enquiries about the treatment of cuttings, he watered them until he replanted them on the Juniper's land.

In an interview Cullity described how the trial vineyard was planted with Ray Jordan:

'Della and I went down there one Saturday afternoon for about two hours. They'd put a disc through that had scratched the surface. And Geoff happened to find a dead cow in the back paddock somewhere, conveniently, you know, when the work appeared. So, he disappeared.

'I thought this is not much good, I'm not going to get anywhere here. Della and I slaved away and I think we planted about ... well I can't remember now, but I remember begrudging the time that I just spent away from my own place. We planted I think about four or five rows and I said to Della, "Why don't you stay here all afternoon and give them a hand?"

'And then Ricky Cullen appeared ... dressed in grey gabardine trousers, with a white shirt and polished black shoes. Didn't look like he was ready to work. He had been sent down by his father, as his father said, "You go down and find out how to do it." So, Rick came down and I showed him how to do this and that and the other thing.

'Della was a good worker ... there wouldn't have been much left.'

As Geoff Juniper was helping the Cullens on their farm, he had access to the tractor and Sue remembers two occasions when the Cullen kids helped them water the vines. 'They used to love the excuse to be able to drive the tractor. That was the Cullens only involvement with that acre of vines.' Stewart and Digby Cullen (then aged thirteen and fifteen) remember those occasions as well, and even more vividly, the blisters they got from hoeing the vines.

On an afternoon in 1967 or 1968, Tom Cullity was with his nephew, Tom, at Vasse Felix when Kevin Cullen turned up in his car and walked to the gate. Cullity immediately launched into a vehement and voluble string of complaints about the neglected vines at the Junipers, which he claimed were 'a nest of pestilence and disease' and were not being looked after. He claimed vociferously that they should be ploughed in, otherwise he might go broke because of the threat of disease spreading to his vines.

Cullen rejected this assertion just as vehemently and at similar volume. The argument became more heated and the language more imaginative, colourful and, says the younger Tom remembering in vivid detail nearly fifty years later, increasingly *ad hominem* as it progressed. Remarkably, he recalled, there was not a swear word among the invective. Simply a magnificent essay in argument using the full gamut of the English language or at least that part of the language devoted to abuse, insult and vituperation. At last, the two red-faced middle-aged men retired to their corners, and Cullity returned to digging a hole on his property.

According to the Junipers, the planting was a failure and produced no grapes and so the vines were neglected. 'We had lost interest in our grapes. We are not proud of it.'

One of the claims made on the Cullen website that Sue Juniper was unhappy about was that, "as a result of the success of the Juniper planting, the Cullens decided to plant a larger vineyard on their farm in 1971". Sue Juniper reiterates that the planting failed and asserts that the Cullens planted in 1971 for unrelated reasons. Kevin Cullen says in his autobiography that they were approached by Terry Merchant (who had been working for Tom Cullity) to enter into a partnership with him. Di Cullen told Sue Juniper that she was only prepared to go ahead with the 1971 planting at the Cullen property because of that partnership, as Terry Merchant would have the responsibility for the venture.

Sue Juniper remembers Tom Cullity and Terry Merchant visiting to let her and Geoff know, as a courtesy, that its new owner, Doug Brockman, was going to plough in the unproductive vines.

Some Conclusions

In recounting some of the events of 1966, we are faced, more so than with most other aspects of this history, with the frailty and inconsistency of human memory. Sue Juniper's memory remains acute. The two inaccuracies in her account are due to incomplete knowledge at the time. She knew that Tom Cullity had approached Peter Clews and assumed that he had agreed to plant vines for Cullity. She was unaware of the discussions between Cullity and Cullen in early May and the plans that they made for a trial vineyard.

In 1982, Barry Brady wrote 'Di believes she helped plant the first vines in the area on a friend's property.' This is a far cry from her claim of twenty years later.

Similarly, Tom Jenkins in his 1997 book *A Vision of Fine Wine* says, *The Cullens knew that people were experimenting with wine. Di remembers 'Joy and Bill Minchin planted some vines in Jindong in 1966. Tom Cullity had trial planted vines near Bunbury. Kevin's maternal grandfather had grown vines on land that is now Clark Street and a sports oval in Bunbury. So, once they got interested, Tom and Kevin went around digging holes in all sorts of places, looking for the best soil. Kevin also tried to get other people to plant, to get an industry going'.*

In his autobiography published in 1994, Kevin wrote: *Before he sold out, Geoff, in partnership with us, had previously planted Margaret River's first acre of wine vines.* In interviews conducted in 1997 and 2000, Di claimed that the Cullens had planted on Juniper land in 1966. Because these views have been given wide currency, we believe it necessary to make it clear that we do not believe these claims can be substantiated. Furthermore, they could be interpreted as casting doubt on Tom Cullity's status as the viticultural pioneer of Margaret River.

Like John Gladstones, we see the passing of time and the tricks that memory plays as the most likely reasons for these views to surface.

Chapter 11

Vasse Felix: Dawn of a New Era

Dr Tom Cullity worked full time as a cardiologist at Royal Perth Hospital and was able to have most weekends off. He would leave Perth shortly after 3.00am and make the slow four-hour trip to Cowaramup, ready to start work on Saturday with the Rossis on the vineyard then drive back to Perth late on Sunday night. For years, he'd make this 600-kilometre return trip more than once a fortnight.

He needed someone to supervise the property when he wasn't around. 'Geoff Juniper lived directly opposite and was prepared to keep an eye on things while I was away. I used to sleep in the back of a Valiant station-wagon in the Junipers' front yard until a shed was built. The Junipers were kind friends. I remember for some reason a bowl of stew and dumplings that Geoff's mother, Linda Osborn, made for him when he was a temporary bachelor and of which I had the benefit.'

Tony Rossi and his sons, Joe and Dominic, had worked with Cullity on the Burekup vineyard and Tom was quick to realise that their skilled labour would be 'utterly essential' if he was to achieve anything from Perth. They became the core of his workforce at Vasse Felix, driving down from Brunswick Junction to meet him at 8.00am on weekends and holidays.

The corrugated iron machinery shed, which was finished in 1968, included a two-by-five – metre room as owner's quarters. The building became the winery in 1971. The Rossis also slept in the shed. Cullity commented that 'they'd rise as soon as the sun came up and as soon as the sun went down, they'd come back to the shed—they brought most of the food—and they'd cook up spaghetti.' Daughters Veronica and Jude Cullity still remember their father talking about the Rossis—what they ate; how much they ate; and their home-made sausages and pasta (scarcely traditional Aussie fare in 1966). They remember, too, his tremendous respect for them: he had met no-one who worked so hard.

Tom Cullity's home away from home—the machinery shed at Vasse Felix. Photo courtesy Vasse Felix

His wife, Veronica, visited only rarely because there was nowhere suitable for her to stay. On those occasions, they would stay at the Margaret River or Geographe Bay Hotels and she would make pasties and sausage rolls for the group. The two older girls, Veronica and (especially) Jude, came more often. Jude remembers being pressured to accompany her father. 'I think he wanted the company although he would hardly talk on the way down and when we got there would send me off to amuse myself.'

Cullity reflected on the enormity of the task ahead: 'There was no back-up, no-one in the area with the slightest reliable knowledge about grapes or wine, and I knew nothing about gardening or horticulture, or wine-making. It was a long haul as adequate wine cannot be made until the vines are four years old and wine-making mistakes cannot be corrected for another year. There are many critical links in the chain and I had to work from the book and from seeking professional advice. This is no way to pursue a trade, an art, or a profession.'

He started to prepare the land for planting late in winter 1966. The Rossis began by building a rabbit and cattle-proof fence. Peter Middleton, an architect on legendary town planner Professor Gordon Stephenson's staff at the University of Western Australia, suggested the site of the future shed and small winery and laid out a plan for vine plantings as close to contours as possible. The land was then ripped by Stewart Melville with a three-pronged ripper to a depth of two feet to bring up stones and roots. About six trees were uprooted and removed. 'This was done in case the clay was compacted by cattle and also because any significant piece of wood could carry fungus infection in that high rainfall area. It was not uncommon to find a dead vine and, on digging beside it, a piece of wood with mushroom-like growths on it, and a characteristic odour. Fortunately, this was not often enough, in our case, to pose a real problem. The roots were burned and stones removed, which was quite a job. An Italian gardener, Claude Delfante, came down with me, an ex-miner, to explode and remove some larger granite. The land was also later ploughed with discs and harrowed to make a planting bed,' Cullity said.

Plastic drains were used in several of the wetter areas. 'I remember having my first attack of rapid cardiac arrhythmia on the riesling patch digging a drainage trench in the summer with a shovel.'

In August 1967, Thomas Brendan Cullity planted seven acres (2.8 hectares) of vines on the eight acre Vasse Felix property at Wilyabrup. The initial planting was four acres (1.6 hectares) of riesling, two (0.8 hectares) of cabernet sauvignon and a half-acre of both malbec and shiraz. He took Bill Jamieson's advice on what to plant. 'I had no knowledge of what varieties would be most suitable and I daresay nobody did, or even would until somebody did it and tried it out. I was the bellwether and the vineyard was the district's feasibility study,' he said.

Tom Cullity among the new vines at Vasse Felix.
Photo courtesy Vasse Felix

They made a fuss of the planting of the first vine. Cullity offered his 10-year-old daughter, Jude, the opportunity to plant the first vine. 'Tony Rossi dug the hole, cracked open a bundle of cuttings and handed me one. I put it in the hole, stomped it down and was told to walk away. I remember thinking, what's going on, and the men saying, "You mustn't look" One of the men performed an ancient fertilisation rite to launch the Margaret River wine industry.

The cuttings from the Swan Research Station had been quarantined and dipped in lime sulphur solution before planting and sprayed with wettable sulphur. Although they were not rooted cuttings, 98 per cent of them took. Cut-worms were discovered on one occasion and resulted in a widespread infestation. To combat this, the ground was dusted with arsenic.

In 1971, Cullity obtained, by conditional purchase, an adjacent 1.6-hectare block that had been a shire council gravel-pit and included some land that was suitable for viticulture. In 1973, he bought an adjoining block (5.6

hectares) to the west. The average price of the land for Vasse Felix, fenced and under pasture, was about $185 dollars per hectare ($75 per acre). Following the original 1967 plantings, 11.5 acres (4.6 hectares) of cabernet sauvignon was planted between 1970 and 1972. Under Cullity, Vasse Felix would have 7.5 hectares under vine by 1977, a winery shed, cellar, machinery shelter and manager's house.

Aerial view of the first three plantings of Vasse Felix, taken in 1985. Photo courtesy Vasse Felix

The Local Reaction

There was a lot of unwarranted cynicism in the region about viticulture, grapes and the doctors. Bill and Marian Leiper were cattle farmers and neighbours who became friends with Tom Cullity. In the early days, he would call in and have a beer with them. Bill used to spend the odd day 'ripping or ploughing or harrowing' at Vasse Felix. The Leipers attended the famous party he gave in 1972 to celebrate the first vintage. When he called in on his friends not long afterwards, Cullity asked Bill, 'What did you really think when I started here?'

'I thought you were stone raving bloody mad!'

'What do you think now?'

'Well I know who was mad, and it wasn't you!'

Those who knew Tom Cullity less well were more suspicious. 'I know that I was thought to be starting a wife-swapping colony, or a nudist colony. Or maybe both. I don't know.'

Shelley Cullen recalled a story from the early days which gives an indication of local sensitivities. Dry weather was vital to the success of the hay cutting season. Yet Cullity, who was a devout Catholic, told the locals that he had been to mass to pray for rain for the vines. They were hopping mad. As Shelley remembers, the rain descended for days on end ... the hay was ruined. Cullity's popularity plummeted even further. One incident remained a painful, lingering memory. 'I remember leaning on the fence one evening and I was dead tired. I was leaning on the fence and a car with two locals went past on Harman's Mill Road [now Tom Cullity Drive]. The husband was driving and there was a sort of a Doppler effect as his wife leaned out of the passenger-side window and called out, "Useless baaaastaaard". It was a bit discouraging. Because I was a useless bastard. I didn't know anything about anything. I had to learn.'

The Beginnings of an Industry

Tom Cullity said he initially thought of making enough wine for a family—'about 900 litres per year'. 'Only gradually did it become obvious that the cost and necessity of tractors, equipment and labour and everything else meant that a larger area had to be planted, for the same cost, if it was not to be only a millionaire's hobby. At that time, I was far from being in that category and was completely uninterested and far from skilled in financial matters.'

It was at this point that Tom Cullity moved from being 'a bellwether' and his vineyard from being the district's feasibility study to becoming the region's viticultural pioneer—its first vigneron; the pioneer who planted its first grapes, built its first winery and made its first wine. While others had planted grapes and made wine—from the Bussells in the 1830s to Bill Minchin in 1966—no one before Tom Cullity had possessed an understanding of what would be necessary to establish a viable wine industry and to articulate that understanding. It is noteworthy that those who followed immediately afterwards—the Pannells, the Hohnens and Margaret River Land Holdings, the

Cullens, Sandalford and Leeuwin Estate—either planted sizeable vineyards or extended their initial plantings as quickly as they could.

'Obviously I had to travel up and down and insist on detail and somebody had to be prepared to do it. The attitude suitable to intensive agriculture and critical wine-making procedures is foreign to the instincts of people who graze cattle and milk. The fact that we made any reasonable wine at all says more about the region's potential than if it had been started by seasoned professional winemakers.'

The Lagans

John Lagan and Eithne Sheridan emigrated from Omagh in Northern Ireland in 1967 and settled in Margaret River when it was a 'small, quiet, run-down, one-horse town, with a library, a few stores and a bank.' They serviced the town as its only resident doctors until 1998. The Lagans became part of the second wave of vignerons in Margaret River when they established Chateau Xanadu (now Xanadu) in 1977.

In his autobiography, John Lagan writes:

My first meeting with Dr Tom Cullity typified the man.

Eithne and I had been in Margaret River only a few days when he came striding through the door to introduce himself to Margaret River's new doctors, dressed in dirty trousers and shirt, and covered in dirt. He looked strange—up to his eyes in muck and dirt, as we would say in Ireland, and not like any cardiologist I'd ever seen. Unbeknownst to me at the time, he was on his way back to Perth having worked all weekend in his vineyard. He introduced himself, welcomed us to the region and we became firm friends.

We got to talking about wine, the Gladstones Report and the South West as a premier wine-growing region. Tom was a convert.

'Lagan,' he said, 'this is the future, buy a bit of land here and develop a vineyard. It will be difficult to do properly, but if you don't do it properly, don't do it at all.'

It was good advice.

The Difficulties

The Western Silvereyes were the big problem at first but it varied from year to year depending on when the marri trees came into blossom. If the marris flowered in time, the birds would leave the grapes pretty much undisturbed. Malbec was the first variety attacked at Vasse Felix. An indication of the birds' variable impact: in 1973, the grapes yielded seventy gallons (318 litres) of malbec whereas the following year, a miniscule seven gallons (31 litres) was vintaged.

Norman Robinson, who had degrees in modern languages and music from Cambridge, and was the CSIRO specialist in bird song, spent some time at the vineyard. Tom explained, 'We recorded a silvereye's feeding cry, devised a system of speakers to project it over the vineyard and hoped to jumble up their communication system. The neighbours didn't like it much and it didn't work. We also planted figs trees and early ripening grapes—malbec and red cardinals—around the vineyard as an offering to distract the birds from the more highly prized varietals.'

The best-known silvereyes story concerns the use of a hawk (brown falcon) to scare them off. After undergoing the requisite training, the hawk was released for the first time but disappeared never to be seen again. The story became part of local folklore and the central feature of Vasse Felix's emblem. A far less romantic version sees the hawk, which was raised on fresh chicken, taking to the skies in the direction of the nearby McClearys' farm. When Cath McCleary tells her husband that she's seen a hawk in the chook run, the farmer grabs his shotgun and the rest, including the hawk, is history.

Endlessly Inventive

The first vintage, off four-year-old vines, took place in 1971. The winery vats and machinery were built or purchased in the preceding months. There was nowhere locally Cullity could source equipment so he became endlessly inventive, even if there were occasionally chaotic results. His daughters thought their father hoped to revolutionise winemaking but they had their doubts. Jude remembers him having a large stainless-steel lid fabricated in Perth for the vats. When they drove down the next weekend and turned into the property they discovered the lid missing. Cullity apparently muttered an expletive and said, 'It was there at Harvey [130 kilometres north].' They found the lid there, 200 metres into the bush.

Cullity also asked the technician in the Surgery Department at RPH to devise an airlock to the 18-gallon (82 litres) metal beer keg in which the red wine was fermenting. It was fashioned from an intravenous drip and it needed to let the gas from fermentation escape without allowing any air into the tank. One Sunday morning after vintage in 1971, the Rossis and Cullity were sleeping in the shed when Tom woke and realised that something was wrong. He couldn't hear the 'tick, tick, tick' of the gas escaping from the keg. He tried to unscrew the attachment without success. He then hauled it outside onto the gravel area in front of the shed and set to it with a hammer and chisel. There followed a tremendous explosion, sending the lid of the cask cascading into the air and drenching Cullity and the shed bright pink with much of the crop of 1971 Vasse Felix Cabernet. When the Rossis emerged from the shed and saw Tom, they feared the worst. The problem was a grape pip, which had become stuck in one of the pipes.

The two pumps were old stainless-steel mono-pumps from the hospital heart lung machine. The crusher had hand-operated rollers and was bought second-hand in the Swan Valley. Cullity added an electric motor and made a small, stainless steel hopper. The crusher was small yet effective and prized for the gentle manner of its crush. David Gregg insisted that it was the secret of the Vasse Felix rieslings made up until 1978, when it needed to be replaced to accommodate the increased size of the crush. Gregg was far from happy about this and believed that the new machine was at least partly responsible for the diminished flavour of the rieslings.

In February 1971, the dual-purpose ferro-cement fermenter and storage tanks were made in Perth at the family firm, Cullity Timbers. It followed a Bordeaux design suggested by Bill Jamieson (double-walled to enclose a space for iced water to act as a coolant). This haphazard method of controlling temperature depended on the availability of ice, which had to be fetched from Margaret River ten kilometres away. In spite of this, they remained in use until a major revamp of the winery in 1985. David Gregg believed that one of their virtues was that they suited the soft, full-flavoured style of cabernet made at Vasse Felix. The skins were plunged three or four times a day for three days, during which time the seeds fell to the bottom of the vat. The winemaking team were careful not to disturb or crush the seeds, which would release their bitter tannins. The vats were kept covered to stop contamination from vinegar flies.

With the help of local Louis Bessetti, they build an extension to the shed with a gantry. This would lift the lids up and down. Terry Merchant recalls the lifting of the first tank with him in it. 'Then it comes off the gantry, didn't it? It bounced about six times so I don't know how I wasn't killed.'

Cullity had high grade stainless steel vats made by Mercury Metals, which were split into two 4,500 litre open fermentation tanks which could be converted for storage by bolting one on top of the other. Cullity decided on stainless steel tanks with a lid floating on top of the wine—an idea borrowed from Bordeaux. It was a good system to accommodate variable amounts of wine in a tank. It left a small gap around the edge, which was sealed with Ondina 18 a high purity paraffin oil. The problem was, as David Gregg commented later, how to get rid of the paraffin once the tank was emptied. He stored the paraffin oil used to seal the 1973 riesling and about two years later, short of bar oil for the chainsaw, he turned on the chainsaw and all around were these incredible riesling perfumes. Until that moment, he had always been disappointed at the lack of bouquet on the 1973 Vasse Felix Riesling. Tom Cullity was eventually convinced that closed stainless-steel tanks would be an improvement.

The Managers

After the Junipers sold their property and moved, Cullity employed Terry and Geraldine Merchant to manage the developing vineyard. They worked on it part time from mid-1968, and full time for a short period in 1971 after the manager's house had been finished. Terry Merchant had worked with John Kosovich in the Swan Valley and believed that viticulture and horticulture were pretty much the same thing. 'I mean, if you can grow flowers and vegetables, you can grow vines.' The Merchants were important pioneers in Margaret River not only for their role at Vasse Felix, but they also planted the first vines at Cullen and, in the nursery at Cullen, cuttings for the second planting at Cape Mentelle. They also had a vineyard of their own for a short time. Tony Rossi taught Terry to prune. 'He was a marvellous old fella and a great worker. It was pretty tough. His first lesson: never look up.

You keep working and then suddenly there are no vines in front of you. You've finished that row and so you get onto the next'.

Terry Merchant was teaching at the time but he and Geraldine would work for a couple of hours before school and about three hours afterwards. He remembers hoeing between the rows. 'Tom wanted all of the weeds out and didn't want chemicals used.' He also cleared the gravel pit, firstly of trees and then 'of hundreds and hundreds of tonnes of granite', which was later used by David Gregg for much of the construction work around Vasse Felix during the 1970s. They facilitated the clearing using home-made explosives of ammonium nitrate.

The Bellwether

Things were tough in the early days of Vasse Felix. The 1971 harvest was a disaster due to bunch rot and botrytis in the riesling and the marauding silvereyes. Tom Cullity recalled, 'I will not forget the exhaustion and disappointment [of that vintage].' A tiny amount of cabernet was bottled from the beer kegs in December and underwent the malolactic fermentation in bottle. It was eventually drunk by friends.

From a small crop the following year, Vasse Felix released its first wine—the 1972 Vasse Felix Riesling. It won a gold medal at the 1972 Perth Show in the small winemaker's class and a silver in the open division of the dry white wine class. This success created the 'bellwether' Cullity had yearned for: a wine that proved the region could produce quality table wine and vindicated John Gladstones' theories. 'It caused quite a stir at the Perth Show and the subsequent publicity brought Margaret River wines to the attention of the Australian public,' Cullity said. It was certainly something worth celebrating with a huge (or as Cullity put it, 'modestly famous') party. Gladstones had made a rare visit to Margaret River to help with the bottling of the 1972 Riesling and he returned for the party. He had to leave to drive back to Perth but slept in his car before setting off. Gladstones described the gold medal winner as 'a big wine with lovely aromas, reasonable body and a soft, balanced palate'.

According to local farmer Bill Leiper, Tom had invited 'half the district,' including the sceptics and the beer drinkers. The Minister for Agriculture, H.D. Evans, local politician Barry Blaikie, the committee of the Cowaramup Club and John Gladstones' parents were also in attendance. Garry Cullity writes that the 1972 Vasse Felix Riesling was presented in a tractor scoop packed with ice and available *ad libitum.* It was a hot night and the wine was drunk by many as though it were beer. Some of the farmers needed assistance to regain their homes. Stewart Melville said, 'It was like putting rocket fuel in my tractor.' Sue Juniper remembers that Clem Ryan was driven home to Cowaramup. 'We got him to the front door standing upright. His wife opened the door. He fell flat on his face.'

David and Anne Gregg

Cullity needed help with spraying for powdery mildew in January 1973 and so Bill Pannell introduced him to David Gregg. Shortly afterwards, Gregg applied for the advertised position of manager/winemaker and Cullity hired him. Gregg was born and raised in England's Lake District, studied dairy technology with a major in cheese production, and had worked for ten years with multinational food company Unilever. His professional life meant that he knew biochemistry and saw many similarities between cheesemaking and winemaking. 'As with cheesemaking, you prepared your starters and added it to the wine.' He studied with Dr Emma Mason, a microbiologist at the Lancashire County Institute of Agriculture, who was passionate about fruit wines. 'I learnt a tremendous amount from her: about flavour, balance and what preserved wine—tannin and acidity. Consequently, I made heaps of fruit wines before coming out to Australia.' Family stories had given him a fascination with Western Australia so the Greggs emigrated in 1971 to take up a farming venture in Busselton. David was thirty-one. When that venture failed, the Vasse Felix opportunity opened.

Gregg and wife Anne, pregnant with their second child, arrived on the vineyard on Sunday, 4 March in his potato truck with all their furniture on the back. He was up at 4.00am the next day to weld a refrigeration unit and be ready for the grapes to arrive at 6.00am. He worked for ninety-two hours in that first week. Frank Wilson's two key workers, Tony Rossi and Claude Delfante, came from Brunswick Junction and picked the riesling within a week. Tom Cullity noted that 'from the arrival of David Gregg as manager, my worries diminished'.

David Gregg, left, Coonawarra viticulturist Bob Hollick (Mildara) and Tom Cullity inspecting

some overly vigorous vines. Photo courtesy
Vasse Felix

It was an extremely hard life for the Greggs. The pay wasn't great: $60 a week with free accommodation in the manager's house and a modest allowance of wine ('carefully monitored' by David Gregg). He was clear on what his role was. Although his job was management he also needed to weld and use a brick trowel. 'But I certainly enjoyed it, and had great confidence that we could make some good wine,' he said later. From the 1975 vintage onwards, he was acknowledged on the wine labels as joint winemaker with Tom Cullity.

Anne Gregg worked alongside David doing anything that needed to be done: pump overs in the winery; tying up in the vineyard; serving at the cellar door; on the bottling, packaging and distribution of wine; researching for the mailing list. After five years of unpaid work, Anne gave Cullity an ultimatum and he agreed to pay her a modest wage.

Life at Vasse Felix in the 1970s

Like much of the work in preparing wine for sale these days, applying labels to bottles is automated. For the Greggs at Vasse Felix it was a painstaking and time-consuming process. Anne had to apply the glue on one side and then the other; leave it for about two minutes for the moisture to expand the label. 'If we put them on straight away, you got a creased label on the bottle. Not a good look. Wait two minutes and as the glue dried, it tightened the label up and you got a perfect finish.' She eventually managed to label 1,200 bottles (100 cases) a day.

Anne and David Gregg

At that time (and until 1976), the Western Australian Government Railways (WAGR) had a monopoly on transporting freight to and from Perth, which meant freight could not go past a railhead. Freight from Vasse Felix had to be collected from the Busselton Railway Station. When their first delivery of empty bottles arrived, the stationmaster rang up and said 'Your bottles have arrived. You'd better come and pick them up.' What he failed to mention was that the pallet had burst and the Greggs had to pick up the individual bottles off the platform. With that same delivery, came a package of thick plastic capsules that we were to be fitted over the corks. The parcel had about a dozen addresses on it, all of which had been crossed out, except for Vasse Felix. Anne Gregg commented, 'Eventually, it dawned on us that the package had been rejected by a dozen wineries and that we were the end of the line. When we started using them, we rapidly realised that because there were no airholes on the top, the capsules pushed corks into the bottles.'

David came up with the idea of a piece of wood with three nails that would enable them to pierce the top of each capsule. The subsequent aeration would enable them to fit the capsules without pushing the cork into the bottle. As Anne said, 'We occupied ourselves for several evenings with this chore. People would not believe that sort of thing these days!'

By 1976, Vasse Felix was handling significant quantities of bottles so David Gregg managed to persuade freight company TNT to tussle with WAGR. It broke the embargo on northbound freight and then extracted permission to bring a full load of empty bottles across the Nullarbor by rail then to Margaret River by road from Perth.

The Greggs were particularly envious of the Pannells at Moss Wood because they had these 'beautiful stainless-steel tanks'. Vasse Felix, on the other hand, had the ferro-cement fermenting vats with the moat around the outside. Twice a day, Anne Gregg went into Margaret River (an hour's round trip) to visit the fishing tackle shop, the only place in town that had an icemaker. She would return with large blocks, which would be dropped into the moat to keep the white fermentation cool. David Gregg eventually hit on a time-saving solution and obtained a cooling coil similar to that used by dairy farmers. The coil would be lowered into the vat to keep the wine cool. When money allowed, they bought a refrigerated 650-gallon (2,954 litres) milk receiver (for $1,200), filled it with water boosted by a touch of alcohol (so that it didn't freeze) and pumped it around the whole winery.

Anne Gregg recalls that in the mid-1970s, they were getting a lot of important visitors from the Eastern States and overseas. She and Sandra

Pannell would often share the entertaining, alternating between handling lunch and dinner. On one occasion, when Kiersten was a baby and Joanna was two, a note came from the winery: 'Len Evans and four others for lunch in 20 minutes'. Evans was writing the 'Indulgence' column for *The Weekend Australian* at the time, so the pressure was on.

'He had been at the Pannells in Busselton the night before and they had been crabbing on the foreshore. He arrived with a bucketful of crabs and invited me to cook them. And, for good measure, he poured two bottles of champagne into the pot in which they were to be cooked.' Anne was aghast. 'We were just about on the bones of our butt at the time and I couldn't believe the champagne was being used for the cooking. We were nothing if not versatile.'

The Vineyard Workforce

Vasse Felix employed two 'permanent casuals' to help David Gregg in the vineyard and winery. Joe Palandri started in 1974. Like his cousin John at Moss Wood, Joe proved indispensable for his skills as a pruner, his dependability and his ability to build in the local stone. Al Gillespie, who still works as a viticultural contractor, was in his twenties when he began at Vasse Felix in 1976. At the time, he was also planting his own vineyard at Witchcliffe on the family farm. He produced outstanding fruit, much of which was snapped up by David Gregg, and by the 1980s he was releasing impressive cabernets under his own Gillespie label. Gillespie had worked as a cellarhand for Jack Mann at Houghton and was described by David Gregg as capable, skilled and 'smart as paint'. The three of them managed the vineyard and winery as well as all the construction and maintenance work at Vasse Felix. They began with the building of an underground cellar in 1974 and moved on to the construction of a larger winery building, which was functional by 1980.

David Gregg talked about the adoption of mechanical harvesting. 'The first machine used was at Cape Mentelle, which is when Alistair Gillespie got interested in it. His father-in-law, Jim Archibald, invested in the machinery and Al got into harvesting on a contract basis and we used him. The famous Alston cartoon was published, illustrating how we would be without a labour force if the surf was up.' So, the move to mechanical harvesting was a necessity. The yield factor was as good as hand-picking and it was delivered at the right temperature.

Improving Quality

When Robert Mondavi and his family were involved with Leeuwin Estate, Robert, Tim or Michael would make an annual visit to Margaret River during vintage, doing the rounds of the established wineries—Vasse Felix, Moss Wood and Cullen. They were interested in local developments and happy to share their experiences of making wine in California. David Gregg noted, 'We watched them keenly and listened to them and adopted many of their techniques—cooler fermentations, more desirable yeasts—and came to understand better the importance of the malolactic fermentation in reds.

I had a lot of respect for Tom [Cullity] and his approach to winemaking ... However, I think we could have adopted stainless steel more readily than we did. We continued to take care with extraction by macerating the fruit as little as possible, and were ever alert to controlling tannin levels in reds. We increased the amount we spent on refrigeration and this gave us greater control over the fermentation temperature, which enabled us to reduce sulphur dioxide levels. The use of better quality oak also improved the wines.'

Releasing the Rabbit

David Gregg commented on the advice in Dorham Mann's article, *The Function and Use of Sulphur Dioxide in Western Australian Winemaking:* 'We used to really lash in with sulphur dioxide, so there was no chance of any malolactic taking place. But in fairness, the purity of the [1973] wine was fantastic. It gave such an immediate impression.'

The secondary or malolactic fermentation is almost always encouraged in red winemaking as it converts malic acid into lactic acid and carbon dioxide. This softens the acidity of the wine and adds complexity and stability. In most wine regions, this is not an issue because the malolactic yeasts are present in the winery and automatically trigger that fermentation. The newness of the wine industry in Margaret River meant Vasse Felix had what David Gregg called 'a virginal cellar' and so the malolactic fermentation could only occur if freeze-dried yeast preparations were used.

In 1977, the problem was solved when Tom, through Cullity Timbers, bought French oak from St Emilion's Chateau La Tour du Pin Figeac. When they had arrived, David Gregg filled one of the hogsheads with Vasse Felix Cabernet. Within a week the bung had blown and a viable imported yeast culture had colonised the cellar. Margaret River had its first malolactic yeast bacteria. Gregg described it as like 'the release of the rabbit in Australia'.

The Wines

Vasse Felix prices were high by industry standards. Australia's largest-selling wine, Lindemans Ben Ean Moselle, sold for forty-six cents a bottle in 1973. Vasse Felix asked for, and got, $1.80 for its riesling. The 1978 Late-Picked Riesling cost a great deal to produce as only a third of the usual volume of fruit was picked to make the wine. It was sold by the bottle in a wooden box. Once people had tasted it, no questions were asked about its $7.50 price tag.

The Vasse Felix Rieslings

David Gregg became aware that some of the vines planted as riesling were, in fact, chenin blanc. He thought that these may have contributed as much as fifteen per cent to the wine and so influenced its character. In fact, there was enough chenin for David Gregg to make a varietal chenin blanc in 1976. He believed that, while the 1972 Riesling was an outstanding wine, the others made until 1978 were less distinguished. After that, he regarded the quality as ordinary and he discontinued the wine in the 1980s. Botrytis infection was a constant problem. James Halliday is kinder in his judgement, believing that the 1977, 1979 and 1981 Vasse Felix Rieslings were all 'beautifully constructed'. The 1981 and 1982 Vasse Felix Rieslings were rejected by the judges for District Certification as 'lacking flavour, having a hard palate and a bitter finish'.

The Vasse Felix Cabernets

In 1972, the cabernet was picked early (probably to avoid the onslaught of the silvereyes) and so was unacceptably acidic and had an oxidised character. It was undrinkable. The 1973 Vasse Felix Cabernet was picked later and three barrels were made. Although it was described by David Gregg as 'fat and jammy', it won a gold medal at the Perth Show, underlining the success of the previous year's Riesling. The 1974

Cabernet showed the style evolving as the winemakers searched for the ideal picking date. James Halliday felt that it had 'power and richness' but was unbalanced by 'stalkiness and strong drying tannins'.

David Gregg was happy with the 1975 and 1976 Cabernets, which showed softness and balance, and indicated that they were achieving the style that he and Cullity had been seeking: a red 'light in the mouth, of modest alcohol content, and a character resembling a good Bordeaux rather than a powerful Australian red'. It was a blend of cabernet (70-75%) with shiraz (10-15%) and malbec. The percentage of malbec (which added softness and colour) increased when a second planting of the variety became available in the early 1980s.

After a vertical tasting of eight of the Vasse Felix Cabernets (1974 to 1981) James Halliday described the wines as lighter and more elegant than many in the region. He commented in 1982 that 'the beautifully made whites and reds of Vasse Felix put the final stamp of quality on the Margaret River region'.

The first great red from Vasse Felix was the 1979 Cabernet, which was shown at the New York Wine Trade Fair and rated second to the cabernet of the reigning champion, Napa producer Stag's Leap. The *Washington Post's* James Conway reported on a blind tasting of cabernet sauvignons, including Bordeaux first growths, 1979 Haut Brion and 1979 Mouton Rothschild; and two Napa superstars, 1978 Beaulieu 'Georges de Latour Private Reserve' and 1978 Heitz 'Martha's Vineyard'. Conway commented, 'I found the 1979 Vasse Felix to be a lovely wine with good fruit and tannin and a lingering finish, with the heat of some other entries. It was the least expensive entry and, for me, one of the most attractive.' This international exposure helped Vasse Felix make some impact on the tough New York market.

The other great Vasse Felix Cabernet Sauvignon of the early years was the 1985, which won a trophy as the Best Red Wine at the 1987 World Trade Fair in London.

Leeuwin Estate was having trouble selling its Cabernet at the time and sold eighty tonnes of its fruit to Vasse. 'It was just the sweetest deal we ever did because Woodside Petroleum [now Woodside Energy] had signed the North-West Shelf joint venture agreement in 1985 and wanted this wine to celebrate the delivery of the first LNG cargo from the Shelf to Japan in 1989. They said we'll pay you progressively.' The authors shared a half bottle of the wine with current owner Paul Holmes à Court and winemaker Virginia Willcock to celebrate the release of the 2013 Vasse Felix 'Tom Cullity' Cabernet Malbec at Tom's former home in View Street, Peppermint Grove, in 2016. It had been purchased in Toronto in the late 1980s and was still in superb condition more than thirty years later: powerfully concentrated, velvety smooth, and wonderfully alive.

Classic Dry White

Since 1983, Vasse Felix had been making a Semillon Sauvignon Blanc with Al Gillespie's fruit from Witchcliffe. The

Oak Barrel in Sydney was handling their wines at the time and David Gregg believed that they should be moving more of the white. Nick Forbes from the Oak Barrel told Gregg the company's bestseller was the Wolf Blass Classic Dry White. 'People think your wine is Margaret River riesling. Why not change the name to Classic Dry White?' he said.

David Gregg checked with Wolf Blass with whom he was on good terms, and was told there was no reason why he shouldn't use that name. The label and the name were changed and, within a month, the wine went from selling a case a week to a pallet a week, with Peter Doyle's fish restaurant at Watson's Bay a huge supporter. We believe this was the first semillon sauvignon blanc blend from Margaret River released as a Classic Dry White. The style has proved enduringly popular.

Working with Tom

There was some ambivalence in the relationship between Tom Cullity and David Gregg in the decade they worked together. At its core was the fact that Tom wanted to be in control of everything, or at the very least everything to do with winemaking. However, that was impossible while he lived in Perth and worked as a cardiologist, especially as Vasse Felix grew.

There is no question that David Gregg's drive and determination to succeed was the major contributor to Vasse Felix's evolution in the decade from his arrival in 1973. Wine writer James Halliday referred to him as the 'very able and fanatically dedicated winemaker' in 1982, while in 1985 he commented, 'Twelve years after arriving, the highly intelligent and motivated David Gregg is still hard at work in the vineyard, experimenting with trellis systems, canopy control and summer hedging.' Tom Cullity's comment seems aposite: 'The Greggs were very good. If it hadn't been for David Gregg's industry and his atonishing approach to things, I couldn't have survived.'

Gregg felt that there was little friction between him and Cullity on the technical side except possibly over his eagerness to introduce more mechanisation and to use stainless steel rather than concrete tanks. However, there were differences of opinion over marketing. David Gregg had been professionally trained in marketing by Unilever in England and enjoyed being involved in production to the point of sale. While there was no question that retailers enjoyed the opportunity of meeting the founder of Vasse Felix, Gregg felt that Cullity was a liability on such occasions. For example, on arriving in a store to show their wines, Cullity would say, 'We were in the district and took the opportunity of calling on you,' instead of, 'We've come up specially to see you.'

Tom Cullity commented years later:

'The whole thing was very badly conceived ... what I did was impossible. If you're not living on the place, I'd say it's quite impossible. Unless there is some sort of corporate management, the only way to run such a place is by owner-occupation. In fact, to follow my belief that great wine requires personal, individual control, the latter method is the only way to go. People like the

Cullens, the Pannells and the Devitts have followed this route. They live on the land and in the district. They educate their children to take over. I see a minuscule number who can go successfully beyond two generations but I hope that even if this be so they find adequate reward for their pioneering work and aching scars in the noble wine they make, and their pride in it, for at least two or three generations.'

As Vasse Felix increased in size and complexity, there was tension between Cullity wanting things done his way and realising the need to give Gregg the freedom to make decisions. As he approached his sixtieth birthday, Cullity realised he could no longer manage the work he had previously done in the vineyard and winery. Even with the winemaking side of things, not living in Margaret River meant that he had to relinquish 'too much control'. He also realised that he was much more interested in winemaking than in running a winery and a wine business. He commented, 'I had nothing to do with marketing, did not have a cheque book and had nothing to do with financial control, except my accountant's annual assessment.' Moreover, he was keenly aware that proper management of the business was vital to the winery's success.

Reflecting on the moment he decided to sell Vasse Felix, Cullity said, in essence, that he had achieved what he set out to do. 'Well, I was down there about twenty years and I think that was enough.' He was a sophisticated wine lover with an impressive knowledge and understanding of European wines. His aim in going south had been to prove that high-quality wines could be produced in the Margaret River region. By the time he sold in 1984, Vasse Felix and the other pioneering wineries had established an enviable reputation. In James Halliday's words, 'one of Australia's finest wine areas'.

A view of Vasse Felix's winery and cellar door in 1985.

End of the Beginning

In March 1979, Tom Cullity and David and Anne Gregg entered into a joint venture for two years. In 1981, Cullity agreed to lease Vasse Felix to the Greggs for four years (for $35,000 a year according to Cullity). In 1984, Tom decided that it was time for him to leave Vasse Felix altogether and so the Greggs bought it from him. 'Any major decision from 1979 on was ours,' David Gregg said. Cullity said he sold it to the Greggs for $360,000 and they subsequently sold it to the Holmes à

Court family four years later for $1.25 million. There's more than a hint of irritation in his comment: 'During his time as my employee he could not have worked more effectively, and I am happy to say could not have been more adequately rewarded.'

We believe this comment is unjustified and suggests that Tom Cullity did not understand just how hard and how thoughtfully the Greggs had worked to make Vasse Felix a viable business for them all. Nor did he realise how the financial circumstances and their personal situation had changed since he had sold Vasse Felix to them.

The Greggs worked tirelessly in the four years they owned Vasse Felix, selling their Busselton house to invest in the business. They purchased a new bottling line from Italy costing $380,000 (plus fourteen per cent because Australia devalued its currency while the machine was on the water); and they sourced three-phase power for the winery, which meant it was then available for other Wilyabrup wineries. There was a need for capital growth: trellising needed to be replaced and much of the equipment needed to be upgraded. As David Gregg said, 'Once we owned Vasse Felix we realised that, for us to survive, we had to increase production. We couldn't buy land: we had to buy fruit. We tripled the output.'

They had had to borrow heavily to buy Vasse Felix and could not have anticipated interest rates rising from fourteen to twenty-two per cent. All this was exacerbated by the Greggs' family situation. They were unhappy with the education their oldest daughter, Joanna, was receiving in Margaret River and believed they needed to enrol her (and eventually her sisters) as a boarder at a private school in Perth. This would be beyond the capacity of the income generated by the vineyard. David Gregg also believed he was showing signs of burnout from the fifteen hours a day he was working.

Gregg believed the district was waiting for them to crack. 'The rumour was going around to just wait for a bit, there'd be a cheap vineyard coming up soon ... Where that came from we didn't know, but we suspected. We had an old Holden station wagon that was playing up so we decided we would change it for an old Merc, which cost us dearly in repairs but it was well-polished and it sat outside the vineyard. It killed the rumours immediately.'

The Sale

The Greggs decided to sell the business: 'We put it on the market in February 1987, and said if it doesn't sell by 28 February midnight, it's off the market. Full stop. One month. We selected 500 names and mailed out a brochure. It was news in several major newspapers but that's all and we got enquiries from overseas. After about a fortnight, an enquiry came from [Robert] Holmes à Court. They choppered down, examined the papers and three days later we got a call saying, Mr Holmes à Court would like to see you in his office. We made an appointment and didn't see him. He was with Rupert [Murdoch], talking newspapers. Apologised profusely ... He and Janet said basically, we're not going to buy it without you two. You'll go on a three-year contract. So, it was all agreed. It took a month to settle. We were well paid. I stayed for five years, Anne for three. But selling Vasse Felix was the best thing we ever did. We secured our future and put our kids through school.'

In 2016, Janet Holmes à Court recounts the episode.

'Over breakfast one morning in the dining room at Peppermint Grove, I saw a news item announcing that Vasse Felix was for sale. We knew the winery and drank some of their wine so I said to Robert, Vasse Felix is for sale. That would be interesting to buy.'

At the time Holmes à Court was mounting a multi-billion-dollar bid to take over Australia's biggest company, BHP. Despite this distraction, he replied, 'Well, why don't we.'

Said Janet: 'We flew down in the Channel Seven helicopter with our young son Paul [now the owner of Vasse Felix] who was still at home then. We were thrilled by what we saw. On the way home, the pilot flew directly west, turned right at one of the local beaches and we flew the whole way back to Perth hugging the coastline. It felt to me like about fifty metres above the sea. It was exhilarating and showed me just how much natural vegetation there still was along the coast. When we got back to Perth I said to Paul, "Wasn't that fantastic?" His reply was a stark: "I've never been so terrified in my life. I thought that if I put my foot out the door, it would have got wet, we were so close to the sea".

Following the sale to the Holmes à Courts, the changes came. Within six months about $380,000 was invested in major extensions to the winery and a whole series of tanks were installed. Small problems—such as David Gregg's failing car—were addressed.

Burnout

Anne Gregg believed that living on the property meant they were constantly on call, and once wines were being exported, the nights were constantly interrupted. If David Gregg was showing signs of burnout before the sale, things remained strained afterwards. 'After we sold out, the leaves started falling off.'

Constantly having to refer to Perth was an issue.

There was an incident which was seminal for David Gregg. An additional internal track into the cellar was needed. The stonemason had some time available and so Gregg authorised him to reroute some drains and add some concrete stairs. There were questions from the accountant and then the auditor in Perth that Gregg regarded as a rap on the knuckles, which left a sour note. 'I never got over that, to be honest.' Anne Gregg was understanding of the Holmes à Courts' position: 'They were really cash strapped ... but half the problem was that it was quite difficult going from owning a place to then being owned.'

On the question of burnout, when Anne resigned after the agreed three years, the general manager (John Ilbury) discussed holiday pay with her. She explained that she'd never had a public holiday while at Vasse Felix. 'The cellar door's always open, so you had to look after that. Those are the things that really lead to burnout because we were always working.'

Chapter 12

Moss Wood and the Region's First Great Reds

Moss Wood played a seminal role in the Margaret River story because they made the region's first great reds. Bill and Sandra Pannell were second only to Tom Cullity as pioneering vignerons when they planted vines (1969) and built a winery (1973) at Wilyabrup. Their 1975 Moss Wood Cabernet Sauvignon, from six-year-old vines and the winery's third vintage, was unquestionably the outstanding wine of the region's first decade. The best bottles are superb and, even at forty years of age, a well-cellared bottle can give great delight. The best bottles from 1975, 1976, 1977, 1979 and 1980 have been outstanding cabernets by any standards. The 1976 was the first wine from the South West to win a gold medal in open classes at the Perth

Show. At fifteen years of age, the best bottles of the 1973 Cabernet 'showed sound fruit in good condition'. A bottle taken by Peter Forrestal to the fiftieth anniversary celebrations at Vasse Felix in May 2017 showed splendidly, defying expectation, with intense fruit that was pure and vibrant. The Moss Wood wines showed clearly at the time, and prove conclusively now, how well suited the Margaret River region is to cabernet sauvignon.

Bill Pannell's fascination with wine was triggered by his Professor of Paediatrics, Bill MacDonald. As part of his medical course at the University of Western Australia, Pannell participated in what were known as 'co-mingle days'. These were instituted so trainee doctors could develop interests and associations outside the medical profession. On several of these days, Bill MacDonald took a group of fifth-year medical students to Houghton in the Swan Valley to meet winemaker Jack Mann. At the time, Mann was serving on the Grape Industry Committee investigating the suitability of the Mount Barker area for table wines. Mann spoke enthusiastically about the wine potential of the State's southern areas and the young Bill Pannell thought, that would be interesting to get involved in.

He described his first taste of the 1962 Penfolds Grange as 'a defining moment in my life'. The occasion was a dinner in 1966 with Sandra at the Garden Restaurant in Perth's Parmelia Hilton on their first wedding anniversary. In his autobiography, *Once More Unto the Vine,* he comments *Such richness! Such complexity! Such balance! I believe that, at that point, I determined to somehow make a wine of comparable quality.*

Pannell took up an RAAF cadetship in 1964 at the end of the fifth year of his medical course. He spent 1966 as a resident at Royal Perth Hospital (RPH) and went to Victoria as an RAAF medical officer in 1967, before returning to the RAAF base at Pearce in Western Australia the following year. While the Pannells were in Melbourne, they took advantage of living close to the wine regions of Victoria, South Australia and New South Wales to improve their knowledge of wine and its production, with a view to establishing a winery of their own.

They enjoyed their forays into country Australia visiting producers such as the Purbricks at Tahbilk, John Brown at Milawa, Max Lake in the Hunter Valley and Ross Heinze, the Seppelt vineyard manager at Drumborg in Victoria's south west. Pannell discussed his idea of starting a small winery in Western Australia's South West and found them supportive. Heinze had scouted vineyard sites in Western Australia and believed Mount Barker would be more suited to whites, while Cowaramup would be better for reds. This advice delighted Bill. He was more interested in making reds and his parents had a holiday house at Dunsborough in the northern reaches of the Margaret River area. This, he realised, was a much better option for him.

He had made enquiries of the WA Department of Agriculture and was sent a copy of Gladstones' 1966 paper, which directed Pannell's gaze to the area around Cowaramup (more commonly referred to as Wilyabrup today). Bill and

Sandra Pannell spent many weeks in 1968 combing the area looking for land that would be suitable for viticulture. Naturally, they were equipped with a trusty shovel to check out soil profiles whenever a paddock looked promising.

In 1966, Pannell attended a retirement function for Royal Perth Hospital consultant physician Dr Ernest Beech and spoke with Tom Cullity about the increased interest in a quality wine industry in the South West. He recalled Cullity commenting that he 'was doing something about it'. 'The significance of his remark became apparent in 1968 when we came across Tom's first planting at Vasse Felix while criss-crossing the Naturaliste-Leeuwin Ridge looking for a site for our own vineyard. I can remember it like it were yesterday. It was summer and everything was browned. It was quite a surprise as we were not aware that anyone else had embarked on a similar enterprise.'

Six kilometres to the north of the Vasse Felix planting, the Pannells found their perfect site on Metricup Road. It was in the drainage basin of the

Wilyabrup Brook on gently sloping land with gravelly loam over yellow clay soil. The property was owned by Jack Guthrie and his family. While the rest of the family were reluctant to sell farming land, Jack's father, Alan, the patriarch known to all as 'The Sheriff', insisted that if they wanted to encourage progress in the region they had to give opportunity to people with ideas. (Alan Guthrie had bought 6,000 acres [2,428 hectares] in the 1940s and only needed the land for its timber rights for his milling business. These rights were ten shillings an acre but he decided to buy the freehold [at £1 an acre] because he was looking to the future and his four children. In addition to Moss Wood, the Guthries' land became Lenton Brae, Moss Brothers [now Amelia Park], Driftwood and Cape Lodge.)

Young Vines
Young Vigneron!

Bill Pannell, shortly after establishing Moss Wood. Photo courtesy Moss Wood

On a handshake, the Pannells bought twenty-six acres (eleven hectares) of the best viticultural land from the Guthries for 'the huge sum' of $200 an acre. At the time, Bill Pannell was doing his residency at RPH and King Edward Maternity Hospital and $5,000 was a considerable sum of money for a junior doctor. When his parents, Nita and Jim Pannell, visited the property, Nita commented that the peppermint trees at the entrance to the vineyard reminded her of an estate in England owned by a friend. The estate was called Moss Wood. Sandra and Bill had agonised about what to call their vineyard and both realised instantly that their search had ended.

After finishing his residency, Bill Pannell with wife Sandra and sons Stephen (five) and Daniel (two), moved to Busselton in 1970, where they eventually built their own home. Nicholas was born that year and Emma in 1973. Pannell joined Kevin Cullen's medical practice. Money was tight and (at least in Sandra's memory) they lived on wild duck and rabbit from the Moss Wood property.

Setting the Scene

Keith Mugford, who joined Moss Wood as winemaker in 1979 and who, with his wife Clare, took over from the Pannells in 1984, summarises the scene in the early 1970s as he saw it, when the wine industry was struggling to become established:

'When Vasse Felix [1972] and Moss Wood [1973] made their first vintages, there were a huge pile of things stacked against them. The Western Australian wine culture wasn't aligned with high quality table wine. They were branching into a viticultural activity that wasn't part of the living memory in Western Australia.

'In terms of the national context, it was also revolutionary because the wine industry in South Australia was a monolithic, moribund entity that didn't think broadly. The idea that winemakers would go outside the established regions there, to places like the Adelaide Hills, was bizarre.

'Thinking about doing it in the south-west corner of Western Australia would have been considered complete madness ... the intellectual pressure would have been enormous: people would have looked at them and thought that they were really foolish. Once they got going, there was interest. The wines were so good, too.

'It's not a surprise that people like Tom Cullity, Bill Pannell, David Hohnen and Kevin Cullen were determined, driven people. You had to have an intellect to be able to cope with the debate. You had to have huge energy and focus to be able to get things done in the circumstances.

'The pressures on the pioneering vignerons were immense. Some of it came from the job itself. Some came from the dream "We are going to make Chateau Margaux in Margaret River" and its complementary reality, which is that viticulture is agriculture and, with it, comes agricultural risk—and all the problems that come with growing a crop safely.

'In the early years, they didn't know what was coming next. There was always something looming ... to blow them out of the water.'

It's hard to imagine what it was like at the time. The pioneering vignerons had land, cuttings and some basic tools. That was it. As Bill Pannell said, 'In the early days at Margaret River, there was nobody who could give you advice. There was no established infrastructure ... Nobody knew about barrels, or machinery, or tank seals.' The exceptions included Tom Cullity, who used to call in on his way down. Pannell said they grew 'reasonably close'. 'He was very encouraging and I was coming in completely blind. He was hyper-critical and believed that the similarity between winemaking and medicine was attention to detail.' After the Pannells had planted the first five acres of cabernet themselves, Cullity made his vineyard team of the Rossi brothers available to the Pannells for the second planting.

Pannell also praised the support of State Viticulturist Bill Jamieson, 'who was around all the time and was wonderfully helpful. He didn't perceive any conflict of interest with what his departmental superiors or the government might want and you felt relaxed with Bill. It made talking about the industry and wine a joy.' When it came time to plant the main vineyard, only Tom Cullity, Bill Jamieson and Dorham Mann came to give them a hand.

Jack Mann was an enthusiast for cabernet sauvignon. Shiraz was unfashionable, so Bill Pannell chose to plant cabernet sauvignon. The cuttings were sourced from Houghton, courtesy of Jack, and planted on a nursery block at Moss Wood in the spring of 1969. The Pannells put in a rabbit-proof fence and began clearing the ground of rock and roots for the first five acres (two hectares) of vines.

'We used to blow up the rocks with gelignite. The kids and I would be hiding behind bushes, and there'd be rocks flying everywhere,' said Sandra. Bill recalled: 'We planted the vines using bush posts [split jarrah posts], which were terrible things to handle, full of splinters. We set up some trellising and eventually trained the things up. We learnt by our mistakes, largely. The locals thought it all a bit of a joke. They used to hang over the fence and laugh at us, and say: They'll never ripen here. One of my enduring memories is of Sandra, near term with Nicholas, drenched with insecticide from a ruptured spray line, vaulting a barbed-wire fence and shedding clothing in her desperate urgency to immerse herself in the nearby creek.'

The Winery

In the absence of a local winery at which to process fruit, Bill Pannell chose to build a tiny winery for the five tonnes of grapes from the 1973 vintage which yielded 2,000 litres of cabernet juice. He mixed the mortar, local tradesmen laid the bricks, and they put the fibro-cement roof overhead. His one extravagance was a Celestin Coq crusher which he bought on Dorham Mann's recommendation. Dorham had stressed the importance of having a crusher of that quality because it would destem the bunches and crush the grapes without damaging the pips and stalks. As a result, Pannell avoided the production of unacceptable levels of tannin.

The wine was fermented (using a cultured yeast from the Department of Agriculture) in concrete cattle troughs which Pannell had sealed with paraffin wax. The grapes were pressed with a small basket press from Italian food importer in Perth, European Foods. The wine was aged in American barriques as he was unable to source French oak at the time.

A cask room was added to the fermentation cellar in 1974 and a further eight acres (3.25 hectares) of cabernet sauvignon was planted, along with 240 semillon vines and one hectare of pinot noir. There were two clones of pinot cultivated at Moss Wood: D2V4 'droopy' and D5V12 'upright'. Bill had been keen to plant chardonnay but was unable to get any cuttings until 1976 and so was looking for another suitable white variety. He rejected the commonly held belief that riesling would suit the region. He considered that the area was not cold enough for the variety. Dorham Mann recommended semillon and he was able to source cuttings for Moss Wood. In 1977, Bill made a small quantity of semillon in a beer keg. He commented:

Keith Mugford and a young Nicholas Pannell in the winery. Photo courtesy Moss Wood

'It looked beautiful and had magnificent fruit. I still think semillon is one of the best white varieties in Margaret River. It did, however, prove rather difficult to sell. People weren't familiar with semillon and weren't comfortable with buying it.

'We tried wooding it, and that seemed to kill the fruit. Semillon seems better tank fermented and tank cured and bottled fairly early. The Margaret River semillons, in particular, have this lovely figgy, spicy character, which I find beautiful with seafood. It took a while for that to gain acceptance.'

Chardonnay cuttings (of the Mendoza clone) were obtained in 1976 and a tiny, non-commercial crop was made from the 1980 vintage. Bad weather for the next two harvests meant there was no commercial crop of Moss Wood Chardonnay until 1983.

A stainless-steel tank was purchased in time for the 1975 vintage and was used for fermentation and storage prior to the wine being aged in French oak. The cancellation of an order for French oak in South Africa resulted in Pannell managing to source some from the barrel maker Scharhinger, and was delighted with its quality and the impact it made on the Moss Wood Cabernet. The contact enabled them to secure quality French oak for future vintages.

Ingenuity in the Winery

Innovation was the name of the game. Cooling was introduced for the 1974 vintage using a system Pannell devised with an old Kelvinator air-conditioning compressor. These were used in coldrooms and so were readily available. The coil was set up so that it cooled water in a chilling pit. The refrigerant was then pumped all around the winery and onto the tanks through polyurethane pipes. The tanks had gutters on the base to collect the water and return it to the chilling pit. Keith Mugford later explained: 'It meant that we could take the refrigerant anywhere we could lay poly pipes. We could lay it out ourselves, repair it ourselves. This system, which could circulate water at about 4°C, worked perfectly for controlling the temperature of the fermenting juice in tanks at about 15°C. The only drawback was that we couldn't cold-stabilise below about 4°C because the water would freeze. As a result, the early Moss Wood wines were relatively tartrate unstable. It only affected the physical appearance of the wines and was not a quality issue.'

Using open fermenters is fashionable now but not in the early 1970s, except for Pannell. Finding a cooling mechanism to chill down an open fermenter was not straightforward. Bill adapted the tank technology so that he could also use it in open fermenters. The coolant was circulated through a stainless-steel coil which was immersed in the open fermenters to lower the temperature of the juice. According to Mugford, 'It worked like a charm.'

The set-up for the small hand-bottling line was similarly ingenious. Mugford said: 'It was set up on the kitchen table and was then put into the winery. The floor wasn't level so Bill set up some nuts and bolts, so that we could make the filler level. We sterilised the old plate filter using low pressure steam from a specially made boiler that sat on a simple gas stove ring and ran off bottled gas. Despite its simplicity, it was a masterpiece and would easily sterilise things: a classic example of how Bill could work things out from first principles. The actual process was similarly well conceived. A low speed pump pushed the wine through the sterile filter and into a hand-operated siphon filler.

'Whoever was working on the filler put bottles on and off the machine in pairs, basically continuously filling four at a time, at about fifteen dozen an hour. As they took a pair off, they passed them to the person sitting next to them, who operated the corker. This was also a manual process, where the operator put a bottle on the machine, pressed the pedal and the cork would be plunged in. It was all very gentle on the wine. Those Moss Woods from the 1970s and 1980s bottled under that regime stood the test of time. It was, however, a very slow, labour-intensive process and, as our volumes grew, we had to go over to the larger automatic bottling lines run by Portavin.'

Learning the Ropes

Cape Mentelle's David Hohnen commented on the challenges of the early of viticulture in the region: 'Everything seemed to be different from what the textbooks told us.' Similarly, Keith Mugford found problems with slavishly following advice:

'We tried spraying with the systemic fungicides for powdery mildew in 1981. They were relatively new and we decided that we were going to use lower rates than were recommended.

We were going to stop our sulphur program earlier to minimise the risk of residual sulphur on the grapes at the time of fermentation. After we realised that these fungicides were ineffective in controlling powdery mildew in our region, we worked on attempting to find out why. We gradually realised that the disease pressure on powdery mildew in Margaret River was way above anything that they had to deal with in South Australia, where the chemicals were initially trialled. We were taking advice on the rates and timing of spraying which weren't going to work for us. We learnt the hard way that, in a new region like Margaret River, not everything worked according to traditional or accepted methods.'

Bill Pannell also noted: 'What we didn't appreciate is that you couldn't use the new fungicides in isolation. You still had to maintain a sulphur program on the vines.'

Getting the Wine to Market

Glass manufacturer ICA had a monopoly on bottles and was notoriously difficult for small wineries to deal with. In the early days, because it didn't believe its packaging would cope with bottle scuffing in transit, ICA would only make their bottles available to West Australian vignerons in cardboard boxes. This was time consuming, cumbersome and more expensive than buying pallets of empty bottles. Moss Wood were small customers compared to the large-scale wineries of South Australia—just one to two thousand bottles an order: ICA were dismissive of any requests they made. However, by 1979, as the local wine industry grew, Margaret River producers were able to buy pallets of bottles.

Sandra Pannell and children Daniel, left, Nicholas, Emma (in Sandra's arms) and Stephen circa 1975. Photo courtesy Pannell family

As revealed in a Chapter 11, WAGR had a monopoly on transporting freight to and from Perth and freight had to be delivered to the Busselton train station for forward delivery. For Moss Wood, this meant Sandra Pannell loading sixteen-kilogram cartons of wine onto their ute and driving the twenty kilometres to Busselton. Once there, she had to unload them, case by case, and stack them into a railway wagon. She remembers most vividly that it was always 'while the railway employees looked on', even when she was eight months pregnant. Anne Gregg at Vasse Felix had a similar experience.

Over a decade at Moss Wood, Sandra Pannell cut and bundled at least 40,000 cuttings a year over twelve years (sold for twenty cents each) to enable her to buy household items such as a fridge, washing machine and a dishwasher. They had little money and were regularly called upon to entertain visitors. Lemons were always in plentiful supply and so an ice-cream maker could quickly and cheaply produce lemon sorbet. Similarly, a pasta machine would allow Sandra to whip up fresh spaghetti bolognese with alacrity. The cuttings enabled these purchases, too.

Early Opinions from the Outside

Not everyone who visited was supportive. John Stanford, a wine consultant from Sydney, told the Pannells that he thought the 1973 Moss Wood Cabernet tasted 'like duck's guts, like Tabasco'.

'Just what we didn't need at that stage,' said Bill Pannell. 'In the early days, we did feel that Hunter Valley people couldn't stop themselves criticising everybody else's wines. So, we learned, after a while, to show them a Hunter Valley wine that they could vent their spleen on, and then we showed them ours.'

Their spirits were lifted after the visit of respected English wine writer Edmund Penning-Rowsell, whose book *The Wines of Bordeaux* had been published in 1969. Penning-Rowsell tasted the 1975 Moss Wood Cabernet and was impressed. He said that if Margaret River could make wines like that, it had a great future. In response to the criticism often levelled at Moss Wood—that they were too soft—Penning-Rowsell stated: 'Great wines are drinkable when they are young.' As Bill Pannell said, 'This boosted our confidence, and everybody else's.'

Growing Up on the Vineyard

Stephen Pannell spent much of his childhood living in Busselton and growing up on the Moss Wood vineyard. When he left university, he made a conscious decision not to become a winemaker, yet he took up a job at Halvorsen Cellars in Sydney. Stephen enjoyed the wine industry so much that he changed his mind and accepted a scholarship to study winemaking at Roseworthy College. He had a successful career in corporate winemaking with Hardy's before establishing his own label. Stephen and his wife, Fiona, have lived in McLaren Vale for more than twenty years, where their label, S.C. Pannell, now has a cellar door, winery and vineyards. Among a raft of other achievements, Stephen was the 2015 *Gourmet Traveller Wine* Winemaker of the Year. He is widely regarded as one of Australia's finest winemakers.

Stephen Pannell gives an insight into life at Moss Wood in the early days:

'It was an intense period. Dad is very much focused; he's a perfectionist; it's what he does, he doesn't stop; he has a determination that is steely. It was full on. He will never fail. His motto in life appears to be, If things are getting you down, just work harder and harder.

'As kids, Mum used to make our undies out of my grandfather's tank tops. We were poor; we weren't badly off at all. It was hard. We all pulled our weight in every way possible.

'Everything was done by hand, everything! Hand bottled, hand corked, packed in the bays, we polished every bottle, hand capsuled, labels applied by hand, then into the box. Very labour intensive. We spent our lives doing that. I wasn't cognisant of the winemaking process, I was just, sort of, present.

'We all had our jobs. At night time, we used to have to write people's names and addresses on boxes and put them on the back of the ute to be sent around Australia. On other occasions, we'd be doing cuttings. We weren't there all the time but whenever we were there, it was work. We'd work hard, I suppose it was good in that that work ethic is still with us. But it was an interesting childhood, that's for sure.

It'd be seven at night and you'd be screaming at Dad, "Can we please go home? I'm hungry. I'm tired. I just want to go home".

'The only way of getting out of going to the vineyard was playing sport. I played a lot of sport. In winter, I played hockey and football and, in summer, two grades of cricket.

'To get to Moss Wood from our house in Busselton was a 20-kilometre drive and a third of that was on a gravel road. We had a Mazda ute: the front seat was so full, Daniel and I and the dog were in the back bouncing along.

'I used to shoot silvereyes. It was my job mostly to keep the birds away from the vineyard. I was paid five cents a bird, for silvereyes especially. I'd be sitting there all day, just shooting birds. Perhaps it's not so politically correct these days but that's how it was done then.

'We became very resourceful as kids. I used to make my own money by catching octopus and selling it for bait. I had my own pots and that enabled me to buy my own sporting gear. I did a lot of stuff in the sea. It was an interesting life.

'Dad's work ethic, I've never seen the like in anybody. Nowadays, I work hard during vintage but there will be periods when I stop. He would never stop. Never stop thinking. Never stop working. He was actively involved in building every part of the winery. From putting in the electric cable to whatever needed to be done. He always took great joy in learning a new skill. It was relentless, overwhelming.'

Integrity Established: The 1978 Dry Red

The problem with the cabernet in 1978 was not the vintage, which produced lovely fruit, but the yeast culture acquired by Moss Wood from the Department of Agriculture that year. Pannell explained: 'It was a different yeast [from usual] ... which produced hydrogen sulphide [rotten egg gas]. The winery stank when we used it. Anyway, I just wasn't happy with the wine. We copper-fined it and salvaged what we could.'

The wine was declassified and sold as the 1978 Moss Wood Dry Red at $2.50 a bottle. Bill Pannell's friend, chemist and winemaker Gil Thomas bought a quantity of the wine and released it under his Thomas label. He entered it in the Perth Show where it won the Stewart Van Raalte Trophy.

Said Pannell: 'Oddly enough, that did us a lot of good because we developed a reputation for integrity. We said that we weren't prepared to sell that as Moss Wood Cabernet. And I think that stood us in very good stead ... but it nearly killed us financially.'

At a major vertical tasting of twenty vintages of Moss Wood Cabernet held at Bill and Sandra Pannell's house in Dalkeith in July 1990, attended by both authors, the one disappointment in the tasting was the 1978 Dry Red.

There was a sequel to the story which came when Keith Mugford received a letter from a Canadian wine lover in 1993. He wrote that he had purchased a case of the 1978 Moss Wood Dry Red in 1980 for the bargain price of $2.50. He explained that he had thoroughly enjoyed the wine, had just consumed the last of it and wondered if there were any left. If so, he mused, was the price the same.

Moss Wood Cabernet Vertical Tasting

At that vertical tasting, the Mugfords and the Pannells presented eighteen vintages of the Moss Wood Cabernets. It was comprehensively documented in the Moss Wood Newsletter (Winter 1991) and in *The West Australian*.

Ray Jordan writes:

At one end of the table in a slightly dusty unlabelled burgundy bottle was the wine that started it all in 1973. At the other was another unlabelled burgundy bottle—representing the story so far. And at one end of the table was Bill Pannell, the man who created the story in 1969, while at the other was Keith Mugford, the man who is adding the latest chapters.

In between was every cabernet made in the 18 vintages of Moss Wood—21 wines in all and among them, without doubt, some of the greatest wines ever made at Margaret River.

The significance of the event was not lost on those of us who gathered round the table. Here was every cabernet sauvignon made from one of Australia's greatest vineyards and the two men who either singularly or in tandem had made those wines.

Four hours later and still on a euphoric high I could only marvel at the consistent quality of the wines. There was not a bad or tainted wine in the lot and the only one I felt disappointed with was the 1978, which Pannell himself rejected and reclassified before release because he felt it was not up to standard.

These wines from the 1970s, from immature vines, were still staggeringly youthful and alive. Sure, they had developed excellent aged characters but they were not tired or over the hill. I suspect they will be ticking over for a few years yet.

The 1975 was a classic—one of the most beautifully perfect Australian wines I have tried. The rich opulent flavours of an aged wine were in perfect harmony with lovely long and broad sweet berry fruit.

Afterwards Keith Mugford admitted that the tasting showed a consistency of style which even he had not realised was quite so strong but, just as importantly, was the fact that it was becoming clear that these wines had great longevity and there didn't seem to be a marked drop off in quality with the older wines.

No Cellar Door

Keith Mugford reflected on the quality of Moss Wood wines which 'made people sit up and take notice' from the first vintage in 1973. 'As the decades rolled by, the quality of the wines improved and the interest of the outside world in Margaret River increased. In 1979, if we got three or four visitors a week, we had a busy week at Moss Wood. We have never had a cellar door but we get more visitors now than we can cope with, and they come from all around the world. We have to employ people to look after them. That's all happened in one generation. Remarkable really.'

While Moss Wood may not have had a cellar door outlet, there are some fascinating yarns about those who have visited the winery. Bill Pannell remembered two occasions vividly:

'One day in 1976 there was this almighty clatter and a Navy helicopter suddenly appeared over the trees, hovered a bit and then landed in a clearing. We were completely baffled until an officer got out, took off his helmet and explained he had come from an Australian ship offshore to buy some Moss Wood wine. They'd heard it was good. They loaded five cases of Cabernet on board, sent the dust flying and took off. It was a good sale.

'Keith and I were working out in the vineyard and Sandra was at the winery when there was the roaring of engines and a whole mob of about twenty bikies swept in. We got up there as quickly as possible, fearing the worst, then found they were from the Ducati Club and were some of the most knowledgeable and pleasant customers we had had for ages.'

Keith Mugford recalls some of the famous people who visited. 'Australian pop icon John Farnham spent a couple of hours talking about wine with us; just a friendly, easy-going bloke. We have a cricket bat at the winery which we get all these famous people to sign: Phil Kearns, Dennis Lillee, Ian Brayshaw, Alicia Molik, Michael Thomson and more ... always a thrill for us.'

Keith noted: 'Michael Palin's visit was particularly memorable because some of the most famous *Monty Python* sketches had become part of our winemaking lives. Often as we moved around the winery floor, someone would start and we would meander through one of the Python sketches. 'The Dead Parrot' and 'Cheese Shop' were favourites. I can still recite that stupid parrot sketch. Michael Palin had difficulty getting his head around the idea that people could make wine while walking around the winery echoing 'Remarkable bird, the Norwegian Blue, idn'it, ay? Beautiful plumage!'

Promoting the Region

While Bill Pannell was the inaugural President of the Margaret River Grape

Growers' and Wine Producers Association (now Margaret River Wine Association), a meeting was held to decide on the name of the region. The mists of time seem to have clouded the details of that meeting held in the Cowaramup Hall in (about) 1975. There were five members present: Kevin Cullen, David Gregg, Mark Hohnen, Bill Pannell and one other. Kevin Cullen, whose winery was called Willyabrup Wines at the time, was a strong advocate of the name 'Wilyabrup' and Mark Hohnen was equally vociferous in support of 'Margaret River' because the town's beaches were getting a worldwide reputation as a surfing destination. 'Why reinvent the wheel?' he posited. Bill Pannell supported 'Margaret River' because he said all the great wine growing regions of the world were either on rivers or in valleys.

The meeting paused for a libation with Wilyabrup having the majority support. Fierce lobbying during the break swung the day and the wine region became Margaret River. The name was registered the next day.

Another matter that concerned Pannell was what he saw as parochialism and self-interest among his fellow vignerons. 'At the time, we were criticised because people couldn't find the wineries they were looking for. It was quite a large area and quite remote and the small number of vineyards were widely dispersed.' In the Hunter Valley, he had noted that on most corners ... and the winemakers would hang their signs on steel pickets directing visitors to their wineries. Bill liked the idea and raised it at the next Growers' Association meeting. He was told that, as Moss Wood was (then) the northern-most winery, 'everybody would see it first'. His rejoinder 'Does that matter?' was not well received and he eventually dropped the matter. His rationale seemed perfectly reasonable: that for a region to succeed it needed to be promoted as a region. His belief that no wine lover would drive 300 kilometres to Margaret River to visit a single wine producer seems equally valid.

Even at the end of the 1970s, all cellar doors were open by appointment only except for Cullens, which was open two afternoons a week. The Pannells had seen a place in Beaune with upturned barrels which served as an informal regional tasting centre. When Busselton's Prospect Villa became available, Bill suggested the idea of using it for a similar purpose but received no support.

Marketing Margaret River

While the early days had their difficulties, Keith Mugford believes that marketing the area was not one of them.

'Margaret River, despite all the complications, when it got going made some fabulous wines and that coincided with a market that was keen to receive them. There wasn't anywhere near as much competition as there is these days so the opportunity to get Margaret River wines selling to the wider world was good. It seemed you could just turn up in Melbourne and Sydney and sell your wine. The wine merchants would stock them and get on the phone to their clients and push them. At the time, it didn't seem easy but that part of producing and selling wine was much easier then than it is now.

'To be frank, if the pioneers of the time had faced the market as we have it now, I don't know how successful we would have been. It got a moment in the sun which allowed the region to consolidate its place in the market. I think that's important.

'Looking back at the commentary from the wine writers and the show judging results, the industry got a dream run through that first decade. The chardonnay, the cabernets, even the pinot noir. With the 1981, Moss Wood made arguably the country's best pinot noir to that stage. We got a lot of positive support at the right time.

The Western Australian market is fabulous for Western Australian wines: the locals really warm to Margaret River. They drank its wines and were happy to celebrate its successes. When it went interstate, there were buyers, retailers who bought the story, bought the wines, bought the whole thing. They all lined up.'

Burnout

In 1970, it was just Bill Pannell and Kevin Cullen in the medical practice in Busselton. It was worse on weekends when the doctors in Margaret River and Augusta were not on call and the two of them had to service medical emergencies south of Bunbury and as far as Augusta. It was hard in the early to mid 1970s, running the practice by day and delivering babies by night. All that, and Pannell, in his spare time, establishing the vineyard and winery at Moss Wood while living twenty kilometres away in Busselton.

Pannell quoted one of the great French chefs who, on achieving his third Michelin star, commented that it didn't seem worthwhile, it was just too hard. He attributed this hard graft as part of the reason that he didn't look back on their time in Margaret River with great fondness.

He remembered all too vividly the family leaving Busselton for their first holiday in the five years since they had arrived. 'I was driving out of town and we came across this horrific motor accident in the tuart forest near Capel. It was a head-on smash with fatalities among the five children and several adults involved. I had to just try and sort that out. It was the kind of unending pressure which I just got beyond coping with. I was getting burned out.'

He took a year off from the practice in 1976 to give his full attention to Moss Wood. While having the time to focus solely on the vineyard and winery made for a much less stressful year, he came to realise the strength of his attachment to medicine. He then needed to look ahead to the time when he was once again doing two full-time jobs. He realised that he would need to scale down his involvement at Moss Wood.

By 1978, he commented, 'My tongue was dragging on the floor really. I had become physically and mentally exhausted and realised that I simply could not carry on as I had been doing. In short, I needed help.' He began looking for a qualified winemaker who might ease his workload.

Enter Keith Mugford

Bill Hardy spent quite a bit of time in Western Australia after his family company had bought Houghton in 1976 and had visited the Pannells in Margaret River several times. Pannell recalled Hardy's support and enthusiasm for their work. 'So, I asked him if he knew of anyone who might be interested in working at Moss Wood.' He mentioned that a family friend of his, Dr Keith Mugford, a McLaren-Vale based orthopaediac surgeon, had a son (also called Keith) who was finishing his winemaking course at Roseworthy College. Bill was happy to recommend him.'

Keith and Clare Mugford at the time they bought Moss Wood from the Pannells. Photo courtesy Moss Wood

Keith Mugford, for his part, had been mightily impressed with a bottle of 1977 Moss Wood Semillon that two West Australians, fellow students at Roseworthy, had shared with him. They were John Elliott (who subsequently enjoyed a successful career with the WA Department of Agriculture) and Mike Peterkin (who worked with the Cullens in 1979 and 1980 and launched his Pierro label with a 1979 Cabernet made from Moss Wood fruit). Mugford had applied to half a dozen wineries for employment as a winemaker and had received a positive response from

Lindemans at Karadoc near Mildura in the Riverina. He also received a letter from Bill Pannell. He remembered that 1977 Semillon and was attracted by the fact that Moss Wood was situated in an emerging wine region. When asked about the lure of Margaret River, he also admitted that he was a keen surfer.

The Pannells visited the Mugfords in McLaren Vale to reassure Keith's mother, Lillian, about his chances of surviving the wilds of the South West. Keith lived with the Pannells in Busselton for a time and Sandra felt it was rather like gaining another son 'with dirty clothes all over the floor'. Bill Pannell knew Keith was 'still pretty green' but he loved his 'great enthusiasm and tremendous sense of humour'. Theirs was a close friendship.

In those first few years, Keith Mugford believed he was a sounding board for Pannell and could reassure him about what they were doing, as well as talking about what Moss Wood could do. While Keith felt that, in 1979, Bill was 'perhaps, running a little low on enthusiasm and in need of help' but was still intensely passionate and determined. 'He would not give in.' Mugford also gained much from Bill Pannell: 'I had all the technical background from Roseworthy but that's not the end of winemaking. Bill had a substantial influence on me—one of his great strengths as a winemaker was his ability to interpret style.'

Mugford arrived shortly before the 1979 vintage and so the two winemakers looked at each vintage of Cabernet that had been made at Moss Wood. They agreed that the 1975 was, as Pannell put it, 'the rather more refined style that we wanted to go for', and the 1979 was made in that mould.

They were both delighted with the 1980 Moss Wood Cabernet Sauvignon and decided if a small portion (200 dozen bottles) were kept in oak for a second year 'it might turn out quite well'. That wine is now selling at auction for more than $500 a bottle. The wine was labelled Moss Wood Special Reserve Cabernet Sauvignon and became the prototype for the treatment of Moss Wood Cabernet in the best vintages (1980, 1983, 1987, 1990, 1991 and

1994). A Special Reserve was not made from the exceptional 1985 vintage because of the low volumes of that year. In 1995, the Mugfords decided that all their Cabernets would be given the same treatment as the Special Reserves—two years rather than one in oak—and released a year later than previously. This practice continues.

Why Margaret River Flourished

Keith Mugford is a thoughtful and articulate vigneron who has spent most of his working life in Margaret River. He is able to be involved in the region's affairs and yet comment on them in a rational and dispassionate way. He says:

'The area blossomed because of the unique collection of individuals who shared the common goal of making the best possible wine, and that one day Margaret River might rival Bordeaux. If they hadn't been so committed and capable, the region's development may have proceeded at a much slower pace and may not have been as successful.

'Certainly, with the honourable exception of people like Max Lake, Murray Tyrell and Ross Brown, there was, at best, polite indifference from the big companies based in south-eastern Australia, so commitment from that side of the country was, and remains, almost non-existent.

'To be honest, this was probably a benefit. It meant this region didn't carry with it the historical biases that in my view still plague that side of the country. It started with a clean slate and the pioneers weren't encumbered by existing or traditional ideas. I worry this individuality is being lost. Perhaps it's just commercial reality but it seems to me we're 3,000 kilometres away from the industry hub and need to understand that our isolation gives us a chance to differentiate ourselves.'

End of an Era

Bill Pannell and Keith Mugford enjoyed a convivial and productive partnership between 1979 and 1983 (Pannell's last complete vintage at Moss Wood) and made outstanding wines during this period. While there is little doubt that having Mugford share the workload made a difference, by 1984 Bill accepted that he 'was becoming extremely tired and needed a break'.

'The intensity of their lives was extraordinary ... Not only did both have time-consuming day jobs (Bill as a busy local GP and Sandra with four young kids and a busy husband) but they threw themselves into the work in the vineyard and winery, refusing to compromise and all the time focusing on making Moss Wood the best it could be. I have great admiration for what they achieved but it was tough.'

Like the Greggs at Vasse Felix, the question of the children's education came to the fore. It was time for them to move to Perth to complete their education. It was a question of breaking up the family or taking the major step of moving back to Perth. In 1984, Pannell had decided that he wanted to move on. He had canvassed their children's future interest in taking on Moss Wood. Although Stephen and Daniel have had successful careers as winemakers and Emma has married a winemaker, none at the time said yes.

Bill and Sandra Pannell discussed the leasing of Moss Wood with Keith and Clare Mugford. Keith had gradually assumed greater responsibility for running the vineyard while they shared the winemaking responsibilities. The Pannells were relaxed and happy to see Moss Wood take a new direction. Mugford said that they were very generous in their lease negotiations. When the business was settled, Sandra and Bill headed for France, where they took time to regather themselves. They had been going to France regularly since 1980, were loving Burgundy, and Bill was falling under the spell of pinot noir.

In September 1984, they returned to Western Australia and shortly afterwards announced to the Mugfords that they wanted them to buy Moss Wood. Again, the Pannells were generous, offering the Mugfords vendor finance until they were able to reduce the loan to a size where they could obtain a bank loan. They chose to sell to the Mugfords believing that they would continue Moss Wood in the spirit in which it was established. The Mugfords took this injunction seriously, believing their work at Moss Wood has served to preserve the legacy of the Pannell years.

Ray Jordan posed the question 'Why sell a vineyard of such quality?' in a 2008 interview with Bill Pannell. 'There is a lot of personal involvement in something like this and I suppose you just run out of that spark and the energy to keep going. I think it needed someone with the vigour that I had in those early days. I'm very pleased to see that Keith Mugford is doing what he is doing because that's really the way I wanted it to go. I could have got a lot more for the place if I had sold it to a bigger company but I know they would have changed things and that's not the way I wanted it to happen.'

Keith Mugford on Pannell: 'He is an incredibly deep thinker and able to use his intellect to understand a problem and then work from first principles to develop a solution. A rare skill indeed. No doubt my view is biased, but both Bill and Sandra's contribution to the Margaret River region is way beyond what most people know. In many ways, Bill's intensity was a blessing and a curse. It gave him the drive that was so fundamental to his success but could also leave him in a situation where he put people off. Sandra had perhaps the more difficult task of all, keeping the peace, working on the vineyard project and running the family.'

Bill Pannell has an astute palate and a wonderful knowledge of the wines of the world especially those from Burgundy, Bordeaux and Champagne. He also has a generosity of spirit that has often been manifest in the understated way he shares the finest bottles from his cellar with those he believes are keen to understand better the world of fine wine. He is well deserving of the recognition he has received. In 2003, Bill was made a member of the Order of Australia (AM). In 2002, the Wine Press Club of Western Australia honoured him with the Jack Mann Medal for distinguished service to the West Australian wine industry.

Chapter 13

Cape Mentelle and the Coming of Age

Congratulations for what you built at Cape Mentelle. The place looks like a subsidiary of Paradise!— **Joseph Henriot, Veuve Clicquot Ponsardin (1990)**

Beginnings

While the Cape Mentelle venture is a story of the Hohnen family, it's certainly not a family story like any other. It is driven throughout by the fortitude and talent of David Hohnen and by the intelligence and financial acumen of his brother Mark. Their father, John Hohnen, kick-started the operation, with the Salmon and Le Soeuf families making noteworthy contributions as partners in Margaret River Land Holdings—the corporate structure from which Cape Mentelle was formed. Mark's Scottish friend, Simon

Fraser, was the investor vital to the realisation of the dream.

John Hohnen was a mining engineer with a lifelong interest in fine wine cultivated as a young man during his time working in the French overseas territory of New Caledonia. He later spent twelve years working for New Guinea Goldfields based at remote Wau in the Highlands. He survived the rigours of the inhospitable terrain with the help of small barrels of Hunter Valley shiraz regularly shipped to him by Sydney wine merchant Douglas Lamb and bottled on arrival. At least partly because his children were at secondary school in Victoria, he moved to Melbourne as Managing Director of Rio Tinto, where he worked with West Australian iron ore miners Lang Hancock and Peter Wright. After Rio Tinto merged with Consolidated Zinc in 1962, he was offered the position of NSW manager but chose instead to move to Perth as Director of Operations (WA) of CRA so that he could remain involved with the exciting developments taking place there. He was a driving force behind the establishment of the

Hamersley Iron subsidiary, and spent a great deal of time being flown (often at improbably low heights) around the North West by Lang Hancock to examine his mineral discoveries first hand. One of John Hohnen's stories sums up Hancock, whom he regarded as a bushman and pilot par excellence.

'We were flying north to look at the Mount Goldsworthy area ... when, forced down to almost ground level by rain clouds, we landed on a large, wet clay pan. After coming to a stop, I mildly commented that we might have stuck fast or, worse still, gone down on the nose. Lang gently explained that there was no danger, one could see where the kangaroos had been crossing—by their tracks.'

When his children were teenagers in Perth, wine played a part in the family's everyday life. Before dinner, John Hohnen would take a small red jug, made by David 'while he was in prison' (Geelong Grammar), and blend the Swan Valley favourite, Valencia No.1, with a Grenache from Sandalford for the family to drink with the evening meal.

John Hohnen and Tom Cullity were neighbours who lived on opposite sides of View Street, Peppermint Grove. In 1964, Hohnen had a massive heart attack in the middle of the night and was carried downstairs by his sons (David later recalled how heavy he was). Margaret Hohnen knew Tom Cullity was a heart specialist and so, as Mark colourfully put it, 'the old girl bolted across the road and grabbed Tom at about 3.00am.' He took over and, in David's words, 'with his skill, my father's life was saved.' John Hohnen remembers Tom saying, 'Fight, John, fight' and 'applying an electric shock to my heart which must have done the trick'. After that, the two men began spending more time together, sharing their mutual interest in fine wine and many of their finest bottles. Giles Hohnen recalls going with his father, probably in 1965, to visit Tom Cullity at his trial vineyard at Burekup.

In 1965, John Hohnen bought Wallcliffe Farm, a small (110 hectares) holiday block on the last reach of the Margaret River before it joins the Indian Ocean. It was adjacent to the imposing

Wallcliffe House, which was built by Alfred and Ellen Bussell in the early 1860s. There were two titles on the block, both of historic significance. One included a farmhouse (the Dairy) which had originally been part of the Bussell property. The other had been awarded by the State Government (or possibly by Alfred Bussell) to Sam Isaacs in recognition of the part he had played in the 1876 rescue of the passengers of the *SS Georgette* which sank off nearby Calgardup Bay. The $30,000 block was close to the small town of Margaret River, then with a population of 400. It had very sandy soils and was considered scarcely arable by Giles, Mark and David. John Hohnen thought that its white sands resembled the soil of Champagne and Mark commented that 'he had the crazy idea he could grow grapes for a sparkler there'. Although a feasibility study in 1972 flirted with the notion, it was never tested.

The property, with its galvanised iron garage affectionately known by the family as The Shack, was a significant impetus to the founding of Cape

Mentelle. As David commented, it started the family going to Margaret River because 'we would stay in the little shack, drink beer, shoot and eat kangaroos and have a great time'.

Following a second heart attack, John Hohnen retired in 1969. He became marginally involved in the wine industry when he was on the board of Sandalford as the representative of the local merchant bank, Westralian International. He was also friends with John Roe, whose family had owned Sandalford's Swan Valley property for more than 100 years and still retained a small share in the business. In the late 1960s, Sandalford were looking to expand and approached Denis Horgan about the Maplestones' property that he had acquired. They eventually bought Maylem's Farm, a property that Tom Cullity had persuaded an American friend, Jim Morrison, to buy. John Hohnen had a significant influence on Sandalford's decision to make the purchase.

Margaret River Land Holdings

Mark Hohnen saw his father as a forward thinker who became interested in the possibilities of viticulture after discussing the Gladstones paper with Tom Cullity. The Wallcliffe Farm block, however, was south of the area described by Gladstones and so when he turned his attention to making use of the land, John Hohnen decided that, given current high prices, beef cattle would offer a better return than viticulture. He bought what became the Wilderness Block, which ran from the Shack Block to the south of Caves Road and south of Wallcliffe Road adjacent to the golf club. He was thinking big and had his son Mark investigate the possibilities of amalgamating several properties into one large contiguous farm. After checking with locals on the suitability of the site, Mark also negotiated with the local shire to put in an airstrip on the property. What was originally proposed was a 'magnificent' farm of 1,000 acres (400 hectares) of pasture, with 800 acres (325 hectares) of uncleared land. The latter would offer tax deductibility as it was converted to pasture.

John Hohnen saw the potential of Margaret River. Photo courtesy Hohnen family

Troubles loomed for John Hohnen in 1970, with his investments in Fiji and in mining plummeting and the bottom falling out of the beef cattle market. His financial resources were stretched to the limit, yet he forged ahead with a revised plan for amalgamating the Hohnen, Salmon and Le Soeuf families' properties. Together it totalled 3,000 acres (1200 hectares) under the corporate umbrella of Margaret River Land Holdings (MRLH), which was incorporated in February 1970. Each family was given shares (valued at $1) depending on the value of the respective properties. The Hohnens received 50,000 shares, the Salmons 66,000, and the Le Soeufs 123,000 shares. They decided to hold the value of the shares to $1 for a year and after that they would take on the agreed market value.

The company began with the farming of beef cattle and, to a lesser extent, sheep. With the fall in the price of beef, John Hohnen quickly saw diversification into viticulture as likely to provide a better return on investment for MRLH. From this time on, the business of MRLH was extended to include the establishment and running of what became Cape Mentelle Vineyards and, after Mark Hohnen became Managing Director in late 1973, the sale of 'non-viable' farming land owned by MRLH, either through subdivisions or the selling of individual blocks (for between $6,000 and $18,000 each).

During the first few years, John Hohnen needed to inject $70,000 into the company to keep it afloat. The Salmons were unhappy with the way things were going, so quit the company in 1973. They sold their shares to John Hohnen who bought them out at par, even though the shares were only valued at 63 cents at that time.

Mark Hohnen met and became friends with a wealthy Scottish aristocrat, the Honourable Simon Fraser, Master of Lovat, while working in London. Fraser, who was with Hambros Bank, visited Margaret River in 1973 and became a significant investor in MRLH from 1974. The company was in difficulties and Fraser offered to take up to 48.6 per cent of the capital. He did this on the condition that the founding shareholders sold a total of ten per cent of the company's shares to the managing director at a negotiated price, thus giving Simon Fraser and Mark Hohnen control of the company.

Dr Leslie Le Soeuf was Chairman of the MRLH Board from 1970 to 1978 and had an increasingly fractious relationship with Mark, who commented: 'It worked for a few years then it didn't. There were too many different personalities.' The Le Soeufs sold their shares to Simon Fraser in March 1980 for the price they asked of $3 a share.

MRLH remained the dominant shareholder in Cape Mentelle Vineyards (CMV) until 1986. Tiny volumes of the first three vintages from the Wallcliffe Vineyard were released under the MRLH label. However, those involved with the operation of the vineyard from 1974 to 1976—Mark and Giles Hohnen and Simon Fraser—realised that it was time to move to the next stage. David Hohnen was scheduled to return from Taltarni in August 1976 to make the wines and supervise the vineyard; a corporate structure was necessary with a name and label. The building of a winery or tractor shed was scheduled for 1977 and there was discussion about the name for the winery. The latter was solved easily after Giles Hohnen suggested Cape Mentelle, which was a landmark nearby, just north of the mouth of the Margaret River.

As a result of the 1801 Baudin expedition, it had been named to honour two brothers who lived in Paris during the eighteenth century: geographer and historian, Edmé, and cartographer François-Simon Mentelle.

Cape Mentelle Vineyards (CMV) became incorporated on 1 September 1976. The vineyard's labels were designed by local artist Gary Mann, who had helped plant the first vines.

Planting the First Vines (1970)

John Hohnen approached Dorham Mann to help them find a suitable vineyard site for a proposed planting. Dorham inspected a number of the MRLH's properties with John Hohnen, Sam Salmon and Leslie Le Soeuf. From a vinicultural perspective, the Hohnen land near the Margaret River on the west side of Caves Road was mainly weak and sandy; similarly, Sam Salmon's land, also on the west side of Caves Road, was unsuitable; while the Le Soeuf property to the south of what is now the winery did not appear ideal. They found an area on Salmon's North Farm with plenty of good Marri trees and a desirable soil profile. This became the site of the first planting of three acres (1.2 hectares) on what is now the Wallcliffe Vineyard.

During 1970, Sam Salmon, farm manager for MRLH, and farm hand Stan Clews fenced and cleared 27 acres (11 hectares) and planting began in August. Leslie Le Soeuf noted in his diary (October 5) that he had seen three acres (1.2 hectares) of cabernet vines, plus rabbit-proof fencing, which had just been finished. Four thousand shiraz cuttings had also been propagated in a nursery on the airstrip block. He indicated that the planting had been done by the Hohnens and their friends as well as the Salmons and the Mitchells.

Gary Mann is a lifetime friend of Giles. As he recalled in 2016 'I was one of the gang from the Western Australian Institute of Technology [now Curtin University] who went down to Margaret River during the term vacation to help prepare the ground and plant the vines under Sam Salmon's direction'. He recalls that the idea of the tree-line label came during that planting.

A feasibility study was commissioned by MRLH and presented in 1972. It looked at the conditions for successful grape growing in the region and considered how suitable the land owned by the company might be for viticulture. In the light of what transpired during the early years at Cape Mentelle, it was noted that bird life—in particular, silvereyes—was likely to be the major pest. Mention was made that this was only likely to be a problem in the years when the marris (red gums) did not blossom naturally. David Hohnen was later to complain that, early on, that occurred three out of five years. The 1972 report suggested several methods to reduce the bird problem—none of them were to prove successful.

While the first plantings were being established the three Hohnen sons were studying: Giles was doing his final year at art school, Mark was in England and David in the USA.

Left: Brothers JR and David Hohnen with friends David Sands and David Paterson (Giles Hohnen has been pushed out of the picture and only his feet are visible.) Right: Giles in his rightful position in the vineyard. Photo courtesy Cape Mentelle

Giles Hohnen

Giles returned from two years of National Service in Vietnam at the end of 1969. After finishing art school in 1970, he spent 1971 and 1972 travelling, working and playing in Europe. He then worked in the vineyard from 1973 to 1976 and played a leading role in building the rammed earth machinery shed (1976) and winery (1977).

Mark Hohnen

Mark Hohnen studied agriculture at Shuttleworth College in Bedfordshire in 1969 and 1970. He then worked in London as a stockbroker between 1970 and 1973, after which he returned to live in Western Australia. Simon Fraser's first visit to Margaret River in 1973 was inauspicious. He came from England with Mark and stayed in Bunbury while they visited the group's properties. To Mark's horror, someone had let the cattle into the vineyard and they'd flattened the vines. Mark spent his time between Perth and Margaret River until he married Cate De Witt in 1974. Then, as he was Managing Director of MRLH, they went to live on the farm.

Mark Hohnen circa early 1970s. Photo courtesy
Hohnen family

Guy Grant worked with Mark at Oceanic Equity for many years and was on loan part time to Cape Mentelle during the glory years, when he was the genius behind *Mentelle Notes.* He tells what is surely an apocryphal tale though swears it paints an accurate picture of Mark Hohnen, the businessman:

'Mark and Simon Fraser were exporting calf dairy heifers from England, Canada and, on one occasion, from Margaret River Land Holdings to the Shah of Iran. That shipment of live cattle went from Perth on a DC10, refuelling in Singapore and Mumbai en route to Iran. They arrived in India on the day the government nationalised the banks. The pilot, a cowboy American, had a wallet which flipped open to reveal upwards of twenty-five different credit cards.

"Take whichever one you want. Just refuel the plane," he commanded.

"No, no, sir. We need to be paid cash."

'Mark Hohen had a few hundred US dollars. The pilot had some, too. 'The Indian official said "Regretfully, I'm sorry your cash is not good. It's not Indian money."

'So, there they were with the heat rising and no prospect of refuelling the plane. 'Mark asks to see the Airport Manager and explains to him, "Look, we need to refuel this plane. You're the one who makes the decision about it. Right now, there are twenty-five cattle with me. If we can't start refuelling the plane within half an hour, I'm going to bring the cows out the back of the plane and, one by one, I'm going to cut their throats on the tarmac."

'With cows being sacred in India, the plane was refuelled promptly and flew off to Iran.'

Guy Grant comments, 'In terms of sheer cunning, he is hard to beat.' As a result of this jaunt, David and Mark Hohnen were invited by the Agricultural Bank of Iran to visit Shiraz to advise the Iranians on producing shiraz wine.

David Hohnen

In 1967, after finishing secondary school, David Hohnen worked as a jackaroo in the remote West Australian outback. He was based at Sturt Meadows, a million-acre sheep station near Leonora more than 800 kilometres from Perth. He earned $12 a week working as part of a team of six who operated the vast property. A wide-ranging skills set, ingenuity and adaptability were necessary to keep the station's equipment functioning.

After that experience, he enrolled in engineering at the University of Western Australia, largely because he believed that this was what his father expected of him. It didn't take him long to realise that this was not the career for him. He contemplated his future, thinking that something in agriculture might suit him—as long as it didn't involve animal husbandry. The idea of viticulture and winemaking appealed. A family friend introduced him to Henry Martin, who offered him a job in the winery at Stonyfell, near Adelaide. It piqued his interest and he decided to explore formal studies in winemaking. Some success with the stock market had enabled him to buy a BMW motorcycle which he drove up to Roseworthy College to investigate Australia's best-known educational institution for winemaking and viticulture. The visit convinced him that he would be better off studying elsewhere. He examined the options available in the United States and contacted the University of California, Davis, and Fresno State College (now California State University, Fresno). He was encouraged by the latter's response and so enrolled there for the academic year beginning in mid-1969.

David Hohnen rode his bike to Sydney where it was taken on board the P&O's *Orsova* as personal baggage. After the voyage from Sydney to Oakland, the bike was off-loaded and David noted there was still petrol in the tank, so he rode the bike over the seven-kilometre Bay Bridge and up to Fresno. He was able to secure off-campus accommodation 'at very, very low cost, living with a small group of 'radical, peace-loving non-conformists'. This was the time of the anti – Vietnam War protests and the killings at Kent State University, so colleges and universities were volatile places. Fresno, on the other hand, was a conservative farmers' town producing almonds, grapes and olives, where radicals or protesting students were regarded as 'wackos'.

Students had a great deal of choice about which units they studied. After the first semester, David had a better understanding of the system and dispensed with 'American history and Indian basket weaving' to concentrate on microbiology, winemaking and viticulture. By doing that, he could compress his studies into a two-year course. While this meant that he didn't graduate from Fresno, he had learnt all he needed to begin the task of establishing what was to become Cape Mentelle.

David Hohnen found the practical side of the course immeasurably beneficial. In 1952, the college had purchased a 160-acre (65 hectares) vineyard which they divided into five-acre (two-hectare) lots. The students were invited to make a pitch for a block, work it for the year, sell the grapes, and share the income with the school. David had a five-acre plot of carignan from which he made $900 one year and $1,200 the next—not inconsiderable sums in those days.

He must have made an impression on staff. In his final semester (Spring 1971), the college's vice principal offered David a part-time position as a teaching assistant, for which he was paid $178.93 per month. His total pay for the semester of $1,735, plus what he had earned from the vineyard, less Fresno State's modest fees meant that he 'was doing fine financially'.

Student trips to the wineries of California in a VW minibus, owned by one of the group, may have been somewhat boozy but David believes he learnt a great deal from them. One of the wineries he visited was Chalonne in Monterey. Years later, it was to play a part in the design of the Cloudy Bay label. He credits his student days and the need to 'drink inexpensive' with his interest in zinfandel, which played a role in the Cape Mentelle story.

David returned to Margaret River in mid-1971 and married Sandy McHenry in September 1971. For eighteen months, he proved to be a prodigious vineyard worker: pruning vines at Vasse Felix (1971); planting vines at Cape Mentelle (1971 and 1972) and Sandalford (1972), and doing the undervine weeding at Cullen (1972). The need to wait until the MRLH vines became productive and the parlous state of its finances meant he needed to seek employment elsewhere. An offer of $4,500 a year to manage Sandalford was comprehensively improved on by Taltarni, which paid him $7,000 a year to develop the vineyard and manage Taltarni. He and Sandy left for Moonambool in Central Victoria in

October 1972 and were there until August 1976. When he arrived, ninety acres (36.5 hectares) had already been planted 'in a haphazard sort of a fashion'. By the time he left, Taltarni was well established.

David Hohnen at Cape Mentelle in 1990. Photo courtesy Cape Mentelle

Dominique Portet, who took over from him and became a long-time friend, cannot speak too highly of David:

'He is, and was, an incredible achiever. He was excellent with the Taltarni's staff, very demanding but always showing the lead.

Consider his achievement—from an empty paddock he created life in this part of the world. Before, there was just sheep and trees ... afterwards there were a lot of dams, interconnected to satisfy the vineyard's need for a 23-year supply of water without rainfall; and 120 acres (48 hectares) of plantings of riesling, sauvignon blanc, chardonnay and cabernet. He planted on contours and used new techniques such as drip irrigation. And he was always trying to save a dollar or two.

Taking over from him and continuing his work was easy.'

Building Cape Mentelle

On his return from California, David planted a further ten acres (four hectares) of vines (six acres [2.5 hectares] of cabernet and four [1.6 hectares] of riesling) in August 1971. At about the same time, Terry Merchant had entered into a partnership with the Cullens to plant their vineyard. Helped by David, he developed nurseries for both Cullen and Cape Mentelle on Cullen land. For the latter, six virus-free varieties imported by the Agriculture Department were planted in a varietal block: gewurtztraminer (100 vines), chenin blanc (100), chardonnay (25), zinfandel (50), pinot noir (25), and cabernet (75), all of which did well except the cabernet. It suffered from black beetle.

Dead vines on the Wallcliffe Vineyard were replanted with these cuttings in 1972. After David's return, Giles was employed to maintain the existing vines and to plant a further 27 acres (11 hectares) in front of where the winery would be built in 1978. While he was at Taltarni, David sent a regular cheque home to cover Giles' wages. This helped during the vineyard's most difficult years and it also enabled him to build up credit with MRLH which, in turn, influenced his stake in Cape Mentelle.

Tom Roberts, a friend of David's from his short-lived career as an engineering student at the University of Western Australia, had gone on to study architecture. He took on, for his fourth-year project in 1973, the design of a Margaret River Winery. His tutor, Fremantle architect Rob Campbell, looked at the sketches and said, 'Why not build it from earth?' The 1970s' counter culture and the energy crisis made it an obvious choice for Tom. Thick earth walls provided thermal mass which moderated temperature fluctuations and offered an aesthetic addition to the landscape. With his university project complete and finding little work for architectural graduates, Tom drifted to Margaret River to work for Mark Hohnen on the farm and play football for the Margaret River Football Club. Tom's rammed earth building ideas took on a new urgency during intense Friday night discussions at the Margaret River Hotel. He felt that if he didn't get something built, his ideas would be seen as 'just hot air'. One of the Friday night enthusiasts was a building inspector, Tony Stone, who pointed out that before any habitable structure could be built, a prototype would need to be erected to persuade the shire councillors that bare, unrendered rammed earth walls would be durable and structurally sound.

Adding a rammed earth extension to the Hohnens' shack on the river block seemed a good option. Plans were again drawn up but immediately abandoned when it was realised that the luxurious new addition would sit uneasily with the rustic lifestyle of the incumbent, Giles Hohnen. Then in early 1976, David gave Tom the go-ahead to build a machinery shed (referred to subsequently in Cape Mentelle lore as The Shed) which would serve as a temporary winery. He and Giles set to work willingly, though he writes years later: 'Progress was slow, day one lasting about a week. This was partly due to the laborious nature of the work, and partly to the amount of time spent taking photos.'

The Shed was the first of these ecologically sound structures built in Margaret River and immediately gained an enthusiastic following. The distinctive architectural style which integrates neatly with the Australian bush has become synonymous with Margaret River. The following year, Mark Hohnen managed to find the necessary $14,000 and the rammed earth winery with verandahs on four sides was built by Giles and Tom Roberts.

Tom, who established an architectural practice in Fremantle, went on to design all the additions to the Cape Mentelle winery and all the Cloudy Bay buildings. With the growing interest in rammed earth building and the need for a Perth presence, Giles went into partnership with Steve Dobson, an engineer friend. In 1979, they started Ramtec, a specialist rammed earth contracting company. The pair parted ways in 1982 and Giles formed Stabilised Earth Structures and rammed earth was introduced to the world.

Early Wines

The outstanding Swan Valley winemaker John Kosovich was a mentor for Cape Mentelle and made its earliest vintages of cabernet sauvignon and riesling from 1974 to 1976. The trip taking the grapes to the Swan Valley was measured by stubbies—twenty-four was considered a good run. David remembers Mark transported the grapes for the 1974 Cabernet in the back of his ute. He arrived late at night and decided not to disturb anyone. Kosovich recalls rising early to find the ute at his backdoor with Mark asleep, his head on a slab of beef, and tomato crates in the back filled with cabernet grapes. It was crushed after breakfast, the juice stored in a wax-lined (former) petrol drum, then transferred to two oak barrels for six months maturation in the Westfield cellar. It was released under the MRLH label. Peter Forrestal brought a bottle of the wine along to a function the night before the 1995 Cape Mentelle Cabernet Tasting. He commented, 'At twenty-one years of age, it was quite rich and concentrated, with chocolate, licorice and leather characters, reasonable weight and soft, dry tannins. Not a great wine but one that showed the promise of things to come.'

Overcoming Problems

There were difficulties with viticulture in the early years. As David Hohnen said, 'At the most basic, we were dealing with no local knowledge. In retrospect, somebody will write the Margaret River viticultural manual one day because it's quite different.' The most difficult of all problems was the small Western Silvereye, which is no problem when the red gums blossom at the same time as the grape harvest. However, if the red gums flower early or not at all, the crop can be decimated. At that time, netting was not an option because it was too expensive. It was not until 1995, when affordable nets from China made an entrance, did netting become widespread in Margaret River. David Hohnen commented that there was good basic research into dealing with the birds but, 'There was nothing we could do. It affected the style of wine that we were making. We used to talk about the importance of getting those early characters into our wine, but looking back, it was simply that we were justifying early picking. We had to pick early or we'd get nothing. Hence, the importance today of netting, or having a very big vineyard where the birds don't get into the heart of the vineyard.' The other particularly difficult pest was the black beetle.

Cape Mentelle did manage to avoid the problem of the root rot phytophthora. Not all the early vineyards in the region took as much care to remove all the jarrah and red gum roots when they were clearing the land. 'On our own block, we originally did it with just jelly [gelignite]. Light a fuse, step back a few feet and blow it out with jelly. Eventually we got enough money to rip it with a [Caterpillar] D9, just pulling up all these jarrah and red gum roots.'

The Need for Improvisation

Like the other pioneers of the Margaret River region, Cape Mentelle needed to improvise because there was a dearth of specialised equipment and no contractors available for specialist jobs. They survived with very little capital and a flair for innovation, especially in the winery. Frugality was a Hohnen byword. As late as the mid-1980s, David Hohnen would be visibly affected by the breaking of a burette (worth $35) in the winery's laboratory. (He still shudders remembering.) In 1972, they shared the $200 cost of an undervine weeder with Cullen, and David did all the undervine weeding on the Cullen vineyard. Add together the cost of the cars that he and Giles drove while working for Cape Mentelle in the mid-1970s and you had half the price of one French barrique ($600).

They bought a basket press from Vince Yurisich at Olive Farm in Guildford for $100. It had been locally made, with its central screw and ratchet drive cast and machined at Vickers Hoskins in Bassendean. It was designed to be mounted in concrete with a moulded circular drain on the outside of the iron and timber basket. It had to be jack hammered out of the cement before being transported to Cape Mentelle, where David built a steel catch tray on wheels to enable it to be moved to whichever tank was being processed.

In 1976, Hardys bought the London-based Emu Wine Company and were keen to sell off the shipping containers in which the Houghton wines had been exported in bulk to England. These square stainless-steel tanks served as fermentation vats for Cape Mentelle's early wines. When the

Margaret River factory of the Sunny West Cheese Company closed in 1976, the Hohnens bought the single-skin stainless-steel vats of varying sizes. With some welding ingenuity, they had an assortment of inexpensive storage tanks. Sourcing the bottling equipment meant an overland trip to Sydney for David in Mark's ute, where he found a second-hand dealer selling a bottle-filling machine, a filter, and a corking machine previously owned by Lindemans. The $500 purchase served as the bottling plant at Cape Mentelle for more than ten years.

The Cellar Door

From its inception, Cape Mentelle has been Margaret River's quintessential cellar door, with rugged jarrah and marri gums standing tall over its rammed earth facade. The tranquil bushland setting, with well-trimmed lawns and restrained native bushes, puts the focus squarely on tasting the Cape Mentelle wines. Mark comments: 'David understood very quickly the power of the woman's palate. It rocked us when we started the cellar door to realise the real decision-maker (when it came to buying wine) was the woman. David got an old tractor and built a kids' play area and had a colouring competition in the cellar door. He was the first to acknowledge that if the kids are happy, then the parents are happy, and the wife will make a decision and push the husband to buy something.'

In the early days, they didn't realise a licence was necessary to offer tasting samples to the public. Some tables were set up across the front door, the bird nets were rolled up on one side of the verandah, and they were selling glasses of wine. Author Tim Winton was an occasional visitor to the cellar door in the early days. He writes in *Mentelle Notes:*

Finally, we approached the pretty rammed earth buildings at Cape Mentelle in our overalls (sequined as they were with fish scales) and nervously stepped inside. There were a few sippers and gobbers and a short line of bottles on the bench. We weaved our way through the Panama and moleskin crew and began working our way meekly in the direction of the 1981 Zinfandel. Needless to say, we spat nothing, and found cause to try more than once, just to be fair. We rolled our eyes at each other like cows in deep grass. We murmured, we mooed and shuffled. We blew a week's rent and a fortnight's petrol money on a case of the stuff. Seventy-four bucks! My wife counted the crumpled notes onto the counter, her teeth black and blue with tasting, and I humped the case to the car, hoping for a glimpse of Mr Hohnen perhaps drifting among the tourists, regally accepting the praise and glory due him, hands clasped behind his back like Phil the Greek. No show. Still, we had a real live case of our wine in the boot and a week's holiday ahead.

Giles Hohnen was working at cellar door on the day when in walked two of Australia's greatest artists, Charles Blackman and Fred Williams. Williams looked at the (1980) Cape Mentelle Cabernet label and said, 'That's the best label I've seen.' Giles, a West Australian artist with a fine reputation gasped 'I did it' with a modicum of pride. He and his wife, Eveline Kotai, who is also a well-known artist, had long regarded Williams' label for Rothbury Estate as the finest example of an Australian wine label.

Cape Mentelle Cabernet Sauvignon

David Hohnen believed that Cape Mentelle made a fairly slow start 'because of the intervening years when I was away [at Taltarni]. We made wine in the tractor shed in 1977 with some really crude gear. The 1977 vintage was also devastated by the silvereyes. The small crop that survived the birds' onslaught was the first released under the Cape Mentelle label. It was a pretty good wine.'

Close friends David Hohnen and Taltarni's Dominique Portet share similar approaches to red winemaking. Both believe that tannin is important for cabernets if they are to develop the structure and strength for cellaring and so the reds are given time on skins after primary fermentation before being matured in (some) new oak. The decision about which barrels be included in the final wine has been a key arbiter of quality at Cape Mentelle. David recalls a visit by Portet at the time he was doing the final blend of the 1978 Cabernet. Portet felt the wine needed some shiraz for better balance. They started pulling corks of the Cape Mentelle Shiraz and adding them until Dominique was satisfied. Portet also recommended the French cooper Jean-Jacques Nadalié. For the first time, Cape Mentelle had oak barrels coopered in France. David Hohnen believed that this oak made a dramatic difference to the quality of the finished wine.

As David commented, 'The 1978 Cape Mentelle Cabernet really got the attention of James Halliday and, thanks to his write up we were able to sell that entire vintage.' Halliday declared it his equal top wine of a 1983 masked tasting of all the cabernets from the first four wineries established in the region—Vasse Felix, Moss Wood, Cape Mentelle and Cullens (as it was then known). Halliday, in the *Australian Wine Compendium,* wrote:

The 1978 is a marvellous wine by any standards ... the colour is an excellent red-purple; the bouquet redolent of rich, ripe, complex fruit and sweet oak; the palate has great depth, complexity and richness with the round, ripe-fruit flavours of most of the Cape Mentelle wines; and the tannin has now softened to the point where it is perfectly in balance with the complete wine. Writing about the same tasting, Huon Hooke commented that the Cape Mentelle wines *were among the best for their power and sheer volume of fruit: the 1978 being my top wine.* He also agreed with Halliday that the 1979 and 1980 were spoilt by a *mercaptan-like off-character which marred the bouquets of two otherwise spectacular wines.* A bottle of the 1980, shared by one of the authors with local winemakers in 2017, was in superb condition and showed wonderful purity of flavour. While a bottle of the 1978, tasted with David Hohnen before the 2015 Cape Mentelle Cabernet Tasting, showed a mature red, still with lovely, velvety character.

David Hohnen did the 1978 vintage at Clos du Val. It had been established by Portet's brother, Bernard, in 1972 and immediately made an impact on the Californian wine scene. The flagship red from its first vintage, the 1972 Clos du Val Cabernet Sauvignon, was one of the six Californian cabernets which outpointed six of Bordeaux's finest in the historic 1976 Judgement of Paris Tasting. Ten years later, the 1972 Clos du Val was the top-ranked wine in a rematch.

His time in California influenced Hohnen's views on the handling of oak with his reds. He believes his use of better quality French oak has made a significant difference to the Cape Mentelle Cabernet. While he was at Clos du Val, he was also introduced to machine harvesters. While these were criticised in the early days, with time, they have been more delicate in their handling of fruit. He believes that their thoughtful use has made a significant difference to wine quality at Cape Mentelle and Cloudy Bay.

After a decade of making Cape Mentelle wines, David Hohnen was asked by *Mentelle Notes* which was the most difficult vintage he had experienced. *In terms of trials, the 1981 vintage takes the jackpot. The two previous vintages had been good and we were looking forward to a third which would set us up on a much firmer financial footing. Then came the storms during spring and what looked like it was going to be a bumper crop was cut in half with drastic consequences for our budget.*

The style of the Cabernet was influenced by the late Paul Pontallier of Chateau Margaux, who visited at the time of the 1985 Cape Mentelle Cabernet Tasting. He commented that the Cape Mentelle was too hard on extraction, so David backed off in future vintages. James Halliday lauded the success of two moves to lighten the style: the introduction of merlot (since 1985); and the installation of irrigation in 1988. The latter was designed to reduce stress, increase fruit sweetness and reduce tannin. The use of better quality French oak following the Veuve Clicquot merger has also had a positive influence on the Cape Mentelle Cabernet.

In 2007, David Hohnen won the inaugural *Gourmet Traveller Wine* Len

Evans Award for leadership. In his article amplifying the judges' decision, Andrew Caillard wrote:

Hohnen once said, 'I want to make one of the defining styles of Margaret River Cabernet; a great Australian Cabernet; a wine that outlasts me and helps consolidate the region as a premium wine producer for future generations.' He will argue that his two successive Jimmy Watson Trophy winning wines which put Cape Mentelle on the map—the 1982 and 1983 Cabernets—were unfinished works rather than completed canvasses. For almost twenty years he worked on the development of this important single vineyard wine, even benchmarking it against other great wines of the world (including his neighbours) in his 'annual cabernet tasting'.

The Jimmy Watson Trophy

The Jimmy Watson has gained a reputation as Australia's most prestigious wine trophy and, in its more-than-fifty-year history, Wolf Blass is the only other winery to win in consecutive years (1973, 1974 and 1975). When David was invited to go to Melbourne for the trophy presentation, he said to his brother, 'We don't have the money to go.' Mark's rejoinder was, 'We can't afford not to go.' He was proved right. The Jimmy Watson Trophy gave Cape Mentelle the momentum they needed to survive, prosper and expand.

The first win for Cape Mentelle was impressive but the second clearly marked it as an outstanding producer and the Margaret River as a region of considerable importance on the Australian wine scene. At the 1983 Melbourne Wine Show, all seven of the eligible gold medal winners were involved in a taste-off which, atypically, was won unanimously. The 1982 Cape Mentelle Cabernet won the Jimmy Watson Trophy as the Best Red Wine of the Show.

Sandy Hohnen, Noel Engles and David Hohnen with the Jimmy Watson Trophy in 1983. Photo courtesy Cape Mentelle

David Hohnen commented, 'I didn't really expect to do so well. Because of the prestige and marketability of the award it attracts intense competition. You're up against the best there is: over 200 wines in the one-year-old claret and burgundy classes. We knew we had a humdinger of a wine, and we thought, well hell, we'll give it a go.' He did note that the 1982 was consistent with the style that Cape Mentelle had been making and refining since 1978.

Huon Hooke said in the *Financial Review* that, on returning home, David Hohnen had dispatched a press release vowing there would be no unjustified rise in the price of the 2,500 cases of the wine still available. Hooke continued: *Margaret River wines have been raising eyebrows in the Eastern States for some years, and this award reinforces the widespread opinion that Margaret River wines are top-notch.*

The 1982 Cape Mentelle Cabernet was the product of an exceptional vintage in Margaret River. The grapes were picked at a slightly lower Baumé than usual (between 12 and 13 degrees), and the harvest was later because of a cooler ripening period. The vintage was an unusually protracted one, beginning on 22 March and ending on 7 April. There was a good yield of fruit (three tonnes to the acre) without irrigation.

In contrast, the 1981 Cabernet resulted from a warmer vintage and shows the effect of a severely reduced crop size. It is a very concentrated wine with a higher alcohol reading (13.5 per cent).

The 1982 Cabernet is predictably a more elegant wine. But it is nevertheless surprising that the Melbourne Show judges, who have occasionally been criticised for favouring the most forward 'upfront' wine, have gone for a bigger, more tannic style. The Hohnen wine is a hiccup in the pattern that has been set over the past 10 years.

Cape Mentelle wines have always been unashamedly big. Mr Hohnen believes in extracting every last drop of colour, flavour and tannin from his grapes.

Huon Hooke described the wine: *Its colour is a very deep, concentrated purple/black. The nose is clean, intensely fruity, with enormous cassis-like aromas overlaid with chalky/leafy/grassy cabernet character. The palate is big and sweet, rich fruit and plenty of tannin but quite surprising softness. It is a superb wine, with deeper, finer flavour and less tannin than the 1981.*

Twenty-one years later, Cape Mentelle winemaker Simon Burnell described an in-house tasting of

Cabernets to select wines for a major tasting in Paris. Burnell noted that when he first tasted the 1982 he pointed it as three stars out of five and said, 'Nicely delicate with some hickory, tobacco and barbecued red capsicum followed by dark mint chocolates and a fine lattice of tannin.' He commented that over the next hour 'this wine grew in stature and complexity, showing a different range of aromas and flavours each time I returned to it.' He increased his rating to four and a half stars. David Hohnen said of that tasting that the 1982 had knocked him out, as he had written it off years before.

The 1983 Cape Mentelle Cabernet was quite a different wine from the 1982 as it was the product of a tricky, hot vintage. It was much denser, more powerful and more tannic. Where the 1982 was elegant and herbaceous, the 1983 was more profound and briary and unapproachable as a young wine. It needed a good ten years, or preferably twenty, to be transformed into a good drink.

In its typically blunt fashion, *Mentelle Notes* said the following about the 1983 red releases from CMV:

Two of these wines have already enjoyed some success at wine shows (the 1983 Shiraz, called Hermitage, won silver for second place at the local Sheraton Wine Awards). This has, unfortunately, resulted in them attracting some of that peculiar brand of media hype that is reserved for any wine that wins an award. Long-standing fans of Cape Mentelle wines will no doubt be pleased to learn that, hyperbole apart, these wines are consistent with the big powerful style of Cape Mentelle dry red we have been producing since 1977. Most of the media interest has been centred on our 1983 Cabernet ... which was our second successive Jimmy Watson win and was only significant, from our view point, in that it proved our first win was no fluke.

David Hohnen made the following 'hyperbole-free' comments, on its release:

A hot summer and early ripening resulted in us picking the cabernet over five days. The hard work was rewarded by a wine with good fresh berry character and with no traces of being overripe. It is in the same style as our 1980 and 1981 but has much greater refinement. A big complex wine showing berry character and great intensity of flavour. It needs a few years to open up and will continue to develop for many years. A big but surprisingly elegant cabernet.

What surprises most about the second Jimmy Watson success are David Hohnen's comments that the wine was difficult to sell: 'Sold a little of the 1983, but couldn't sell the rest.' He gives two reasons for this. Firstly, that there was a trend in Australia which favoured white wines over red and this wasn't reversed until the so-called 'French paradox' gained attention, which suggested that there was scientific evidence to indicate that French consumption of red wine reduced the numbers of overweight adults and contributed to a lower incidence of heart attacks in the country. And secondly, the substantial tannins in the 1983 made it appear unapproachable as a young wine and this slowed sales.

Most show judging is of wine that has been finished, bottled, and ready to sell. The conditions of entry for the Jimmy Watson Trophy (until recently) allowed for unfinished and therefore unbottled wines to be entered. This has caused controversy from time to time. What David Hohnen describes below was possible, and happened no doubt on other occasions.

When interviewed by Ray Jordan, David denied setting out to make a show wine:

'In selecting the bottles to send to the Melbourne Show I took advantage of the looseness of their conditions of entry. As I was told, "If you don't shoot, you won't have a chance." They told me that the big companies have teams, not only winemakers in the panels that are going to judge, but teams of two and three just focusing on making show wines. So, do what you have to do to win the medal.

'I used to pick over a range of ripenesses, and there were probably four to six distinct batches of cabernet and thirty to forty different barrels. I'd pick the best barrel within each batch and then line those up and find the best barrel and that went to Melbourne. No different to what they have been doing for years.

'Then no one complained when we made a blend of the 40 barrels ... it roared out the door.

'In the years leading up to 1982, they were planting cabernet in Tasmania because people wanted an overtly herbaceous style. I tell people today that I got the Jimmy Watson because the judges thought it was a herbaceous Tasmania cabernet.

'Then in 1983, I had a great big tannic wine from a really hot year in Margaret River, and it was loaded up with oak, and I chose a good barrel.'

For David Hohnen and Cape Mentelle, it was particularly significant because he believes that without the Jimmy Watson Trophies, Cloudy Bay would not have happened.

'When I got to New Zealand, I had those two Watsons under my belt and they treated me with a bit of reverence and showed me around. When I got back, the Watsons gave the people enough confidence with what we were saying about New Zealand. Cloudy Bay wouldn't have happened if Mark hadn't borrowed a million dollars at an interest rate of twenty-four per cent. He wouldn't have done that if it hadn't been for two Jimmy Watsons. I call the barrel hall the Watson building. Suddenly, Mark was prepared to throw more bucks into wineries.'

From its earliest vintages, Margaret River had produced some very good to exceptional wines which were well reviewed and sold well, especially in Western Australia. It was the prestige attached to the Jimmy Watson Trophy that acted as an imprimatur for Cape Mentelle and the Margaret River region. David commented, 'The local winemakers got together and held a dinner for me because there was recognition that it was just what Margaret River needed. We had a reputation before for being expensive with no substance to those prices. So, it was terrific. Everybody appreciated it.'

Guy Grant and Marketing Cape Mentelle

Before the Jimmy Watson Trophy win, Cape Mentelle was building up some unsold inventory because in David Hohnen's words, 'we were pretty average producers' and had no experience or expertise as marketers. They addressed that by engaging Guy Grant, a jovial Scot with marketing qualifications who worked for Mark's Oceanic Equity. 'We had a person who could help us capitalise on the Jimmy Watson, and that's what made the difference, because as Wolf Blass proved, you can only get out of an award what you actually make of it.'

The mailing lists of Vasse Felix and Moss Wood were the envy of many because, as David said, 'they had access to the medical profession, and, even today, we know those guys are the biggest drinkers in the world'. So, as a first step, Guy Grant bought a list of local medical practitioners from the Medical Board for $1.50 to give Cape Mentelle similar reach. In his quieter moments, he does admit to the politically incorrect editing of the list to remove doctors with names which suggested that they might not drink alcohol. Then he created his magnum opus, *Mentelle Notes.* Its refreshing lack of hyperbole in describing the company's wines, combined with Grant's incisive wit and unmistakeable Scottish accent, and David's laconic observations, made it one of the finest winery newsletters in the country.

A sample of the tone of the publication can be perceived when, after a wide-ranging interview in March 1988, Guy Grant suggested that they have one more before dinner. David Hohnen replied, 'Yes, by all means, have another can, but I would now like you to answer one question. You have been described as "looking like a failed Perth businessman", you are becoming more eccentric, more undisciplined and your stories get worse as you get older, yet four times a year you manage to produce an occasionally eloquent and sometimes even funny edition of *Mentelle Notes.* How do you do it?' 1981 Zinfandel!

When majority ownership of Cape Mentelle changed following the sale to Portfino, Guy Grant faced a dilemma: he was given the option of 'part-time employment with a mob that loved him but paid him nothing, or stay with a crowd that drove him nuts but paid him well'. He made the second and very sensible decision and stayed with the day job.

Guy Grant had documented the winery's history for twenty years until 1988. He handed the reins to Jane Adams who has preserved its tone to this day.

Financing Cape Mentelle

As Managing Director of Margaret River Land Holdings, Mark Hohnen was responsible for organising the finance for its vineyard and winemaking operations. He was very much involved with the day-to-day operations of the vineyard in the early years while David was working at Taltarni. His father-in-law, John De Witt, was senior in Westpac and a friend of the State Manager, Ralph Lindsay. Shortly after he married Cate in 1974, Mark got together with his Stanford-educated cousin, Stuart Hohnen, to formulate a business plan for the winery. The investment they were seeking was to buy winery equipment. Ralph Lindsay told Mark, 'This would be one of the best prepared business plans we've seen. However, you'd need to be crazy to invest in Margaret River. They're either drunk or fishing.' They didn't get the finance.

Cape Mentelle was kept afloat because Mark was subdividing and selling off blocks of land: firstly, the airstrip, and then rest of the Wallcliffe Wilderness, Glenellie and Wallcliffe Farm. As he told *The West Australian: The winery was cash hungry and we had some farming land which was totally unsuited for farming so we subdivided and sold that. That's how I got involved in real estate in the first place.* In 1977, the MRLH board authorised the Managing Director to investigate acquiring a majority shareholding in a publicly listed company for expansion. Mark Hohnen, Simon Fraser and John Hohnen (St Just Investments) took control of Oceanic Equity in 1976. Four years later, it acquired Margaret River Land Holdings by issuing paper—the three investors exchanged their holdings for equity. This gave them majority control of Cape Mentelle, with David Hohnen as the minority shareholder.

Mark Hohnen, the financial mastermind of Cape Mentelle, in 2006. Photo courtesy the Hohnen family

Mark looked to buy the Margaret River Hotel as a source of cash flow to fund Cape Mentelle. Its owners, the public company Auto Investments, refused to sell and so Mark decided to buy them out, no doubt aware of the possibilities offered by their ownership of the Ford dealerships in Bunbury and

Albany. He commented, 'I researched the company and reckoned it was cheap.' MRLH acquired 15 per cent of Auto Investments and Oceanic Equity 19.9 per cent and made a bid for Auto in May 1981 on a five-for-three basis. This bid was contested and not completed until March 1984, by which time Ocean Equity had won the battle for its hotel interests, Ford dealerships and property trusts.

A Parting of the Ways

The tensions between the Hohnen brothers David and Mark are a part of the Cape Mentelle story. As Mark put it, 'There was only eleven months between us: brothers are brothers.' Until 1986, these differences were resolved amicably and the winery benefited from David's work ethic, his single-minded pursuit of viticultural and winemaking excellence, and his refusal to compromise and desire to expand, as well as Mark's talents in money matters and his ability to satisfy the cash-hungry needs of Cape Mentelle while balancing his own ambitions in the corporate world.

At the beginning of the 1980s, a difference between the two emerged that had nothing to do with finance. Mark felt that David needed to make the tough decision to split the jobs of winemaker and wine grower rather than have him continue to do both. They spent time in South Australia looking for someone who could take on the job of viticulturist. Their first choice was Bill Potts, a man with a formidable reputation and close family ties to Langhorne Creek. Potts was keen to take on the job but didn't feel he could make a long-term commitment to Margaret River. Their second choice, Brenton Air, had no such qualms and proved to be ideal. He enjoyed a close working relationship with David Hohnen as Chief Viticulturist for twenty-two years from 1981 to 2003. He still lives, sails and fishes at Augusta.

Mark explained the root cause of the differences between him and his brother: 'David was passionate about producing wine and I was passionate about producing returns and wine.' In

1986, David's decision to proceed with the capital-intensive pursuit of making sparkling wine with Cloudy Bay's Pelorus led to a rift between the two. David described it as, 'Mark and I had a huge biff up.' *Mentelle Notes* commented, *Thank God for family, otherwise, we'd have to fight with strangers.* Mark's view was that public companies expected returns on investment and because wineries consumed too much money, especially in the early stages of development, they were not the domain of public companies. Mark was also under pressure to find capital to fund his commercial ventures.

Consequently, in late 1986, Oceanic Equity, now Apex Pacific, decided to divest its non-core assets including much of its holding in Cape Mentelle because it was still a major drain on funds. MRLH sold fifty per cent of Cape Mentelle to Portofino, a local Perth group led by Leon Ivory and Allan Fletcher, and retained a twenty-five per cent share in the winery. At that time, Red Triangle, a company owned by Tony Fairhead and Mark Hohnen acquired the balance of MRLH including the share in Cape Mentelle.

Portofino had expected to capitalise on the 1987 America's Cup yachting regatta held off Fremantle but the expected windfall did not eventuate. That combined with the 1987 stock market crash, resulted in the company being plunged into dire financial straits. David Hohnen was informed of this while working for Cape Mentelle in London in 1989. He learnt that Portofino would have to sell its fifty per cent shareholding in the winery as Cape Mentelle and Cloudy Bay were the only cashable assets in its portfolio. A prominent Perth businessman had put in an offer, which Portofino would 'have to accept'. David asked for a few months to find an alternative buyer.

Cloudy Bay

David's interest in New Zealand had been piqued by a conversation with respected Australian winemaker Stephen Hickinbotham. Then, in November 1983, a group of New Zealand winemakers—Joe Babich (Babich), Ross

Spence (Matua), John Hancock (Morton Estate), John Baruzzi (Penfolds, NZ), and Kerry Hitchcock (Cooks)—visited Cape Mentelle after the Wine Industry Technical Conference in Perth in 1983. They tasted the range of Cape Mentelle wines in barrel, including a wine that David was particularly pleased with—the 1982 Semillon Sauvignon Blanc—and they left a mixed case of their wines with David. He was startled by the intensity of the fruit character in the sauvignon blancs. John Hancock comments, 'A few weeks later he rang to say ... that he hadn't been able to achieve what he wanted in Margaret River with sauvignon. He was coming to New Zealand to have a look and could we catch up.'

David visited New Zealand in 1984. Long-serving wine judge and lawyer John Comerford organised his trip of the South Island, which ended in Blenheim. He learnt that there were only two or three uncontracted growers in the region. David remembers that it was in Marlborough where he saw brown hills for the first time on that visit. It was then he thought—this is the place! As his small plane took off from Blenheim, he saw the outline of Mount Riley and knew that he had the label for Cloudy Bay in his mind's eye. It was ready next year for the bottling of the first vintage. Later, David recreated that scene and the view he saw when he was interviewed for a BBC television program by Jancis Robinson MW as they took off from Blenheim.

Once the decision had been made to go to Marlborough, it was Mark Hohnen's responsibility to find the money to enable Cape Mentelle to establish the new winery. It was not the most propitious time for such a venture. Firstly, as part of a vine-pull scheme, the New Zealand government was paying $5,000 an acre to anyone who wanted to pull grapes out. And secondly, when Mark came up with the money, the company was paying 23.5 per cent interest on the $1 million loan.

David's next task was to find a winemaker for the project. Both John Hancock and John Comerford suggested Kevin Judd—'a young Aussie guy who had been at Selaks for a few years and had made some impressive sauvignons'.

David stopped in Auckland for the wine show where, at the public tasting, he focused only on the sauvignon blancs. Those he liked best were from Marlborough. While most people were relaxing, chatting and drinking, he noticed one person who was tasting as diligently as he—it turned out to be Judd.

The Judd family migrated from England when Kevin was a boy. They settled in South Australia and Kevin later went to Roseworthy College (1977–1979). He did a vintage at Reynella in 1979 and became assistant winemaker in 1980. He decided to leave Reynella after the Hardy's takeover and applied for a couple of jobs in New Zealand hoping to learn about cool-climate winemaking. He joined Selaks, which was based near Auckland and crushed fruit from Hawke's Bay and Gisborne.

Judd takes up the narrative. 'After the tasting, David Hohnen came over, tapped me on the shoulder and said, "G'day. I'd like to come over and see you next week." He came by the winery and was asking questions like: Where do you live? What do you do on weekends? I was wondering what was going on, so I went home to [wife] Kimberley and said, "I think David Hohnen is going to offer me a job." Sure enough, he rang me about a week later, at the end of his first trip to New Zealand, saying he had plans to set up a new company there and would I be interested in making the wine? I accepted. They had no name for the company, no winery, no vineyard, no office in New Zealand: I thought things could only get better.'

On David's next trip to New Zealand the pair visited Marlborough. 'We drove out to the Awatere and thought that was too far away.' In the interview for this book, Judd chuckled thinking about how times have changed. They meandered around the Wairau Valley looking for a suitable winery and vineyard site. *Mentelle Notes* reports: 'On their last despondent day, Corbans' Chief Viticulturist, Allan Scott, showed them the bare paddock that is today [1988] planted with 110 acres (45 hectares) of vines and is the site of the Cloudy Bay winery.' That parcel of land was owned by Corbans. Scott was convinced it would be suitable for the Cloudy Bay project and brokered the deal.

The purchase was anything but straightforward as the sale of rural land to overseas interests was a politically sensitive issue at the time. David Hohnen called on John Comerford to handle proceedings with the Overseas Investment Commission (OIC) when negotiations became tricky. His application to the OIC stressed 'the wine synergies advantageous to New Zealand with a company producing red wine in Margaret River and white wine in Marlborough'. Comerford continues the story: 'David suggested that a gift of the Jimmy Watson Cape Mentelle Cabernet Sauvignon might assist the application. Despite being cautioned against making such an inducement, David produced the bottles from his satchel when negotiations seemed at an impasse. A week later the application was granted.' The purchase of the property was settled on 28 June 1985. (Cape Mentelle was only the second foreign buyer of land in New Zealand.

West Australian entrepreneur Laurie Connell had bought a North Island horse stud shortly beforehand.)

The OIC limited the amount of land Cape Mentelle could buy to 120 acres (48 hectares) and a subdivision was required to sell off the surplus land. After the sale, David divided off four 20-acre (8 hectares) vineyard blocks which would supply fruit to Cloudy Bay; three were bought by Allan Scott, Ivan Sutherland (Simmerland) and David Leonard (Valhalla); and one was gifted to Kevin Judd (Greywacke). He would take ownership on completing seven years working for Cloudy Bay. The remaining land would become the winery site.

Plans had been made to make a wine with purchased fruit in 1985. Montana, which had the most sauvignon blanc plantings in Marlborough, was not prepared to sell fruit or wine. David negotiated with Paul Treacher (General Manager) and Allan Scott of Corbans, which had a surplus of sauvignon blanc, to supply Cloudy Bay. The fruit was sourced predominately from their Stoneleigh Vineyard in Marlborough.

Corbans were developing Stoneleigh and were keen to crush its fruit on site. Cloudy Bay offered them the capacity to do that from the 1986 vintage and so the arrangement proved mutually beneficial until Corbans built their own winery in 1989. Kevin Judd had resigned from Selaks but because the timing would have left them in the lurch for harvest, he stayed on, and supervised the winemaking of Cloudy Bay by phone.

David Hohnen was in Marlborough when the fruit was picked and followed the truck to Gisborne where it was juiced. Judd suggested exchanging a tiny amount of the Stoneleigh fruit for some of Corbans' barrel-fermented semillon from Gisborne. David thought that would benefit the wine. When asked how much Cloudy Bay was made for that first vintage, Kevin replied, 'We made as much wine as we could from a truck and a trailer load of grapes.' For the more technically minded, *Mentelle Notes* reported that it was forty tonnes.

When the wine was ready for bottling, it was trucked to the Corbans winery in Auckland. That's where Judd met James Healy. Five years later Healy joined Cloudy Bay as oenologist and became a crucial member of the leadership group. The other key member of that team, Ivan Sutherland, joined in 1986 (and stayed for eighteen years) as viticulturist.

The launch of Cloudy Bay on the Australian scene was one of Guy Grant's finest moments. He believed that for the most part it was a waste of time to send samples out to the trade: they wouldn't bother tasting them. He came up with a novel idea: a stylishly presented shoe box with a bottle of the first release Cloudy Bay and a jar of New Zealand green-lipped mussels plus a classy wine glass. It was delivered to all the key independent wine retailers in Australia with a note suggesting that they get some crusty bread, good butter and try the mussels with the sauvignon blanc. Len Evans received the package as a member of the wine media and rang to congratulate Grant on the idea.

'That's pretty innovative for the wine industry,' he said. 'How did it go?'

'Terrible,' replied Guy Grant, 'We got more orders for mussels than we did for the wine.'

Evans appreciated the wit and wrote it up in his influential newspaper column. The campaign was a huge success and the wine sold extremely quickly.

As David Hohnen reflected, 'Cape Mentelle had a very difficult start: with not much capital, hard work, lack of experience, lots of mistakes, and we really hadn't made a cracker. When we went to Cloudy Bay, we utilised everything we had learned.' The key was that the New Zealand label was based, initially at least, on a white wine that could be marketed within six months of harvest. The 1985 was released in mid-1986 and the following vintage in October of that year. The cash flow generated enabled Cape Mentelle to cope with the high interest rates and fuelled Cloudy Bay's growth, including the building of a sophisticated winery.

The following vintages sold quickly. Tucker & Co. in Sydney would release all their stocks of Cloudy Bay on the one day. The retail trade 'would go crazy, if they got their allocation late'.

Veuve Clicquot

Veuve Clicquot Ponsardin (VCP) interest in Australasia was driven by its charismatic president, Joseph Henriot, who wanted Veuve Clicquot to expand, and he considered the price of land in Champagne prohibitive. VCP was a subsidiary of Moët Hennessy Louis Vuitton SE (LVMH) and Henriot was keen do something different from the Moët subsidiary, Domaine Chandon in the Yarra Valley. So, the notion of producing white wine in New Zealand appealed. In winter 1989, Dominique Portet sent a fax to Kevin Judd saying that he was coming to Marlborough with a couple of friends and asked if he could call in. He arrived with Joseph Henriot and Rupert Clevely, Sales Director of VCP in the Asia Pacific. The party dined with Judd that evening at Rocco's restaurant in Blenheim.

Kevin Judd believed the visit to Cloudy Bay was casual and that they were visiting to get a feel for

Marlborough and, specifically, to buy a few hundred acres of potential vineyard land near Renwick. They bought the land which, following the acquisition of Cloudy Bay, became surplus to their requirements. Dominique Portet's recollections are similar to Judd's. He believes that Joseph Henriot had not tasted Cloudy Bay before the visit, though he was very impressed with what he saw: winemaker Kevin Judd, the site, and the wines.

Mentelle Notes offers an elemental view of what transpired:

By habit the production staff were testing the fastening screws on the winery roof. The screws strained as Eric Clapton pounded out across the valley, amplified to rocket lift-off levels. No, it was louder than that. The visitors didn't complain but Judd, a sensitive soul who mumbles a bit, lowered the decibels and replaced Clapton with Vivaldi's Four Seasons.

Barrel after barrel, Judd took the visitors through their paces. One of the Frenchmen, a fifth generation Champenois, was particularly struck. Holding a glass of fragrant barrel-fermented sauvignon blanc he gazed through the window as the valley cast its spell.

'Sacré bleu, c'est magnifique, n'est-ce pas?'

Joseph Henriot ... decided then and there that it was time the widow Clicquot stepped out beyond the confines of her beloved Champagne and purchased a stake in the Wairau.

Both Joseph Henriot and Rupert Clevely were impressed with Cloudy Bay and keen for Veuve Clicquot to acquire it. Joseph Henriot told Judd years later that initially the board of VCP weren't interested in buying Cloudy Bay or a share in it. However, Henriot made it clear that, if they wouldn't buy it, he would.

These events roughly coincided with David Hohnen's search for an acceptable investor to take the fifty per cent stake in Cape Mentelle owned by Portofino. He heard about the Cloudy Bay trip organised by his friend Dominique Portet, so he rang and asked him, 'Why did you go there without telling me?' He got the whole story. 'I want an introduction because we are looking for a partner to take over the equity that's held by a bunch of Perth investors.' As he put it later, 'And so one thing led to another.'

The VCP team initially only wanted to buy Cloudy Bay but Mark Hohnen, who led the corporate negotiations, insisted that they had to buy the holding company, Cape Mentelle, as well.

In concluding the merger between Veuve Clicquot and Cape Mentelle, there were three issues to be resolved: the sale of the fifty per cent shareholding in CMV to VCP by Portofino; the arrangement between VCP and the other shareholders in CMV, David and Mark Hohnen; and an employment agreement with David Hohnen. VCP purchased the Portofino shareholding for $2.9 million; and twenty per cent of CMV from the Hohnen brothers' for $2.2 million. The employment agreement with David Hohnen made the VCP board responsible for the overall strategy for production, distribution, marketing and administration of CMV but gave David Hohnen, as CEO, autonomy in the day-to-day running of both Cape Mentelle and Cloudy Bay.

In February 1990, Joseph Henriot wrote to David Hohnen: 'Congratulations for what you built at Cape Mentelle. The place looks like a subsidiary of Paradise!' A press release in April 1990 announced that VCP had purchased a significant stake (seventy per cent) in a merger with CMV. Joseph Henriot said in a statement: 'David Hohnen, a man of rare gifts and a perfectionist, has succeeded in creating a real work of art in the Margaret River area of Western Australia, and in the Marlborough area of the Wairau Valley, New Zealand. We are particularly happy that he will develop with us these Australasian treasures.'

Jancis Robinson MW, in her obituary of Joseph Henriot who died at seventy-nine in 2015, suggested that the acquisition of Cape Mentelle and Cloudy Bay changed the shape of the global commercial wine map.

The merger necessitated a change of distributors in the United Kingdom as Veuve Clicquot had a major share in H. Parrot & Co. Peter Diplock, who had been distributing Cape Mentelle and Cloudy Bay since the beginning, had no contract beyond a handshake. However, VCP was keen to be seen as honourable in the eyes of the trade and so allowed Diplock to continue distributing the brands for an additional year. With the changeover to H. Parrot & Co., Joseph Henriot gave an undertaking that David Hohnen would have input in setting the UK retail prices. He also recommended that a brand manager be appointed to promote Cape Mentelle and Cloudy Bay. Mark Hohnen believed a marketing manager with a similar bailiwick would make a difference in overseas markets that were increasingly difficult to sell into.

In May 1991, David Hohnen and Rupert Clevely flew to London to negotiate the handover of distribution and release a vintage of Cloudy Bay to the English trade. After that, they took a private jet to Paris, and drove to Reims. While he was there, David mentioned in conversation with a young VCP winemaker that his father would be turning eighty on 7 July. Shortly afterwards, a magnum of recently disgorged 1911 Veuve Clicquot arrived in Perth. It was opened with a pop on John Hohnen's birthday and, David says, still had a natural bubble and, although a touch maderised, tasted delicious. John Hohnen died later that year.

Mark Hohnen (through Red Triangle) remained a shareholder of Cape Mentelle until 1995; as he put it, 'another five years of expanding and never getting a dividend'. Needing to refinance some of his investments, he sold to VCP at that time.

David Hohnen remained as CEO of Cape Mentelle and a minor shareholder until 2003 selling his remaining fifteen per cent of Cape Mentelle in three tranches in 2001, 2002 and 2003. He commented: 'They've been perfect investors. They've allowed us to keep our autonomy. Being makers of champagne, they've not dabbled at all in the production of still wines. They've been extraordinarily supportive. I think everyone in our company has really enjoyed the opportunity to have some exposure to a completely different culture and to work with a traditional French company.'

Interestingly, Veuve Clicquot and, since 2003, LVMH, have left their dividends in Australia and New Zealand, allowing the wineries there to invest in land and develop their vineyards.

Chapter 14

The Cullens

Not Your Average GP

Dr Kevin Cullen was a prodigious worker who loved the challenge of studying. In 1953, he spent three months in Melbourne finding out what would be required to complete the higher degree offered by the MRCP (Membership of the Royal College of Physicians). For the six months prior to leaving for Edinburgh with the family in 1957, he averaged thirty-five hours a week study on top of his usual, not insignificant, workload. Once there, he spent three months at lectures and three months attending clinical demonstrations in general medicine and (his specialist subject) cardiology and worked so diligently that he passed his exams at the first attempt. This was followed by three months working in Professor Derrick Dunlop's ward, gaining practical experience in the field.

When he returned home he threw himself into further studies and, in 1962, he was awarded a Doctorate of Medicine from the University of Western Australia. His thesis was based on his survey into behaviour disorders in 3,440 children from 1,000 West Australian families. Subsequently, he was offered a postdoctoral fellowship from the National Institute of Health in the United States. In 1963, with the family in tow (minus Rick who remained to study for his Junior Certificate at Hale School), Cullen studied at the University of California, Berkeley's Institute of Human Development. This enabled him to undertake future longitudinal population studies. The family returned to Australia via England. Kevin returned to London for three months in 1964 to work at the Child Development Institute and prepare himself for a ten-year study of women and children focusing on the prevention of behaviour disorders in children. He had this in place by early 1966 and it was funded through to 1974.

The Busselton Health Study

Kevin Cullen became aware of the Framingham Heart Study in the United States and decided that Busselton would be an ideal place for such a study. He worked with characteristic energy, involving key medical personnel from Perth's four major hospitals and the CSIRO. Through the Rotary and Apex clubs, he galvanised the local community, enlisting the support of the St John Ambulance, co-opted countless volunteers and canvassed local businesses for funding. The work of examining people at night began over three months in 1966. A large medical team from Perth spent a fortnight handling questionnaires, and taking blood pressure and blood samples. Many staff from the Medicine Faculty at the University of Western Australia gave up two weeks every three years over the following eighteen to work on the Busselton study. They encouraged significant numbers of their students to work on it as well. The flood of papers in medical journals which followed established a reputation for the

Busselton Health Study and eventually the funding came.

The population study became Kevin Cullen's grand obsession and his lasting legacy. Medical surveys of more than 20,000 people over 50 years have measured the health of the population of the town. As well as this, much has been contributed to our understanding of common diseases and health conditions. Importantly, the study empowered participants to take an active role in their health and wellbeing. The study, which still charts the health of the population of the town, has attracted worldwide attention and generated more than 300 research papers.

Margaret River doctor John Lagan described the study in his autobiography in his own flamboyant way:

Kevin and the other participating medicos he had corralled, began collecting blood samples, weighing, measuring, swabbing, sleep monitoring, delving deeply into family health histories and examining the very environment the 'guinea pigs' lived in. Some of the things they put those good folk ... through were incredible ... The results showed that the large Busselton test group had a much lower death rate than the Western Australian average, vindicating Kevin's view that people live healthier lives if they simply know the results of their medical tests.

How Kevin Cullen found time to remain at the energetic heart of the project, to work as a busy GP, and to become involved in other community matters beggars belief.

Working the Land

The Cullens had bought some coastal land in the 1950s and following their time in California in 1963, where they saw the rising value of coastal land, they borrowed money, as Kevin put it, 'to buy what we could lay our hands on at Wilyabrup'. Although this strategy was successful in the longer term, land values did not rise as much as he had anticipated during the 1960s. Having to find $2,000 each December to meet interest payments meant that money was tight for the family during the late 1960s and 1970s. He was delighted in the year he won the Faulding Research Award as it was worth $2,000. However, he was always looking for opportunities to sell some of their blocks to meet the interest payments.

Ironically, this led to two attempts to sell what became the Cullen vineyard block in 1971. The first of these came in 1966 when Cullen was helping Tom Cullity in his search for a suitable site for his vineyard. As he said in his autobiography, 'The Department of Agriculture's Bill Jamieson had advised Tom to buy the land we had offered him (which later became the first site of our vineyard).' Tom Cullity decided against the offer and bought a nearby plot on the Osborn farm—with help from Kevin Cullen.

In 1968, Cullen offered the site to Godfrey Hatton, a strawberry grower from Nannup. He didn't have the necessary cash and wanted the Cullens to give him a mortgage to buy the land. Looking back on these events twenty-five years later, Kevin says, 'Again, we were in luck as we refused to sell it to him on these terms and took it off the market.'

The Cullen family in 1978—Vanya, Ariane, Shelley, Di, Kevin, Stewart, Digby and Rick.
Photo courtesy Cullen family

Although Di Cullen was no longer practicing physiotherapy in 1966, she led the busy life of a mother with six children—Rick (19), Shelley (16), Stewart (13), Digby (11), Ariane (10) and Vanya (7)—and had responsibility for running the 800-hectare family farm at Wilyabrup, a half hour's drive over a partly gravel (and sometime impassable) road from their home in Busselton.

Ariane Cullen wrote:

Di was organising the farm including clearing the land ... which was done in barbaric fashion with chains suspended between two bulldozers, creating a swathe of destruction in their path. Di understood the critical mass concept as applied to natural biodiverse regeneration of bushland, so insisted on leaving largish stands of remnant virgin bush wherever possible...

Dairy farmer Bill Russell, who worked for the Cullens for eleven years and whom Kevin described as 'a wonderful help in both the vineyard and eventually in the winemaking,' described the property on both sides of Caves Road as 'pretty poor farming country, especially unsuitable for fattening cattle'. He explained how hard it was for Di to get the farm established especially given her lack of experience and her family responsibilities. The farm manager Ray Buck was a willing labourer but knew little about farming so they weren't making much money from the farm.

Santa Gertrudis was a breed of lean beef, originally from Texas which had been farmed in Australia since the 1950s. They were valued for their ability to thrive in harsh climates and the Cullens believed they would be ideal for the Wilyabrup property because they were 'tick resistant, placid-natured and large-framed with plenty of meat'. They paid for Geoff Juniper to attend a course in Harvey on artificial insemination of cattle and purchased a herd of Santa Gertrudis females. However, the process of inseminating the cows proved more difficult than expected. Even the purchase of a Brahmin bull failed to solve the problem and the experiment failed.

Di Cullen looked after the cattle with advice over many years from neighbour Bill Osborn and cattle doyen Billy Leiper. On one occasion, they had breeding cows with baby beef. Bill Osborn and his wife Linda suggested to Di that she take the best money she could get for the baby beef so that the rest of the animals had enough fodder. She and Kevin rejected the suggestion because they weren't happy with the price for baby beef at the time and decided to keep them, finish them off and then sell them. When the calves grew and needed more feed, it wasn't available because there was not enough hay. Later, things did improve, as Ariane Cullen explains, when Di took the good advice of Billy Lieper and settled on a 'small', 300-head of 'good forager, good tempered' Angus!

The Cullens were also interested in breeding Saxon Merinos because of their extremely fine wool. They were impressed by their ability to forage in the harsh conditions in Western Australia's north and believed that they would make good use of this arid coastal land. Bill Minchin and David Harricks fenced 100 acres of Cullen bushland off Juniper Road for this purpose. Kevin was advised to stock it with 100 Saxon Merinos. Against this advice, he put 200 sheep on the block and most of them perished.

Ariane Cullen recounts two stories:

'After clearing the land including the slope immediately north of the winery, we grazed sheep and cattle there, and usually mustered them with horses of varying temperament and quality. A day that stands out in my memory was the day that Kev (not an experienced rider, or a rider at all really) decided he'd muster the sheep on a frankly dangerous old trotter. Red Ned, stood seventeen hands high, was blind in one eye and as mad as a meat axe anyway.

'After a few minutes, Kev was seen thundering up the hillside northwards, the giant animal in full pacing flight and then in a terrifying, lolloping, uneven canter. Dad looked like a flea on the animal—then the flea jumped, at full speed. Our hearts were in our mouths but the rider returned with just a few bruises, stating he'd taken the best option.

'Another close shave for Kev took place in the stockyards that stood immediately north of the current winery entrance road. The Friesian steers from Hutton's next door regularly escaped into our place and created havoc among the vines. Kev and Di were sorting their Friesians within the stockyards when a large steer with huge horns took a dislike to Dad and charged him. Luckily, in his terror, Dad tripped over. The beast cleared his prostrate form with a massive leap, knocking the hitherto solid jarrah fence down and lumbering off, bellowing with rage into the vineyard again! Dad was white as a ghost for three days. I remember realising, perhaps for the first shocking time, that a parent could be mortal, immediately followed by immense gratitude that he had survived.'

For her part, a year or two earlier, in the same yards, Di had been savagely butted from behind by a merino ram, leaving her injured in the stockyard raceway. Being alone, she had to crawl with her badly sprained ankle to the safety of the car. Such was farm life and it is little wonder, perhaps, that Di and Kev morphed their activities towards viticulture and winemaking over the years.

Sue Juniper commented, 'The Cullens were heavily involved in trying to produce fine wool and lean beef. Di often said to us that a vineyard would be another burden in their agricultural pursuits and she was dead-set against the idea.' She was also aware of her limitations. On a separate occasion, Di said to Sue, 'We've failed with sheep; we've failed with cattle: they'll plant grapes on our property over my dead body.' Reminiscing Sue said, 'She knew who would have been responsible for looking after the vines, in addition to her other work on the farm, and caring for her young family.'

In 1969, Kevin Cullen was invited to work for a busy and harrowing three months in South Vietnam with the medical team from Western Australia servicing a major provincial hospital in Long Xuyen. On returning home, he became involved in the second survey of the Busselton Health Study; and, at a national level, with the Royal Australian College of General Practitioners. Concern about the activities of mining companies on the beaches near Wonnerup spurred the Cullens to take leading roles in the Vasse Conservation Committee, which helped establish environmental safeguards for the region.

The Cullen Planting, 1971

There are two, contradictory, versions of how the first vines came to be planted at Cullen. In his autobiography, Kevin Cullen said:

In early 1971, Di and I were approached by Terry Merchant to see if we were interested in planting a vineyard in partnership with him. He had been working for Tom Cullity and we never asked whether he'd been sacked or just left Vasse Felix. We liked the idea as we had been the first to initiate public interest in vineyards, back in 1966.

On the other hand, Terry Merchant said:

'I was still living at the Cullitys—Kevin and Di arrived at the door and said, "Could you come over the fence and have a look at setting up a vineyard over here?" The arrangement was that we were four people in partnership and they provided the land and I provided everything else.'

The plantings were planned and supervised by Terry Merchant and began in August 1971, with Terry and

Geraldine Merchant and Di Cullen doing most of the work. While he was working part time at Vasse Felix from 1968 on, Terry Merchant had been teaching at the local primary school. In 1972, he was transferred to Perth, he suspected 'as punishment' perhaps for the after-hours vineyard work he did, or getting the school children to help in the vineyard. So, most of the planting in 1972 was done by Geraldine, and Di Cullen. By September 1972, sixteen acres of cabernet sauvignon, four of shiraz and half an acre of malbec had been planted. Kevin later commented that Terry planned the 'initial plantings well but the shiraz and malbec took very poorly and we replaced them the following year with riesling'.

Ariane Cullen recalled:

'I was fifteen at the time (in the August holidays of 1971) and remember helping plant some of the vines in the south-west corner near Caves Road: my job was to tamp down the soil immediately after planting. Mum (bless her) had a knack of making it seem interesting. There was always an incredible sense of purpose in her plans and the execution of them. I usually felt very positive and hopeful about what we were doing, including what impact it might have on the district's future. However, even at that age I was subliminally aware there was a financial risk involved for the family (the latter probably from Kev).

'I remember Mum promising me in 1971 that for my 21st we'd be eating our own beef and drinking our own wine—she'd never made false promises before and nor did she this time.'

After almost two years, there was a falling out between Terry Merchant and Kevin Cullen which resulted in the Cullens paying the Merchants $6,000 for the work they had done in planting the vineyard. The Merchants had threatened legal action and engaged lawyer Howard Olney (later a judge in the Supreme Court of Western Australia and the Federal Court) to handle the matter. Kevin Cullen indicated that resolution was held up until Terry Merchant accepted in the settlement the failure of four acres of shiraz. Merchant says that the dispute was resolved, rather dramatically, on the steps of the court house. The Merchants used the money as a deposit for a bank loan to buy a sizeable farm on the western side of the Margaret River townsite. They established a vineyard on the property, which briefly supplied their family wine label. It was on ideal soil but on the top of a mercilessly wind-swept hill and so it was abandoned. The Merchants have since enjoyed a comfortable living thanks to a series of subdivisions of their property.

Managing the Cullen Vineyard

After the Merchants had left at the end of 1972, Di Cullen assumed responsibility for the vineyard. The following quotes from letters to oldest son Rick, in 1973 and 1974, are revealing of Di's state of mind and the family's circumstances. She wrote:

We are in the middle of shearing at present, Bernice Barton and I draughted out the 900 odd sheep today for culls. We should get an extra five bales from less sheep this year at $200 a bale. Dad would rather hang on but I find

500 to 700 sheep enough to run after cattle. I'm sure they help to clean and fertilise the place. The vineyard starting to take shape—so it should—it takes all the sheep's profits.

We can only drive along Caves Road—everywhere else is impassable except on horseback. We now have 126 calves and about 300 lambs, if they haven't all drowned.

VERY busy here, hay, branding cattle, dipping sheep, training vines and trellising ... my fair share of entertaining, endless meals and nightly visitors' beds.

The more I think about it the better I feel about a 100-acre vineyard—not this year though. We hope to get 200 odd bottles of wine in April—grapes have flowers on now and growing apace—so are the weeds! So much to do and not enough time ever.

The halving of the beef price since the previous year's sales led Di to comment, 'Can't see us making a profit this year—ONCE again...'. She noted that 'an army of 14 people were hoeing the vineyard while only two people were looking after the rest of the farm, 700 sheep and 400 cattle'. The sale of a block of land—and the prospect of another sale—made the outlook considerably brighter. 'I still haven't got used to not having to worry about which bills to pay this month. I didn't realise just how much such things have haunted me over the last eight years or so...'

Both 1976 and 1977 were busy years for Di Cullen. To fund the winery developments and the building of their farmhouse, the family sold the Busselton house and she and the children lived in the beach house at Gallows. Kevin stayed at the nurses quarters in Busselton during the week because of the unpredictability of the road. His work at the medical practice remained essential to funding the vineyard and farm. Their house on the farm was finished in 1977 and this alleviated some of the pressures on the family.

Meanwhile, Di was supervising the extensive new plantings in the vineyard totalling nearly nine hectares of chardonnay, sauvignon blanc, semillon, merlot and cabernet franc.

The Department of Agriculture's Ian Cameron responded to Di ordering merlot by explaining that it was one of the most difficult varieties to propagate. Research at the time suggested that merlot was highly susceptible to even natural low levels of chlorine. Graft-take decreased as chlorine levels rose. As the Cullen vineyard was relatively close to the coast, Cameron was worried about the effect of airborne salt on the early growth of the merlot cuttings. Di rang him twelve months later to say that she'd had a terrific strike rate with the merlot of more than ninety per cent. When he visited to check on the planting, he found that almost all of the 'merlot' was sauvignon blanc. The cuttings had got mixed up. The lot of the early vigneron was not an easy one.

Murray Neave had been sacked by Tom Cullity in late February 1972 and, given the shortage of experienced workers in the district, he and his wife Margery were offered employment by the Cullens. His first job was to convert the shearing shed into a winery. It had been the Robinsons' farm house during the group settlement days of the 1920s and Murray Neave had to replace the wooden and asbestos walls with granite as well as stone from the property. This building was replaced by a new winery in 1977 and has been since been subsumed by the current cellar door complex. Those who visit the cellar door and winery today may well marvel at the effort which went into clearing the land around it.

Ariane Cullen described what was necessary:

'I remember huge windrows of felled jarrah logs running parallel to Caves Road and spanning the whole paddock for just about the length of the property. The trees had been ring-barked years before so were bone-dry but still required the lighting of many small fires which then were fuelled with ever bigger logs in order to burn the giant trunks: it'd often take several burns and re-burns over a week or two, to finally clear them.'

During 1974, dairy farmer Bill Russell visited his parents and found Murray and Margery Neave also there. Murray was sounding off about Kevin Cullen wanting twelve months work done in a week. He asked Bill if he had any spare time to help him straighten some trellising that had been done carelessly. That was the beginning of Bill's eleven-year involvement working part time on the Cullen vineyard and in the winery.

The Neaves were less successful in the vineyard than in building the winery, as Bill Russell's anecdote illustrates:

'I remember that, even then, Di and Kevin didn't want to use chemicals on the vines. Murray Neave had a Fergie 35 underground weeder that would pull the weeds away from under the vines. On one of his regular Wednesdays at the vineyard, Kevin came along and wanted to know why Murray wasn't going faster. With Kevin looking on, Murray pulled a vine out and hit the fence post in his haste to go faster. I got that job after a while.'

It didn't take long for Bill Russell to realise there was so much work to do at the vineyard that he asked his mate, Ellis Butcher, to help. Kevin Cullen commented: 'After the Neaves left, we had to get Ellis Butcher and Bill Russell to repair all the errors they had made.

Ellis and Bill brought their wives to help and between them, the two families put us on our feet again.' Ellis, as a cattle farmer, was able to put in more time in the vineyard than Bill, a dairy farmer. As a result, he took over as vineyard manager when Di became winemaker in 1981.

Toilers of the Vineyard

A gathering of a dozen vineyard workers from Cullens in the 1970s remembered the past with boisterous enthusiasm. No shrinking violets here: a collection of strong women remembering how hard it was working from 8.00am till 3.00pm—pruning, planting, weeding, wrapping down in all kinds of weather. Some helped in the winery during vintage, picking leaves out of the crusher, while others specialised in working at the cellar door or in the kitchen. When there was an urgent order, most of the team would give a hand with bottling, labelling and packaging. A common theme was the huge affection the workers had for Di Cullen and the sense of fun that made light of the hard work. The length of time they remained at Cullen underlines the job satisfaction they must have felt.

Annie Russell who worked in the vineyard, cellar and restaurant for seventeen years remembers that, whenever possible, Di would work with the team. 'She would never ask you to do anything that she wouldn't do. We planted and trained the vines, cleared the ground under the vines, kept the weeds down and the vineyard looking pristine. Di was very particular about tidiness'.

For Fran Covell, 'It was just fantastic to have Di as a teacher, a mentor. Nothing was too much trouble, and you know how long the days were that she kept. First there and last to leave'. For Roswitha (Ros) Boros, 'She was one of us and, no matter what, was always there at morning tea.'

Vanda Allen said, 'We worked hard and you did arduous stuff in the vineyard ... but the company was so great. We'd be out there in the rain and come in all wet and bedraggled. Di would have rushed home and made a pot of soup for us ... The laughs and the sharing was very special.'

Both the work and the money they earned (at a dollar an hour) were useful to the women's self-esteem and made a difference to their lives. Teresa Hann said, 'Di had you working because you wanted to do your best. The money was helpful. That's the reason we've got a little property down in Warner Glen Road now. We've got 86 acres [35 hectares] that we bought in 1974. What I earned here helped pay for the groceries and the bills. What my husband was earning helped us pay for the property.' Annie Russell commented, 'When you're farming you never had any spare money. We were dairy farmers and struggling. The pay we got from working in the vineyard helped put us on our feet.'

Ariane Cullen said:

'Mum very much valued the locals' understanding of the seasons and soils and their mostly uncomplicated approach to farming. Not one to take anyone for granted, she treasured, in particular, Annie Russell and Teresa Hann, who were lynchpins in establishing the original vineyard in the early 1970s. Many a time we kids (more often Van and I as the others were at boarding school) joined these wise and hard-working women training and pruning the vines or labelling the bottles, with, of course, everything done by hand. The work was not the chore it could've been, as these stalwarts were cheery, funny, and perpetually grateful. It was a great lesson in life for me and remains a fond memory to this day.'

Margaret Butcher and her husband, Ellis, planted Fire Gully, one of the region's most picturesque vineyards, on their farm. They sold the block that became Fermoy Estate and planted and nurtured its vineyard for three years before handing it over to Fermoy. Ellis was vineyard manager at Cullens from 1981 and worked on many of the local properties. Margaret was involved in the planting of Moss Wood, Sandalford, Wrights, Pierro, Palmer and Woodlands, and picked at Vasse Felix in the early days. She explained that one of her daughters wanted to go to boarding school, so she got a job at Moss Wood.

In the early years, Ellis was involved in dairying and growing maize. He would get up at 4.00am, milk the cows, be at Cullen by 8.00am, and go back home at 3.00pm to do the second milking. As Margaret said, 'It was really full on. Then in the later years we stopped dairying. The men worked really, really hard.'

Not that the women were any slouches! Margaret remembers, 'One day, when the children were going to swimming lessons, and I was working at Sandalford, way out at [the block they called] Siberia. I used to ride a push bike to work at five o'clock in the morning, work for three hours, ride my bike home, pick the kids up and the rest of the kids along the way, take them for their swimming lessons, then drop them off before going back to do another three or four hours work.

Margaret Butcher also talked about making money from cuttings. 'I helped with pruning and then I could go back after I had pruned and use the wood for cuttings. What I cut I was allowed to sell on my own. They were very generous in that respect.

'The first year I did it (1978) my daughter was eighteen. I did enough cuttings to get me to England and back to see my family ... I remember my girls saying, in the season to do cuttings, that they were never going into vineyards "because Mum and Dad work too hard".'

John Locke, who worked at Cullens in the late 1980s, describes how the picking was organised. 'We were working under contract rates which were around sixty cents a ten-kilogram bucket. The buckets were laid out along the rows and you worked with a partner either side of the row; picking any bunches on your side of the vine and fighting over any in the middle, making sure you picked every bunch. Leaving the full buckets, marked in chalk with your number, to be picked up later. The average picker filled eighty to a hundred buckets a day, with the champion, Milly Harvey, tallying about 150—no mean feat.'

Ros Boros described in detail how labour intensive making wine was:

'Harvest was always exciting ... You'd go out with the tractor, throw the buckets off the back for the pickers, and you'd go and pick too. When it was time, we'd pick up the buckets, stacking them yay high on the back of the trailer and take them straight to the back of the winery where we put the grapes fresh from the vineyard straight into the hand crusher. You'd have a person either side to pick out all the leaves and sticks. Di was very fussy. She wanted her product to be the best.

'End of the day, all the tubs were stacked high and they'd have to go through a washing machine that we had specially made. There were a whole lot of water jets, you put the tubs in from the right ... wash the tubs and just keep pushing them through. A person on the other side would grab the tub, put them upside down for the next morning. That would take you well into the evening because harvest was March and the days were starting to get shorter.

'Pruning was always a funny job. I remember one time it was so cold ... I looked at my colleague and said, "Do you know your nose has turned blue. My fingers are as blue as your nose"

... You had to wear gloves but, of course, they'd get wet and there's no recipe to keep yourself dry when you were out in the rain. You just stayed there. It was a full-time job. With pruning, you are creating for the coming season. You were shaping the wine to make it more profitable or bear enough ... It was very rewarding.

'We'd help with the bottling as well. When it was time to bottle, everyone was on the bottling team. It was a job where you needed many hands. I used to like it when Vanya came out and worked with us. She'd be out there singing and that was a joy to me as she has such a wonderful voice.'

Fran Covell, who worked in the cellar door for thirteen years, remembers the staff picnics at which Di would share the great wines of the world and use it as an opportunity to train the staff. 'We were included in all the big events and it felt like being part of a large family: we were cared for and appreciated. We were tasting in sherry glasses, too ... we've come a long way. It was very exciting and we were all learning as we were going, including Di and Kevin.'

Teresa Hann loved Di, 'she was a beautiful human being,' but had ambivalent feelings about Kevin. 'He was a brilliant doctor and saved my son's life because he diagnosed osteomyelitis and had him operated on quickly ... He was a lot of fun, great guy ... brilliant one minute [but] just switched like that. We used to look forward to Wednesdays. When he didn't turn up, we used to be disappointed. When he was in a good mood, he was just lovely to talk to. But when he was on the other side, god almighty, you never knew what he was going to do. Look he was a lot of fun. I can never forget that plank...'

Bruce Allen, who was also an experienced carpenter, was building the lunch bar and making it separate from the cellar door. When he went home for lunch, he had left a long plank just inside the door. Kevin Cullen came in, saw the plank, and spoke loudly to anyone who would listen, 'This is a winery! This is a cellar door! People come in here. Pick the bloody plank up.'

When no one responded, he picked up the plank. Instead of just walking straight out with it, Kevin started swinging the plank from side to side, eventually hitting the wall on one side, then a table on the other.

Teresa Hann said, 'He wanted to put it somewhere, but didn't know where. I got the giggles. Vanda couldn't stop laughing. Kevin saw us laughing and got mad. We had to walk out in the end because he was going to throttle us. Yet next time when he came in, he was his usual happy self.'

Shelley Cullen's Food Bar

Winewriter Alan Young was delighted when he visited the Cullen cellar door in 1983 and found that the 'jarrah pantry serves home-made cornish pasties, jaffles and banana cake'. At the time, wineries which offered lunch were a rarity. Shelley Cullen was aware of the large numbers of hungry visitors who were driving around the vineyard area with nowhere to stop for food. She began in 1981 by serving plates of cheese and biscuits and gradually increased the offerings. Shelley comments, 'It took us a year to work out a menu that didn't require a chef and that a few of us (Mary Wise, Jan Bowes and the veteran Elaine Goode) could churn out quickly when we were busy.' The formula was fresh and simple: consisting of the best in local crusty bread, cheeses, honey-cured ham, a port-infused pâté and either a pumpkin or sweet potato soup in the cooler weather. Mary Hirschmann's Swiss father was a chef who taught her the art of display, which came to the fore in the Vineyard Platter—a constant feature of the menu for the fourteen years that the lunch bar remained open. Along with Belaroma coffee, there would be Annie Russell's carrot or apple cake and lavender biscuits. Bill Russell reminisces in 2016, 'I still miss the ploughman's lunch.'

As Shelley Cullen observed:

'Not that running a busy lunch bar was without incident, especially with neighbours like Boodge Guthrie.

'The staff were seated next to the main northern doors chatting quietly over morning tea. A huge shadow filled the entrance, the teeth-jarring roar of a Rolls Royce engine shattered the tranquility. Boodge Guthrie had arrived in his home-made plane to scare the wits out of us ... and he succeeded. Not that the staff should have been surprised. Boodge would often cut the plane's engine, glide in over the vineyard, and when he was overhead a group of workers, restart the engine with a huge roar and give them a scare.'

Shelley Cullen's lunch bar—a Margaret River institution. Photo courtesy Cullen family

Shelley mused on the staff's 'relationship of sorts' with the shire health inspector, 'a nice man' called Jim.

'There was a running joke, especially on busy, long weekends, for one of the group to say loudly, "Oh, hello Jim!" While the lunch bar might not pass the rigorous standards of health departments these days, back in the 1980s there was more room to move as the shires encouraged a small industry to grow.'

She also recalls hosting a famous Burgundian winemaker and his conservative wife. 'We were short of staff and so one of the guests offered to set the table ... unfortunately with plastic knives, forks and spoons. This was only noticed as the food came out—the soup, the ham and the cake. All was forgotten or forgiven over a glass or two of chardonnay and some hearty country fare.'

Kevin Cullen

Anyone who worked at Cullens had a story about Kevin. Bill Russell says:

'Kevin wasn't able to spend a lot of time at the winery but he was there every Wednesday. We had enormous respect for Kevin, you had to like him but we would wonder what he'd come up with this week. I thought of Kevin as eccentric and impulsive: he'd have an idea and wanted you to act on it right away. But you had to go to Di first to get her OK before you'd do it.

'One anecdote from 1976 is perhaps typical. Kevin came around one Sunday morning and said, "Do you have a shovel and tape measure?" We went out to the block and Kevin said, "I'm thinking about building a house."

'Digby and one of the other boys was there. Kevin climbed on the hill, got out the tape measure and said, "This is how long the house should be." We measured it out. "This is how long this room should be. That's the kitchen area. That's the living area. Right, Digby. Shovel. Start digging a trench where the walls are going to go." He started a house like that. One minute we were all there standing around. Without any hesitation, he started. That's where the house went.'

On another occasion:

'One of his patients, Joe Bell, had a sore knee and booked an appointment to see Kevin who, at the time, was trying to get community support for the medical centre. He welcomed Joe and persuaded him to sign the petition and said, "Thanks for coming in to sign the petition."

'Joe's reply was a plaintive, "I've come about my crook knee!"

The Early Wines

The lack of a trained winemaker until Mike Peterkin took the position in 1979 was a problem for the fledgling winery. Kevin Cullen commented, 'We had to depend on Bill Jamieson for advice on grapes and wines,' while Di declared, 'One could not speak too highly of the effort put in by Bill Jamieson, mostly in his time off.'

Ariane Cullen said:

'They were convinced even then that to succeed one had to produce only premium wines, preferably using only classic varieties, and never, ever sacrifice quality. Needless to say, this policy was costly at times when mistakes were made along the steep learning curve, and I remember Di discarding whole vats or barrels of wine if she thought them not up to standard!'

The first crop in 1974 suffered significant bird damage: half a tonne was picked, it was hand-and-foot crushed, and tipped out. There were 160 dozen bottles of cabernet sauvignon made from the 1975 vintage.

In an article on the early days, David Hohnen describes one of the first wines made at Cullen—a rhine riesling:

Stainless steel, de rigueur these days, was very expensive and, more often than not, tanks were made from concrete culvert pipes coated internally with paraffin wax. Cullen needed a lid for their pipe fermenter, so one was fashioned from resinous boards which could be lowered by pulley to interface exactly with the fermenting wine.

The day arrived to sample the newly fermented riesling. Much fanfare, a pipette and ... grimaces all round ... Margaret River's first and possibly last retsina was poured into the Wilyabrup Book.

This disaster gave way to the joys of success only a few years later when the 1977 Wilyabrup Wines Riesling won the only gold medal in the 1977 Dry White Class for Small Vineyards and then the Robert Bryce Trophy as Best Dry Table Wine in the Small Vineyard Classes at the Canberra Wine Show. The judges included John Vickery, Tim Knappstein, Wolf Blass and Karl Stockhausen.

The winemaker, then, was Bruce Allen who had taken the position in 1976 and worked for Wilyabrup Wines for three vintages until July 1978. A native of Durham in England, he had a degree in agronomy from the University of Durham and had lived in Kenya, where he was a dairy farmer. He came to Western Australia and joined CSBP as an agronomist before moving to Sydney where he worked as a wharfie. Bruce became a farm management adviser for the Warialda area in New South Wales and then returned to the West as an agricultural adviser with Cresco Fertilisers. He bought eighty acres (thirty-two hectares) of coastal virgin bush off Juniper Road to the north of Gracetown in Margaret River. Over the thirty-year period he lived there with his wife, Jan, they built two houses, including the spectacular, environmentally sustainable Mataranka House. Although he had no background in winemaking, he took up the challenge of making the wines at Cullens with great enthusiasm.

Winery records suggest that 450 dozen bottles of the 1976 and 1977 Cabernet Sauvignon were made and 500 dozen of the 1978. James Halliday commented favourably on the 1975, 'a strong yet smooth wine with considerable complexity'; the 1976, 'a round, sweet and soft fore-palate, followed by a long, slightly dusty finish with soft but persistent tannin evident'; and the 1978, 'a youthful, deep and complete wine with a very long finish, with soft tannins.' The 1976 won a gold medal at the Hobart Show. The 1977 suffered badly from bird damage.

It quickly became obvious that a larger winery would be needed and work commenced on that in 1977. It was organised by Bruce Allen, helped by the winery team—Bill Russell, Ellis Butcher and David Weightman—with the hard-working and strong Bob McCleary taking responsibility for the largest rocks. Stonework was an important part of the structure, with most of the rocks coming from the property. Finding rocks with flat sides was always challenging. With minor modifications, the 1977 winery has stood the test of time. Kevin Cullen was so happy with the stonework that he had the winery team do the stonework for the family home on the other side of Caves Road.

Cullen vineyard circa 2014 with a healthy cover crop of broad beans. Photo courtesy Cullen family

Like the other pioneering wineries, Cullens had to improvise with equipment. Having staff who could weld and were accustomed to mixing cement was also invaluable. At first, they bought (unused) septic tanks and treated them with paraffin wax. Then Kevin Cullen was able to obtain some 1,000-gallon stainless steel tanks and Bill Russell made stands for them. He also built some cement rainwater tanks. They used perforated poly pipe for the cold water to trickle down the sides and cool the tanks. A blood filter was found to be suitable for filtering wines as long as the pads were changed regularly.

Working in the Winery 1979–1980

Bruce Allen was not employed on a full-time basis. After bottling had finished and he had topped up the barrels of 1978 Cabernet, Bruce finished up as winemaker at the end of July 1978. At that time, the intention was to re-employ him at the beginning of 1979. Mike Peterkin's work records show that his first task at Cullens in 1980 was on the 15 January and the last on the 12 November. One can only speculate that Bruce Allen was not employed fulltime as a money-saving measure.

Peterkin sets the scene:

'When I arrived in 1979, Cullens were definitely in the second rank behind Vasse Felix and Moss Wood. Prior to 1979, to my knowledge, Cullens had only produced one wine that had received any public recognition. That wine was the 1977 Riesling which had won a gold medal in the Small Vineyards Class in the Canberra Wine Show. [It also won a trophy]. Despite these successes, that wine showed evidence of a major winemaking fault in excessive levels of volatile acidity. [In 1978, they also won gold in Hobart for their 1976 Cabernet Sauvignon.]

'When I took over the role of winemaker at Cullens in 1979, I replaced Bruce Allen whom I believe had held the winemaking role for the previous three vintages ... he was the first to admit that his knowledge of winemaking was extremely limited. Kevin and Di, at that time, had very limited knowledge of winemaking practice and theory. Kevin had read a textbook on winemaking and possessed a keen palate but had no aspirations of becoming a practical winemaker. Di's role was mainly in the vineyard at the time.'

Peterkin's view is supported by South Australian winemaker Brian Walsh who visited Margaret River in 1975 and in 1976 or 1977 with Hunter Valley winemaker Ian Scarborough. He commented in 2014: 'We visited both Vasse and Moss Wood ... There was probably nothing else that was really firing. Both Cullen and Cape Mentelle were doing stuff but the winemaking was pretty rudimentary in both places.'

In 1979, there were very few people with formal winemaking training in Western Australia: Bill Jamieson and Tony Devitt at the Department of Agriculture, Dorham Mann (Sandalford), Bob Cartwright and John Brocksopp (Leeuwin) and David Hohnen (Cape Mentelle). Peterkin believed that, at that time, as much as fifty per cent of wines had obvious, common winemaking faults, and it was particularly the case with white wines.

Peterkin's comments are supported by the then Deputy Premier and Minister of Agriculture W.R. McPharlin in a ministerial note to Premier Charles

Court, in November 1974. He firstly explained that the comments of the Chief Judge at the Perth Show related mainly to the classes reserved for West Australian winemakers producing less than 90,000 hectolitres.

Faults evident were generally associated with bad wine-making techniques. Many faults could have been overcome if the winemakers had more technical skill and modern equipment...

Many local vignerons, however, have little formal training in winemaking principles and are operating properties which are too small to justify purchases of modern equipment such as stainless-steel centrifuges, ultra-coolers ... This is reflected in the quality of the product that can be achieved.

On completing his medical qualifications, Peterkin went to Roseworthy College in South Australia and completed the three-year Diploma of Oenology. His training was enhanced by doing vintage with experienced winemakers Dorham Mann in the Swan Valley and Tim Knappstein in Clare.

In 1979 and 1980, Peterkin worked in the winery with Bill Russell and David

Weightman. He explained that, during vintage, the three of them put in extremely long hours. David Weightman talked about regularly being home at 10.00pm. The work was physically demanding as their little press only held three-quarters of a tonne and the total crush was around 100 tonnes. While the winery was satisfactory for its time, it was poorly equipped by today's standards and required constant attention to keep it operational.

From the 1979 vintage, Peterkin won a trophy with a new style of wine—Semillon Sauvignon Blanc—when the 1979 Cullens won Best Full Bodied Dry White at the Perth Show. The 1979 Cullens Riesling (largely made with Frankland River fruit) won a gold at the Mount Barker Show while the 1979 Cullens Cabernet Sauvignon won gold at the Perth Show in the following year.

Bill Russell says, 'Bruce Allen had been to ag school and read books. Mike had been to Roseworthy and he came back and started to make good wine straight away.'

Peterkin comments, 'One should never underestimate the role of luck in all of this, but in the space of one vintage, Cullens were suddenly on the map and people started taking notice of their wines.'

Semillon sauvignon blanc has since become hugely popular and the region's best-selling commercial style. In recent times, carefully crafted oaked versions of the style have enjoyed critical acclaim and consumer popularity. Outstanding examples currently produced include those from Pierro, Cullen, Cape Mentelle, Vasse Felix, Lenton Brae and Fraser Gallop.

Peterkin said, 'I have never claimed any originality for the idea as I simply borrowed it from the French. What I did do was create a new style which emphasised aroma, freshness and fruit character. When I planted Pierro in 1980, the potential was obvious and I devoted a third of the total plantings at that time to the varieties.'

Blends

In discussing the winemaking at Cullen, Peterkin said:

'This was the era of single varietal wines and blends were unpopular with the public and with most winemakers. Kevin and Di held to the belief of the majority, in single varietal wines. I had to be very persuasive to get them to allow me to make blended wines such as Semillon Sauvignon Blanc and Cabernet Malbec Merlot. Even after the trophy win, they had little faith in that style of wine and let the Semillon Sauvignon Blanc lapse a few years after I left the winemaking role. Di's interest lay in making single varietal sauvignon blanc. She may have blended ten per cent semillon in her Sauvignon Blanc, yet that is not an indication that she supported the semillon sauvignon blanc style of wine.'

Another of the changes that Peterkin successfully implemented in 1979 was to make a cabernet blend: in that year—the Cabernet Sauvignon Malbec Merlot. More generally in future, this was a Cabernet Merlot and a vital part of the Cullen portfolio. From 1982 onwards, the Cullen flagship red—since 2001 known as the Diana Madeline—has been a Cabernet Merlot.

James Halliday commented, 'There is no question that overall the Cullen Cabernet Sauvignons are the firmest of the major Margaret River makers and, indeed, may be seen as too firm by some wine lovers. I like the strength and believe that the older wines do show that patience will be rewarded. However, the cabernet merlot blends made since 1979 may be seen as a more attractive style.'

The authors have been fortunate enough to taste several of the early Cullen reds in the past ten years. That firmness in their youth has enabled the wines to mature admirably and they have drunk magnificently at more than thirty-five years of age.

Di Cullen—Winemaker

Peterkin worked as winemaker for Cullens in 1979 and 1980 without payment. He said that he did that because the Cullens were financially stretched at the time, because of his love of winemaking and of Shelley Cullen (whom he married in January 1983), and because he liked Kevin and

Di. There were times during those years when he could not be at the winery (he spent some time working in medicine and was also consulting to Alkoomi). On these occasions, he returned to the winery in the evenings and/or on weekends to review the situation and set up the work program. Di played a role in ensuring that his instructions were implemented. With a smile on his face, David Weightman talked about having to read reams of notes in a doctor's handwriting.

Peterkin decided that he wanted to spend more time working in medicine and, as Di was keen to take on winemaking, he agreed to help her through the 1981 vintage. He taught her the basic skills and how to implement the procedures that he had set up in the winery over the previous two years. He made himself available whenever the need arose.

Di Cullen had an exhaustive preparation for winemaking. She had been involved in the vineyard for a decade and had supervised it from the beginning of 1974 until the end of 1980 (which included the planting of 8.72

hectares of vines in 1976 and 1977). Her energetic and inquiring mind and the fact that the Cullens were operating a small family business meant that she was always involved, even if, at that stage, it was in a supervisory capacity. Once they started to make wines, she had responsibility for bottling, labelling and packaging, as well as dispatching the wines to market. There was also the cellar door, which was open on Wednesday and Saturday afternoons.

David Weightman commented that the changeover from Peterkin to Di Cullen was seamless because she had always been around and involved. While Bill Russell agreed with this view, he was conscious that it was Di's first time with responsibility for the winemaking and that she was learning in the job.

Di experienced show success in her first year as winemaker at Cullens with the 1981 Cullens Cabernet Sauvignon scoring top points in the open Cabernet class at the 1981 Melbourne Show and the 1982 Perth Show. It was third at the 1982 Canberra Show. There were eighty-six entrants in that class at the Perth Show: the judges' comments read, 'a strong class of elegant cabernet sauvignon with well-handled oak'. At the Canberra Show, Lester Jesberg liked the wine's 'superb blackcurranty fruit and balance' and believed it would age admirably. Writing in the *Epicurean* in 1983, Ian Hickinbottham described Di Cullen as a genius.

The 1982 Cullen Sauvignon Blanc enhanced her reputation and made her the first woman winemaker to win a trophy at the Perth Show. James Halliday commented on the wine:

Diana Cullen has developed her own very distinctive style of winemaking, which is particularly evident with the white wines. All are oak-fermented and she has had outstanding success with several vintages of sauvignon blanc. Her view of this wine is that it really should be made like a cabernet sauvignon, invested with mid-palate weight and pronounced oak.

It does not always work, however, for small-oak fermentation of white wines is a demanding regime. What is more, they are often very difficult to assess when young, needing some time to develop fruit character. This is particularly so in the Margaret River area, where the aroma levels are often reduced and the fruit obscured by the naturally high acid of the young vines.

Len Evans comments in *The Complete Book of Australian Wine* that many critics consider the Cullens Sauvignon Blanc one of the very best wines of the variety in Australia, if not the best, and gives as evidence its performance in the 1983 Sydney Show. Evans describes it as *a highly distinctive style reflecting Di Cullen's unique approach to this variety and her great willingness to experiment with the treatment of the fruit to improve quality and complexity.*

Chapter 15

Regional Certification

Tom Cullity was a Francophile and so it is scarcely surprising that, when he thought of ways to protect the commercial interests of Margaret River vignerons, he turned to the French system as a model. The French notion of appellation suggests a link between quality and a specific place. It focuses on established vineyards and traditional winemaking methods and the certification of wines to guarantee authenticity. Although it is now enshrined in law, its formative years required faith, trust and cooperation between those involved in establishing the system.

Cullity first raised the idea of appellation in a submission to the WA Department of Agriculture in October 1967, shortly after he planted the first vines at Vasse Felix. In advancing his belief that 'we may well have an area as important to Western Australia as Bordeaux is to France' he argued for protective legislation which would ensure that no winery should use the district label unless the wine in the bottle was from the district named.

Following a change in government, Cullity wrote to the Minister for Development and Decentralisation, H.E. Graham, in 1972, suggesting a model of legislation that would involve an independent panel of judges which would guarantee the origin, yields and quality of any wine carrying the district's label. State Viticulturist Bill Jamieson gave a measured response to the suggestion in an interdepartmental memo (dated November 1972), pointing out that the major concern in Western Australia at that time was ensuring unscrupulous vignerons could not make fraudulent claims about the origin of wines. He believed that this could be done by minor amendments to existing legislation. While he accepted that a form of appellation control might benefit the wine industry in the future, he thought the local regions needed to develop a reputation for high quality wine first.

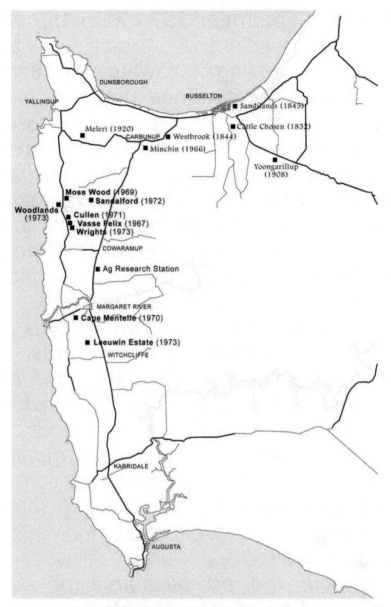

A map depicting almost 150 years of wine
growing in the South West region.

A similar case was made by Len
Evans in a letter to the Premier, Charles

Court, in September 1974 after the two had discussed the topic at the Exhibitors' Tasting following the Perth Wine Show. He summed up:

At this stage, I feel that a start should be made into those specific areas of region and variety. It is most essential that the wines under such control come specifically from one area—good, bad or indifferent. Secondly, that the key variety used on the label is the key variety in the bottle ... In the case of wines that are blends of varieties, the dominant variety must be the first name used (to safeguard the Cabernet Shiraz type of wine in which the truck loaded with shiraz passed the cabernet vineyard.) Control of quality, control of viticultural procedures, control of suitable soils comes later, I think, when we know a great deal more about these matters.

I think the establishment of such laws would be of considerable advantage to Western Australia for a number of reasons:

1. It would encourage local growers to establish more classic varieties and so reap the advantage to be gained from such guaranteed nomenclature;

2. *It would firmly establish the various areas of Western Australia to the wine consuming public;*

3. *It would show a progressive attitude to the wine industry of the State and so steal a march on the older established and better-known areas of Australia;*

4. *It would be of immense, constant promotional value to all Western Australian wine areas—that they could claim to be the first to operate under such regulations.*

The Premier followed up the matter with the Minister for Agriculture, W.R. McPharlin, who agreed that regional authenticity of prestige wines was important and believed that this could be dealt with effectively through the Health Act, which was uniform throughout the country. He thought it important that the wine industry decided what level of appellation control it wanted and how much the various stakeholders were prepared to pay to support its implementation.

When the State Government made it clear it would only act on this matter with representative industry bodies, steps were taken to establish a regional association of winemakers. The Margaret River Grape Growers and Wine Producers' Association was set up in the mid-1970s at the instigation of David Gregg, who became Secretary, with Bill Pannell as its first President. The Government initiated a trial, under the auspices of the Department of Agriculture, which ran in the areas bounded by the Busselton and Augusta-Margaret River Shires for four years from the 1978 to 1981 vintages. It was voluntary and involved fourteen local vineyards. Its focus was on regional certification. A wine needed to specify all varieties contained in the blend unless it contained eighty per cent or more of one variety. As long as the Assessment Panel considered it sound and regionally representative, it was entitled to be labelled 'Certified Margaret River origin'.

It needs to be noted that there were no official boundaries of the Margaret River wine region until October

1996—just the land contained within the two shires.

At a meeting of the sub-committee of the Regional Wine Origin Certification in March 1981, David Hohnen spoke out strongly against Capel being included in the Margaret River region. He believed that because of its different soil type and climate, it should be grouped with Bunbury. The minutes record that the meeting 'was most insistent that the area be properly and definitely defined' and that the matter be referred to the proposed meeting of regional representatives.

At the same time, the Department of Agriculture was running the scheme in the Great Southern. David Gregg commented, 'We had ten meetings and the Great Southern was also drawing things together. In fact, they were ahead of us in many respects. Pretty much what we adopted was actually designed by Tony Smith and Betty Pearse in the Great Southern.'

The Regional Certification of Wines Planning Committee comprised representatives of the Department of Agriculture and the producers' bodies from Margaret River and the Great Southern. It proposed to continue the scheme past the trial period each year from 1982. It would operate within a detailed bureaucratic framework. The wineries needed to:

1. Indicate in writing annually if they wished to continue to be involved in the scheme;
2. Send a plan of the vineyard indicating the varieties planted in each block;
3. Send statutory declarations indicating the weight of the crop by variety and the volume of wine made of each variety.

The plan was that, by 31 July, a departmental oenologist would have visited the wineries involved in the scheme to assess the quality by tasting from each tank. As long as it was considered sound, producers could then have the wine labelled. However, if the Assessment Panel were to find the bottled wine unacceptable, then the producers would be responsible for having the certification logo removed from the bottle. This would have been time consuming, labour intensive and expensive to carry out. It's hard to imagine that any producer would label the wines until the bottled sample had been approved.

Six weeks before any wine was to be released, the producer had to notify the Department of Agriculture. It would then send an inspector to randomly select six bottles of the wine for assessment (three of these would be held at the winery in case of an appeal against the panel's judgement). An independent panel would taste blind. There were several occasions when wines were rejected and at least two occasions when the panel's decision was reversed on appeal. Each winery was responsible for covering the cost of the department's monitoring of their wines. (In 1983, the cost to Vasse Felix to have three wines authenticated was $203.48 plus $36 for the panel assessment.)

One of the disadvantages of this system was that wineries would require two separate operations to bottle and label their wines rather than just the one. The scheme also depended on the support of local producers. David Gregg took some delight in quoting a Champagne producer who said, 'Most people are honest. Others just need a little assistance.' In the minutes of a meeting of the Regional Wine Origin Certification Sub Committee dated 17 Oct 1980, Chairman Tony Devitt reported that the department was having some trouble with illegal labels and that producers should check the legality of their own labels.

Many reasons were advanced for the failure of the scheme. However, the telling blow came when one of the original proponents, Cullens, had a 1983 wine rejected for volatility. Kevin Cullen was angry because the wine had previously won a bronze medal at the Perth Show, which under the system's protocols should have given it certification. So, he decided to challenge the system.

We have sourced photos of the five Cullens labels. The 1979 Cabernet Sauvignon and the 1981 Sauvignon Blanc has the Certified Margaret River Origin stripe across the corner (which was used during the trial) while the 1982 Cabernet Merlot has 'Certified

Margaret River Origin' at the bottom of the label. Two wines released in 1984—the 1983 Cullens Cabernet Merlot and the 1984 Cullens Chardonnay had 'Margaret River Origin' on the front label in the space where 'Certified Margaret River Origin' appeared on authenticated bottles. When this happened, David Gregg decided he could no longer support the scheme. 'It had no bite, no powers, so let's forget about it,' Cullity commented. 'One of the stalwarts bent the rules a little, so it was an interesting exercise but it didn't mean a great deal.' At about the same time, a South Australian producer called Eastough started selling South Australian port which he had labelled as being sourced from Margaret River.

Cullens wines with the official certification labels. Photo authors' own

Keith Mugford believed that the problems were more far reaching. Because the Margaret River appellation consisted of all the land in the two shires, the judging focused on minimal quality. There were also administrative and practical problems such as the occasions when vignerons had to wait too long for the judging panel to process the wines for certification. Moss Wood owner Bill Pannell felt it should have been enough to declare on the label that the wine was sourced solely from Margaret River without any attempt at quality assessment.

Cullens wines from 1983 and 1984. Photo authors' own

By the end of the decade, interest in the certification scheme had vanished: in 1989, only two wineries were interested; by 1990, there was only one.

Chapter 16

Sandalford: The Tyranny of Distance

The authors believe that Sandalford's decision to take fruit from Margaret River and make wine in the Swan Valley has meant that they have marginalised themselves from the Margaret River story.

In 1840, the colony's first surveyor general, John Septimus Roe, received a land grant of 510 hectares on the banks of the Swan River. He named it Sandalford after the family estate in England. The property was largely neglected until the early years of the twentieth century when John Frederick (Fred) Roe decided to grow table grapes for the export market. After World War II, Fred Roe's sons David and John decided to begin commercial wine production with the former as winemaker and the latter as viticulturist. The unhappy relationship ended sadly in 1969 with David's premature death.

After that, John Roe sought increased advice from the Department of Agriculture and its Viticulture Adviser Dorham Mann. In June 1972, he wrote to Bill Jamieson requesting assistance in establishing his Margaret River vineyard. A file note on this correspondence from Jamieson asked officers within the department to assist.

To fund expansion, Roe sold seventy per cent of Sandalford to private investors who were bought out by London-based Inchcape in the late 1970s. They bought the company outright in 1991 but a year later sold to a group of Perth businessmen, including Peter Prendiville, who became the sole owner shortly afterwards.

Tom Cullity had encouraged his Californian friend, Jim Morrison, to buy Maylem's Farm for $40,000. When John Roe was looking for land, Dorham Mann suggested this impressive vineyard site. He was able to procure it for $90,000.

With a new vineyard, increased production from the Great Southern and more fruit from the Swan Valley, Roe approached Mann to become full time winemaker, which he did at the end of 1972, staying at the helm until 1987.

Sandalford became the biggest vineyard in the region with about 120 hectares acres under vine. One of those involved in initial planting was a young David Hohnen. Mann recalls Hohnen's prodigious work ethic in being able to work from dawn until dusk and beyond with nothing more than a cut lunch to keep him going.

The first wine from the Margaret River vineyard was an unoaked cabernet in 1975. Such was the quality of the 1976 that Mann advised Sandalford's hierarchy not to release it, but wait until the 1976 was ready. The publicity surrounding this release was such that when the 3,000 cases were released, they sold out in six weeks through the cellar door.

One of the strong varieties from Margaret River was verdelho, and in fact both authors recalled (during an interview with Mann), tasting separately all those years ago, the 1977 verdelho. Mann agreed it was a remarkable wine that created much interest when distributed in the Eastern States.

Under the Prendiville family, Sandalford has refocused its energies almost exclusively on Margaret River, with a range of wines that includes cabernet sauvignon, shiraz and chardonnay.

Chapter 17

The Woodlands Story

David Watson remembers growing up playing football in Darlington with wine industry stalwarts Tony Mann and Ron Page. In about 1967, Watson was invited to a barbecue where he met the Mann family. He was working as a surveyor at the time and remembers quizzing Jack Mann about making wine. Mann invited him to Houghton during the next vintage. Thus began Watson's fascination with wine.

He and Heather were married in 1968, built a house on the top of Greenmount Hill in 1970 and listened to stories about the glory days of the Darlington wine industry in the 1880s and 1890s. John Roe gave him some cabernet cuttings from the Sandalford vineyard at Margaret River and he planted them in white quartzy rock soil in 1972. They didn't grow.

The Watsons spent Easter 1973 at Busselton and called into the local newsagent on the Monday to buy a paper. They saw a notice in the window of Elders Real Estate next door advertising the sale of twenty-four acres (ten hectares) of potential vineyard land in Wilyabrup for $5,000.

David and Heather Watson at the 1982 Perth Show. Photo courtesy Woodlands

'Heather and I raced out to inspect the land, jumped the fence, and dug some holes (being a surveyor, I always kept a spade in the boot of the car) and were impressed by the quality of the soil, the aspect to the south and the cleared area ... I thought this was such a lovely valley that even if the vines didn't work it would be a gorgeous place for a holiday. Five grand—you could buy a small block in the Hills for the same price. Both Heather and I were working.

'I had been involved in land classification in the Esperance area during my time as a staff surveyor with the Lands Department. I knew that the department had records of soil classifications in most areas of the South West and got the site details from the department, which verified my observations and test holes—Class 'A' site. I had also read Gladstones' papers by this time, so was fully aware of the potential.'

The Watsons bought the land from Paul and Hilda Ensor, although firstly, they had to get the permission of its owner, (Paul's mother) Granny Ensor. When they went to see her, the first question she asked them was 'Are you doctors?' When they replied, 'Certainly not!' she said, 'Good, well I'll talk to you.' She agreed to sell twenty-four acres of a sixty acre title that was part of her 1,000-acre (405 hectares) farm. Shire planning rejected the subdivision as too small and so they had to ask the Ensors if they could buy the next paddock. Paul Ensor had said to Watson, 'You know you're buying my best hay paddock.' They also ended up with his second-best hay paddock as part of a 44-acre (eighteen hectare) block.

As he was a licensed surveyor, Watson did the subdivision himself. He realised it would take until the end of the year to complete the process and was keen to get a vineyard underway by planting cuttings in spring. He had met Bill Pannell in 1969 as a patient when Bill was the Ear Nose and Throat resident at Royal Perth Hospital. Watson had broken his nose playing football with Collegians. In August 1973, he rang Pannell and asked for some cuttings. Pannell asked where the cuttings were going to be planted and, understanding Watson's dilemma, offered a spot at the bottom of the Moss Wood cabernet patch.

David Watson commented in 2017:

'We had the best-looking nursery as we were petrified of Bill! He taught me how to drive a tractor. He said, "There's a tractor, an old Massey 135," because he had just bought a new one and we were hand hoeing. I jumped on this bloody thing, not knowing a lot, and bogged it to the eyeballs. Bill was over, ploughing in his new planting on the hill up to Metricup Road, and I told him I'd bogged his tractor. Well, if you've ever seen anyone with steam coming out of every orifice!

'We had enough money to pay Stewie Melville $500 to push over the thirteen huge red gums on the place. Then Heather and I borrowed the tractor ... because the red gum roots were twenty feet long in the clay. We'd set this big Fiat tractor up past there with a rope and jerk it to slip these long roots out. It took a while. So, Heather and I dug all the roots out by hand. It was a tough job.'

The land was ripped and ploughed ready for planting in 1974. They took Pannell's advice and began with a small planting of cabernet sauvignon in a three-acre vineyard. They chose what became Block 1, which still produces their Reserve Cabernet. Watson believes that it was the best site because it had 'deep pea gravel laterite topsoil over clay at depth'. They planted pinot noir

(1974) and malbec and more cabernet (1975). They were preparing to make their first vintage in 1976 when neighbour Boodge Guthrie's Black Angus invaded the vineyard and laid it to waste. Watson described the action of a cow eating: 'They have long tongues that they whip around the vines and strip every leaf.' It took the vines two years to recover and so their first (small) crop was in 1978.

Watson commented, 'It was those times when we're all young and keen and eager, and setbacks didn't seem to worry. Like the cows: just put up a fence, because no-one had fences.' (This wasn't quite accurate. David says, 'The old fences around the property were built by Granny Ensor and were falling over. We fenced off the new planting area to protect it, but when we expanded the plantings in 1975 we took the fence down. So, when the cows got through the old boundary fence they could wander at their leisure through the new vineyard. Boodge's cows were scrawny Aberdeen Angus that were pretty wild.')

After buying Woodlands, the Watsons stayed at the tiny group settlement cottage (now at the entrance to Brookland Valley) courtesy of the Ensors. In 1974, they built a transportable tractor shed—now part of the house and winery complex. They had to drive the tractor out to set up their beds. Power was provided by a kerosene fridge and a Tilley lamp. The upgrade in accommodation came at the end of 1984, after which they had power, flushing toilet and 'all mod cons'.

Perhaps the most amazing thing about the Watsons is that they have made the round trip to Margaret River from Perth pretty much every weekend since 1973 to work at Woodlands.

David explained it: 'I'd always driven. I spent my previous life as a surveyor. We'd work nine-day fortnights, come back Thursday night, go back Sunday night. I've just driven long distances pretty much all my working life, so it didn't really worry me.'

There was, however, one occasion on which he did weaken. He drove down with Tom Cullity for a meeting of the Margaret River Grape Growers and

Wine Producers' Association that probably went late on Sunday night. They both bunked down in the Vasse Felix winery, and got up at 4.00am for the drive back to Perth.

David Watson in 1979 with baby Stuart, who is now chief winemaker at Woodlands. Photo courtesy Woodlands

Watson remembers Tom saying, 'You're driving'.

'I don't know how I survived—I can recall driving this old Peugeot and Tom's nodding off and I'm trying to stay awake ... It was terrible. I would get to Tom's place where I left my car to go down. Veronica was such a lovely lady. I would have a shower there, change, she'd make breakfast, then I would head off to work.'

Another of the things that was different about the Watsons is that they had five years to establish Woodlands before their first child was born—Stuart in 1978. He was followed by Andrew (1981) and Elizabeth (1983). All were given two weeks before they began spending their weekends in Wilyabrup.

Watson made the first vintage of Cabernet at Woodlands in 1978 and followed this up by making 100 cases in 1979 and 125 cases in 1980. Fortunately, there were 250 cases of the 1981 Woodlands Cabernet Sauvignon, which won trophies as Best Red Wine at the Perth, Canberra and Mount Barker shows. The authors thought it a stunning red and would rank it among the finest dozen cabernets ever produced in Margaret River. The 1982 won trophies and gold medals. Production was doubled in 1983 and the 1985, 1986 and 1987

Woodlands Cabernets won gold medals. By any standards, it was an impressive first decade.

Very little wine appeared under the Woodlands label from the end of the 1980s until 2001 and Watson commented, 'We basically disappeared out of the wine industry. It was just too tough.' The demands of family life and the financial strain of putting the children through private school took their toll. They still made the trip each weekend but hired former Sandalford vineyard manager Barry Thompson to help in the vineyard and winery from 1987 onwards. In 1992, he was responsible for the planting of the malbec and merlot, and in 1995, the chardonnay.

They sold grapes to Peter Pratten at Capel Vale (1988 to 1991) and then to Di Cullen (1992 to 1997). Woodlands was leased from 1998 to 2000 before reverting to family ownership. Eldest son, Stuart, moved to Woodlands and took over the winery and vineyard in 2003 and his brother, Andrew, made a commitment to the family business two years later. Finances were tight and getting back into the market difficult. David Watson would go into a shop where he hadn't been for ten years and the retailer would say, 'I remember your wine. Whose should we take off our shelves for yours?' Consequently, they sold ten tonnes of fruit to Houghton for five years from 2002, albeit for very good prices.

Since the second generation have taken control, the quality of the vineyard has enabled Woodlands to secure a place among the top rank of Margaret River producers. In fact, each year their top cabernet sauvignon is one of the most keenly sought-after Margaret River red wines and receives wide critical acclaim from wine writers and industry professionals.

Chapter 18

Leeuwin Estate: The World Discovers Margaret River

In the history of the West Australian wine industry, few people have seen opportunity and grasped it with such zeal as Leeuwin Estate founder Denis Horgan. Possessed of an acute business brain and a keen understanding of premium product marketing, spliced with a little good fortune along the way, Horgan built Leeuwin Estate from a cattle property in an unproved wine region, to a position of pre-eminence for its quality and style.

From its ideal location, just south of the Margaret River township, to its modern winery, to its impressively marketed range of wines in which its Art Series Chardonnay stands supreme, Leeuwin presents as an estate built on meticulous and disciplined strategic execution. Its wines are synonymous with the finer things in life, of which art is a visual expression and the wines an indulgent sensory experience.

Very early on, Denis Horgan brought his professional discipline to the fore. 'Chartered accountants are always taught that you must have a mission statement. Ours was simply: To produce wines that ranked with the best in the world, through the pursuit of excellence.' He recognised that, as a small family operation, Leeuwin could not hope to compete with the advertising budget of larger wine companies, and adopted a marketing strategy around 'fine wine, food and the arts'.

Complementing that was the commissioning of Australian artists to produce the artwork that would adorn the best bottles that became synonymous with the Art Series range. The idea came from a visit to the Bordeaux First Growth, Château Mouton Rothschild, which uses famous artwork on its labels (Jean Cocteau, Georges Braque, Salvador Dali, Henry Moore, Joan Miro, Marc Chagall, Wassily Kandinsky, Pablo Picasso and Andy

Warhol). Never shy to ask the question, Horgan inquired if he could take the idea back to Margaret River using Australian artists. Philippine de Rothschild agreed and Horgan's wife Tricia started buying Australian art with a copyright waiver included in the price.

The first Art Series Chardonnay label featured West Australian artist Robert Juniper's painting, *Caves Road.* In 1982 Leeuwin launched its first Art Series Cabernet Sauvignon featuring a painting by the great Australian artist Sidney Nolan. When initially approached, Nolan advised that he was not a graphic artist and did not paint for wine labels. However, he was known to be a red wine buff and was sent two unlabelled bottles of the 1982 Cabernet Sauvignon—which remains one of Leeuwin's best vintages. He responded, 'For this wine, I would happily provide a painting.' Nolan's *Dolphin Rock* appearing on its label.

The annual Leeuwin Estate Concert reinforces the link between the arts and fine wine. Initially an audacious, crazy one-off idea, it has endured and done as much as any single event to bring a tourism focus to the region and to Leeuwin Estate. In the early 1970s, that was all very much in the future. The reality of Leeuwin Estate's formation is far different from what one might expect: though it is a compelling story nonetheless.

No Grand Plan: It Just Happened

In the late 1960s, Leeuwin Estate was a rather beautiful cattle property in a region of high unemployment. And it may well have remained just that, even after being acquired by the Horgan brothers, Denis and John, had it not been for a profound and unlikely intervention. This involved a chance meeting with investors who had flown halfway across the globe, peddling an idea about a new industry, talking a language that was completely foreign to the Horgans. Moreover, it involved one of the world's most influential wine people, of whom neither the brothers had heard.

Perhaps there is something ironic for such a forward-thinking enterprise that soon after acquiring the property, the Horgans named it *Nagroh*—Horgan spelt backwards. In 1969, when Denis and John acquired the Poll Hereford farm, it was bought through their private company, Prindiville Holdings, as a secondary consideration in an important business deal they were pursuing in their corporate endeavours. Initially it operated as a grazing property and sometime weekend retreat for the two Horgan families, until 1973 when a meeting took place that would change its direction and transform the region from a quiet, struggling rural backwater, with a few promising vineyards, to a wine tourism destination of grand estates, outstanding wines and innovative contemporary food.

The Rise and Rise of Denis Horgan

The chain of events had its genesis in the 1960s when the young Denis Horgan was in his early twenties and learning about the world of global business as a chartered accountant in England. It was there he saw the potential for specialisation in mergers and acquisitions. Stimulated by the concept, Denis wrote to John flagging with him that when he returned to Australia the two of them would set up a company for this purpose. In an interview at the height of his business success in the late 1980s, Denis recounted that his year in London had given him a 'higher macro perspective' that would underpin many of his future decisions.

Horgan has, for much of his life, been a driven man. From the time of his father's death when Denis was just fourteen, he worked as a barman, studying at night and in the early morning to complete his accountancy exams. Horgan's eyes never diverted from opportunity. He learnt quickly and, in the late 1960s, as a young enthusiastic businessman, he began his climb up the corporate ladder. In fact, it wasn't so much a climb as a rocket-propelled launch that saw him become, in the blink of an eye, one of Australia's wealthiest and most successful businessmen, with a personal fortune estimated at $200 million.

Within a few years of returning to Perth, he had his own accountancy practice employing about a dozen people. In 1969, he bought out his biggest client, Prindiville Holdings, which subsequently became the Barrack House Group—the vehicle for later expansion. In that same year, he gained control of local conglomerate Metro Industries Ltd, which under his chairmanship became the third biggest company in Western Australia. Metro Industries grew from a small industrial-based company, headquartered in Perth, to a diverse national group with factories, hotels, retail stores and distributorships in all mainland Australian capitals as well as Singapore and China. John Horgan, who shared an interest in Prindiville Holdings with Denis, was Metro Industries' Managing Director from 1969 to 1984.

To take control of the company, Denis had to demonstrate his strategic thinking and appetite for a public fight. The Press reported daily on his stoush with Alan Bond, another corporate powerhouse of the era who, in 1983, would sail into history winning the America's Cup with *Australia II* on the waters off Newport, Rhode Island. It took Horgan six months to win this old-fashioned corporate slugfest. Horgan wanted control of Metro Industries because it was rich in cash and stocks, and would give them the muscle and flexibility for future growth. This was to include the manufacture of oil platform modules on Woodside's Rankin and Goodwin projects and later a joint venture project with massive contracts in the North Sea.

The Turning Point

Then, in 1969, came the first of a series of fortuitous events that would lead to Margaret River and Leeuwin Estate. The Horgan brothers began eyeing off a business whose premises were close to their headquarters. Mapstone Plumbing was a major industrial plumbing business servicing building developments in Perth. The Horgan brothers saw this as a logical fit with their other businesses. Buying it would give them an integrated entity that would service the growing West Australian economy with its booming demand for commercial and industrial accommodation. There were plenty of bigger deals in Horgan's corporate life but, in many ways, this acquisition was the most enduring and significant in Horgan's corporate career. It would certainly be the most personally meaningful and defining. He just didn't realise it at the time.

The owner of Mapstone also had a private company, which had, as part of its assets, a farm just south of the township of Margaret River. At that stage, it was a grazing property and not much else, but the owner had pumped a lot of money into it. That, in itself, presented some tricky financial considerations. The negotiations for Mapstone became protracted and reached a stalemate. Eventually the owner brought things to a head by demanding that the deal be done within twenty-four hours or he wouldn't sell. The plumbing business was always the primary objective. However, the farming property offered an appealing opportunity to the Horgans. Denis, particularly, was a keen surfer and this property was not far from one of the best surf breaks in the State.

Prior to the sale, the Horgan brothers had discussed the property. With the deadline looming and an accountant sitting in the office poised to do a deal, action was needed. The Horgans' uncle, Harold Dyer, was an Elders stock agent working that day in Capel 100 kilometres away. John Horgan contacted him and asked him to inspect the property. By the time he reported back to them that afternoon, with a glowing recommendation, the deal had been done. When the board of Metro Industries decided that the farming property wasn't a logical fit, the Horgans purchased it separately through their private company, Prindiville Holdings. John Horgan maintained there was no formal ownership arrangement for their new asset. 'It was a handshake deal between two brothers,' he said. 'It was a reasonably-sized property and I became the general manager up until 1977 to look after the stock and other aspects of the grazing property. As it turned out, that was to include the first planting of vines.' John Horgan remained part of the business until 1980.

Along with the property came Henry Kowalski, a Polish exile and long-time farm worker. He became one of the Horgans most trusted and closest friends. He died in 1995 just before the birth of Denis and Tricia's grandson—who was named Nicholas Henry Furlong for him. It was Kowalski who reported to John Horgan one morning that he had found 'all these holes around the property' which he thought 'might be gophers'. The alternative was that they had been made by mining surveyors. It had been mischievously suggested around that time that there was gold on the property and the Horgans had to contend with people jumping the fences to have a look. In fact, John recalled that, at one point, 'there were thirty people out there digging around for gold'. It wasn't quite as far-fetched as it might seem. Small amounts of gold were known to have been discovered throughout the South West. In *Gold in Margaret River,* Tom Wenman writes: 'In 1896, there were reports of six claims on Boodjidup Brook at the southern end of what is now Leeuwin Estate. Unfortunately, the records have been lost.'

Oh, yes, this really was the Wild West and things like that really did happen. At this point it would be easy to say the rest is history, but it wasn't that simple. The next phase in the sequence of fortuitous events was just about to start.

The First Meeting

In 1973, everything changed. A single phone call set Nagroh on course to become Leeuwin Estate. A Seattle-based group, headed by lawyer Robert Lee Ager (a descendant of American Confederate General Robert E. Lee, as he was keen for all to know) and financial analyst Robert Avery, was developing a prospectus for a global wine business and looking to develop a first-class Australian property. The key to the likely success of the prospectus was Californian wine man Robert Mondavi. He would be the public face of the business.

Mondavi was a legend in the United States, having done as much as anyone to introduce Americans to wine. Mondavi had engaged Renmark-based Rev Cant as his viticultural consultant. Rev had been the first Australian to do the viticulture course at the University of California, Davis; had worked at Charles Krug, the Napa Valley winery of Robert and Peter Mondavi; and had married Judy Travers, daughter of the owners of the long-established Napa vineyard, Mayacamas. Judy was a close friend of both Robert and Peter Mondavi's families.

Cant had recommended the Margaret River area as worthy of investigation. He had taken them to visit and buy Margaret River Vineyard Holdings (later Cape Mentelle) which, at the time, had a 3,000-acre (122 hectares) property and a 17-acre (6.8 hectares) vineyard. The deal fell through when the majority shareholder, John Hohnen, refused to sell. Things were looking up for MRLH, with Mark Hohnen agreeing to return from London to manage the company and Simon Fraser happy to invest.

The Americans were keen to look at other properties with suitable viticulture land. The Cape Mentelle group had earlier considered acquiring the Mapstone land for their wine enterprise, so Cant and Mondavi looked at that—it was they who dug the 'gopher holes' on the Horgan property. They were obviously excited by what they saw.

Tricia Horgan remembered the incident. They made the phone call to Kevin Edwards, who was acting for them in Western Australia. He was a friend of John and Denis Horgan from school days and also their lawyer. The Americans asked him if he could do a property search to see who owned the land. In identifying the block, they described the strainer posts in the corner of the paddock as the biggest they'd ever seen. Kevin, who had visited the Horgans at the property with his family, said he had no need to do a property search as he knew who owned the land. There was no mistaking the Henry Kowalski strainer posts.

Denis made it clear the property was not for sale but agreed to meet the Americans. 'As a matter of interest, I asked Kevin Edwards who they were. He said that one was an attorney from Seattle; the other, Robert Mondavi, had been described to him as the most innovative man in the world of wine. I told him to bring them up for a drink after work. That was when we had the office in Kings Park Road. I sent my secretary Paula Willis over to Perth Library to find out who they were and she came back with photos, including the front cover of *Time* magazine.'

Kevin Edwards remembers that those present at the meeting were the Americans, Rev Cant, and the Horgan brothers. Denis recalled, 'We had a couple of drinks and I asked what they were doing for dinner. I rang my wife first because we had three little kids at this stage, so I took them home for dinner. It was really over the dining room table at home with both Ager and Bob Mondavi where they proposed the joint venture or something like that. I said I would think about it and let me find out more.'

The Joint Venture

Later that year, Denis and John Horgan went to the Napa to see the Mondavi winery to understand the scope of the operation and determine if this was something they wanted to be involved in. Denis' comment was simply, 'I was astounded by what I saw.' Subsequent discussions and meetings eventually resulted in a joint-venture agreement between the Seattle Group and the Horgans. And this is where Denis Horgan came to the fore. Enter a viticulturally naïve, business-sharp Horgan, who recognised that you don't fly around the world to rural Western Australia unless you are very keen and you have money to put on the table. Realising that he had been dealt a strong hand, he had the leverage to broker a very clever deal, whereby the Seattle syndicate would have a minority interest and yet fund almost the entire development of the estate. Its vineyard would be planted and winery built with some of the best advice in the world.

Californian winemaker Robert Mondavi in 1980 during one of his visits with Denis Horgan. Photo courtesy Leeuwin Estate

It is almost certain that the syndicate considered that having a substantial (49 per cent) minority interest would give them the opportunity to buy the entire estate later. They hadn't reckoned on the straight-shooting, hard-bargaining Horgan, who also just happened to love the place and never had any intention of selling it. But those tense discussions would come a few years later.

In 1976, Denis Horgan wrote to Premier Charles Court summarising the first meetings with the Seattle group and indicating the significance of the venture.

Approximately three years ago, we were approached by Robert Ager, a Seattle Attorney, and Mr Robert Mondavi, a Californian winemaker acting on behalf of an American syndicate, to purchase our 1600-acre farming property at Margaret River. They had previously thoroughly investigated the potential of this region as a premium wine growing area and were anxious to purchase a property and commence development. After checking their credentials and establishing that they were highly respected citizens in the United States, we were able to negotiate a joint venture.

The arrangement with the American syndicate would give Horgan and his brother, John, fifty-one per cent of the equity in the joint venture while allowing the Horgans to retain ownership of the land; the American parties would contribute to the capital requirements and provide technical expertise. The Horgans would manage the joint venture.

In fact, Horgan structured a very clever deal, whereby the syndicate was required to make regular payments, and if for some reason they did not meet those payment deadlines, then their equity would decrease and Horgan's equity would increase. As it turned out this became fundamental to the acrimonious end to the arrangement a few years later.

In 1976, the Premier, of course, was receptive to the initiative because of its potential to contribute to the State's economy. The letter was following up a phone call Horgan had made the previous week to Court's home. Apart from being one of the State's more influential business leaders, Horgan knew Court well, having worked closely with him as a young man learning the ropes of accountancy.

John Horgan with Robert Mondavi. Photo
courtesy Horgan family

Horgan wrote that what he and his
brother were doing at Leeuwin was *of
considerable importance to the area in
general* and summarised what had led
to the creation of Leeuwin Estate.
Horgan described how he had initially
had difficulty *with the then Labor
Government in Canberra* obtaining the
funding from the American group, but
that this had been secured. Horgan said
that, at that stage, there were 100
acres of vineyard planted and a further
100 would be planted later that year
and another 100 in 1977. The eventual
planting was expected to be 1,000

acres. Subsequently, this was reassessed and Leeuwin was never planted to this extent.

Horgan was full of praise for Mondavi, whom he described as

...a most exciting individual with tremendous energy and enthusiasm for the district and our project ... His interest in Australia stems from the fact that Margaret River fortunately has all the most desirable characteristics and features for producing high quality varietal table wines. These wines, which Mondavi assures us will have their own style and character, will be produced not only for the Australian market but will rank with the fine wines of the world, including the Bordeaux region of France.

He personally intends to supervise and train our staff both here and in California in the early stages of the venture and intends to keep a watching brief as we proceed.

As a clear pointer to where the Horgans would take Leeuwin Estate in the future, he highlighted to Court that *Mondavi is also convinced that the wine and tourism industries have a close relationship. I desire to construct a winery with such aesthetic appeal that it will complement the tourist traffic through the South-West of our State.*

This is such a profound statement from Horgan because it clearly demonstrates how, early in the development of Leeuwin, he understood the synergies between wine and tourism. It is something he almost certainly learnt from Mondavi and a concept which subsequently underpinned much of the development of the region.

Planting the Vines

During the early years, John and his wife Jenny played important hands-on operational roles developing the property. On one occasion, this nearly had calamitous consequences. While accelerating along one of the roads into the property, John lost control of his trail bike as he headed towards an oncoming and formidable hay-baling machine. Something clicked in. He rose from the bike, letting it slip beneath him and plough into the metal and hay. He was thrown free, ripping skin from his arms and legs and knocking himself unconscious. Tamara, Horgan's eldest daughter ran to his wife and pronounced: 'Daddy's dead.' He wasn't. Over a chance drink with former world champion Grand Prix motorcycle rider John Surtees in England a couple of years earlier, Horgan had asked, 'What should you do when you're about to crash on your bike?' Surtees told him: 'You lose the bike from under you by standing up.' That manoeuvre, recalled in a split second, may well have saved Horgan's life.

The meetings with the Seattle syndicate and Mondavi had planted the seed in the Horgans about this 'new thing called viticulture'. It was inevitable that someone with Denis Horgan's instinct for opportunity and timing would switch into gear once there was a sense that there might be an opportunity to be had. Certainly, the meeting with the Seattle syndicate members had both Denis and John Horgan thinking about the concept of growing grapes and making wine. A little bit of research into Mondavi would have told them that if someone of his standing in the world of wine was prepared to get his hands dirty on the other side of the globe, then they had nothing to lose.

Later in 1973, the Horgans made the decision to plant a small nursery of riesling close to the Boodjidup Brook with cuttings sourced mainly from the Department of Agriculture and supplemented with some from Tom Cullity. These vines were planted initially by John Horgan and farm manager Henry Kowalski. They had sought advice from Bill Jamieson at the Department of Agriculture and their consultant viticulturist Rev Cant.

As discussions with the Seattle group continued, Denis Horgan's energy levels switched to overdrive and plans were quickly drawn to plant a staggering 220 acres (89 hectares) of vines. Leeuwin was moving from cattle property to vineyard at a speed and on a scale which dwarfed anything else in the region. Vasse Felix had just doubled its vineyard from ten to twenty acres; Moss Wood was still only thirteen acres and not destined to grow much larger; while Cape Mentelle was in the process of adding twenty-six acres to their existing fourteen. Sandalford, which processed its Margaret River fruit in the Swan Valley, was the only other winery to plant a sizeable vineyard in the region during the 1970s.

It soon became obvious to the Horgans that someone with substantial viticultural experience would be needed to oversee a planting on such a scale. Rev Cant, who made regular trips to Margaret River to advise the Horgans on viticulture, was making his mark in his home state of South Australia. He established one of the first vineyards (now Barrett's) in the Piccadilly Valley shortly after Brian Croser's pioneering planting and he was becoming increasingly busy. Cant recommended another Riverland-based viticulturist, Stan Heritage, for the position of vineyard manager. Heritage arrived at Leeuwin in 1974 to set up the vineyard and stayed until John Brocksopp arrived in July 1979.

Heritage, Kowalski and John Horgan commenced the planting program by preparing the vineyard sites, deep-ploughing, deep-ripping and emptying them of stone. Once they had been measured and pegged, an initial eighty acres (32 hectares) was planted by hand and a detailed contour layout of further vineyard sites was undertaken. John Horgan, businessman, accountant and managing director of a major expanding industrial company was suddenly John Horgan, viticulturist. And a viticulturist with very little knowledge about viticulture. To help, Bill Jamieson gave Horgan a copy of a publication that Australian scientist and oenologist Bryce Rankine had written on winemaking and viticulture.

Fortunately, he had a willing worker in Henry Kowalski, and in Cant and later Heritage, men who knew something about planting vineyards. This was basic stuff. John Horgan said, 'I rented a bulldozer, learnt how to drive it and I ripped. It was a military style operation with about sixty hippies helping us—one was an Oxford professor with three wives—and five local farmers: all salt of the earth guys happy to be earning something because the dairy industry was going backwards. They all had a pretty good time because this was a period of heavy marijuana usage and these guys were often as high as kites ... It was pretty much the blind leading the blind, but somehow we managed to get those vine cuttings in the ground.'

The initial varieties were primarily riesling, cabernet sauvignon and shiraz. A small amount of gewürztraminer was planted, though it was grafted to chardonnay a few years later. With this frenetic period of planting and a winery in the planning stages, Nagroh was coming to life. The Horgans decided that the property needed a name that more clearly reflected its image and by the time winery was built it had become Leeuwin Estate.

In March 1976, John Horgan wrote to Bill Jamieson seeking information on suitable grape varieties for the region. Although his letter doesn't indicate it, he was almost certainly focused on obtaining some of the new chardonnay cuttings that the Department of Agriculture was about to release. Mondavi had made it clear that this was the variety of the future. Horgan indicated that Leeuwin Estate's vision lay beyond the domestic and even national markets: *As suggested by you,*

I have written to Bob Mondavi seeking his confirmation of the varieties recommended in view of the necessity to forecast future American and Japanese market trends. He took the opportunity to mention to Jamieson that *Bob Ager and Bob Mondavi are expected here at the end of this month, and I hope that you will have time to once again meet up with them.*

Obtaining cuttings was particularly difficult for Leeuwin given the size of their planned plantings.

The Mondavis at Leeuwin

In the early 1970s, Mondavi was a leader in modern winemaking in California, with a focus on premium wines. Under his leadership and direction new styles entered the world of wine, including an oak-matured sauvignon blanc that revolutionised the style as fumé blanc, and chardonnay, with which he would have such a profound influence at Leeuwin Estate. The Seattle group saw Mondavi as the industry icon who would attract joint venture partners to its proposed global wine portfolio. As part of the arrangement with Leeuwin, the Mondavis would receive ten per cent of the Seattle group's investment in the joint venture.

During the seven years the agreement lasted, Mondavi advised the team at Leeuwin on the design of the winery, the vineyard and the winemaking techniques. Mondavi and his sons Michael and Tim provided logistical support at vintage for Leeuwin. Bob Mondavi promised to be involved in making the first two Leeuwin Estate wines. Over almost a decade, one of the Mondavis (and on one occasion both Bob and Tim) made the long journey to Margaret River from Napa at vintage time.

Bob Mondavi had a clear expectation that at least one of the Horgan brothers would spend three months learning about modern wines and winemaking the Mondavi way in California. Tim Mondavi recalled, 'John was the one who came over to see us in the Napa Valley, to work with us on designing the winery layout. So, John is the one we worked mostly with in the first years, until Denis started to get more involved. The winery structure was already there. I remember working on the design of the winery and giving criteria for the tanks, valves, mixing apparatus. But at that stage John was really the one who interacted with us on getting it done. I worked with Bob Cartwright, who was the winemaker, and John Brocksopp came on a little bit afterwards. He was the stable guy who oversaw all of it.'

Cartwright did vintage in California in 1978, and Production Manager Brocksopp in 1980. The latter recalled, 'I spent heaps of time with Tim and Bob while I was there. I used to meet Bob for breakfast at the Yontville Diner (a Napa landmark for twenty-five years) and we'd discuss what we were going to do that day. He'd especially talk about how we were going to make wines equal to the best in the world. He was big on that.'

Bob Mondavi wasn't just concerned with the big picture. He was a talented wine man who was happy to get involved in the day-to-day work of making wine. In 1976, he returned to the United States from Leeuwin via Taltarni in Central Victoria. Bernard Portet was a friend of Mondavi and his brother, Dominique, knew Bob from working in the Napa. On the night Mondavi visited, he helped Dominique blend a wine that Bernard and David Hohnen had made at Taltarni using rudimentary equipment. Dominique commented in 2016, 'He had a very good sense of blend and the capabilities of wine potential, which was useful for us for future plantings. An amazing man, a great visionary and very generous.'

Robert Mondavi with his sleeves rolled up in the Leeuwin vineyard. Photo courtesy The West Australian

Similar stories are told about Mondavi and his sons during their visits to other wineries in Margaret River. The local vignerons enjoyed those visits at vintage time and valued the generosity of the Americans in sharing their knowledge.

On one of his first visits to Margaret River, John Horgan had to step in and rescue Bob Mondavi from an embarrassing situation. With no suitable accommodation in Margaret River, Horgan and Mondavi were staying just south of Busselton. 'I think he was still suffering from jetlag because at five-thirty in the morning he decided to go for a swim. Anyway, he left all his clothes on the beach and he headed out into the ocean. The next thing I heard was a frantic Bob Mondavi calling for help. The first thing I saw was a beautiful girl training her horse up and down on the beach, jumping over Bob's pile of clothes. Then I saw Bob well out and over his depth in trouble. I had to drag a naked Bob Mondavi back to the beach. I was more worried that the stingers might get him in his exposed nether region than anything else.'

Mondavi saw that one of his first tasks in Margaret River was teaching Denis and Tricia Horgan about wine. Denis has often described himself as a 'beer drinking surfie' and his knowledge of wine at the time was next to nothing. Mondavi would arrive with cases of wine and think nothing of opening a dozen or so bottles before dinner in the interests of exposing the Horgans to some of the world's finest wines. Denis confessed, 'I used to taste wines that I had never heard of before. But I couldn't bear to spit them out so I would drink them.' Tricia recalled how Mondavi would take them through evening tastings of great chardonnays and proclaim: 'I think that this property can produce chardonnays that rival these.'

Almost from the outset Denis Horgan, influenced by Mondavi's prophetic words, set a course to produce wines that would rank with the world's best. It is difficult to comprehend that this lofty and ambitious aim was set in Horgan's mind when Leeuwin was little more than an early work in progress. Perhaps it was because he knew so little about the wine industry that he could set the bar so high.

Tim Mondavi said that he visited Leeuwin four or five times. 'I would stay for a couple of weeks, and I loved it. The first visit I had anticipated long hours and intensity because we had that in the Napa Valley, but Leeuwin was such a tiny winery that it was a toy, a jewel, and great fun to work in. Just working there was a delight: the spirit was high.'

He recalled his first visit to Leeuwin and the excitement in the air. 'I remember charging down there at some speed in Denis' gold Mercedes and there was a big tasting going on. My father was there and we went through all types of wines. There was electricity in the air between Denis and my father. It was an exciting beginning of that venture ... I think that Denis was a kindred spirit to my father. They saw in each other this dynamism and a commitment to make things successful. Their energy reverberated and people felt it.'

Michael Mondavi had a similar response and yet was prepared to tackle some of the potentially sensitive issues. 'The fun thing was working with Denis—this certified public accountant, business person—who was so enthusiastic. On my second trip, two years after the winery was built, I walked into the cellar—they had bright mercury vapour lights—and thought, oh my god, the nose was saying they didn't spend the time or effort on sanitation. I spent the next five days in the cellar with their employees scrubbing everything.'

The Times Were a Changing

In 1980, John Horgan spent three months at the Stanford Business School, which enabled him to continue his friendship with the Mondavis. Shortly after this, he reluctantly decided to leave Leeuwin completely. Although his active role had, by that stage, diminished considerably, he still admits it was difficult deciding whether to remain with his brother and Leeuwin or to go with Metro Industries. In the mid-1980s, Denis, as part of John's leaving active participation in Leeuwin, made a payment to his brother which allowed him to invest in the Burgundian Domaine de la Pousse d'Or.

The Seattle Deal Goes South

The money had started coming through by 1976 but not long after that Bob Ager stopped making payments and the Horgans had to fund the building of the winery. At about this time, a group of his investors from Seattle ('insurance brokers and people like that ... really lovely people,' said Tricia Horgan) came to Western Australia to see their investment. They had a spit roast at Tricia's Mosman Park home while Denis was in London. She took them to Margaret River and walked them through the vineyard. What astounded her was that they had no notion that Ager was in default of the payments.

When the deal with the Seattle syndicate eventually fell over, the Horgans had ownership of the property and a state-of-the-art winery with an extensive vineyard. There are various versions of how the deal collapsed. Robert Mondavi's son Michael remembers the time when the arrangement collapsed. He said, 'We had a small share in the business of about ten per cent. We did not want to be beholden to one partner or the other. We wanted to do what was best for the wine in Margaret River. A few years later, they agreed to disagree.'

Michael Mondavi tried to get the parties together to resolve their contractual differences but it appeared to have gone past reconciliation.

'We'd done a couple of conference calls and the written correspondence was getting nasty. I called the Seattle guys and asked: "Why don't we go to Australia?". "I won't go down there," was the response. I called Denis. "Why don't you come to Napa or Seattle?" "No, I won't," was the equally emphatic reply. I said: "Listen guys, why don't we meet in Hawaii?"

'We met at the Kahala Hilton for three or four nights. I called it the worst vacation that I ever had in Hawaii. The fellow from Seattle and a couple of his investors were there. Denis was there. They weren't even on speaking terms. I'll give Denis credit. Every free moment we had, he was working either on the winery deal or his other businesses. I would have to go and find the Seattle guys at the swimming pool. Denis and I did not get any sunshine. I gained so much more respect for Denis and I called my father at the eleventh hour and said I'm glad we're not doing business in the Napa with these guys from Seattle. They are not passionate or love this business.

'Denis managed to buy out the partners. I had three separate phone conversations over a day and a half with my father. We gave up our ten per cent so that Denis could buy the business, to make sure that this opportunity could develop. My father admired Denis' entrepreneurial spirit and desire to make good wine. My father and I had a great affection for Denis. He was always straightforward with us. He was a tough businessman and he didn't leave a lot of grey on the table, but he was straightforward and honest. We respected that. And he had that passion for trying to build something.'

Denis explained that by the time of the Hawaii meeting, 'It got to the point where the Seattle group didn't have any equity. Then what I did was pay them back everything that they'd put in. I made sure it went back to the people who had put in the money.

Said Tim: 'We were a part of the Seattle group. They were the ones who contacted my father and it was my father who had the contractual relationship. That was for a small percentage of what was going on. When things went sour between the investors and Denis we tried to be friends with everybody.

'Since we were involved with the Seattle group, and that relationship ended, Denis wanted us to be involved but wasn't willing to give us what our time was worth in terms of equity ... [we had] a lot of things going on. I felt that I would rather do fewer things and do them well. We were busy enough as it was without going all the way to Australia.

'Even though we loved it and still love our relationship with Denis, Tricia and the family. It was great fun for us. Every time we went we would learn as much as we shared ... but to carry it on in a sustained way, there needed to be something because we had more than enough fun in the Napa too.'

While it is clear that the joint venture ended with the meeting in Hawaii, Denis remembers paying Robert Mondavi a fee to come to Margaret

River to consult to Leeuwin Estate on a couple of occasions after this.

Learning from the Mondavis

The Mondavi involvement was critical to the early development of Leeuwin. Robert, Tim and Michael brought an entirely new approach to winemaking and in the young Cartwright and Brocksopp they had willing allies keen to learn and absorb as much as they could. Tim Mondavi said that 'Cartwright had his own ideas, that's for sure, but he was also willing to do the experimental work that we were advocating. Ultimately the wines give the answer and you go where the results are. He was open to that, and Denis, most importantly, was insistent on that.'

John Brocksopp explained how the experimentation worked. 'We wanted to learn about the impact of lees contact on the whites and so we made some batches that were given no lees stirring, some which were stirred every day, some once a week and some once a month. We compared the results of these experiments to see which most suited the grapes at Leeuwin. Similarly, we wanted to find out whether we should move the red wine from the fermenters directly into barrels or not. We tried the direct approach and compared the results to sending the reds from the fermenter into tanks, then settling the wine, and then moved it into barrels. We found that when moving the wine direct from the fermenter to the barrel, we had unclear, leesy wine. However, in the long run, that method produced wine with more body to it.'

Brocksopp believed that they were probably one of the first in Australia to import French barrels from Seguin Moreau. Before that time, winemakers had imported French staves which were made into barrels by Australian coopers. With Bob Mondavi's coaxing, they fermented the 1981 Art Series Chardonnay in a container load of new Seguin Moreau barrels.

Tim Mondavi commented, 'In the early stages, we relied more heavily on new oak than we should have. What liberated us from this over-dependence was being able to care for empty barrels better than we originally did. At Leeuwin, we developed techniques that we picked up in Burgundy and trialled in the Napa Valley, which allowed a gentler oak regimen to be used in the white wine process, particularly.' He realised early on that there was something special about the chardonnays at Leeuwin.

John Brocksopp summed it up, 'We had always considered that white wine had to be fruity and that chardonnay had that beautiful fruit character. He looked at the chardonnays from Burgundy and said, "They are different. They have complexity, are beautifully integrated, have a touch of class." We had some ding-dong arguments. We weren't fully convinced despite the results of his experiments. We adopted it slowly. However, Tim totally changed our way of looking at chardonnay.'

The Partnership

There have been few partnerships so profoundly influential in Australian winemaking as that of John Brocksopp and Bob Cartwright, one which brought technological skill and philosophical depth to the craft. While Denis Horgan provided the vision and the capital, it was Brocksopp and Cartwright who supplied the magic. Without their innate understanding of the vineyards and the wines, Art Series Chardonnay may well have become simply a very good Australian chardonnay. Instead it became what Denis Horgan sought when he put these two together—a great wine of global standing. The pair was the embodiment of an ideal working partnership where the whole is far greater than the sum of the parts. The pair took the raw materials and refined, challenged and analysed them to redefine Australian chardonnay.

Winemaker Bob Cartwright and production manager John Brocksopp circa 1980s. Photo courtesy Leeuwin Estate

For a long period, the fortunes of Leeuwin wines were inextricably bound up with careers of these two men from 1979 until Brocksopp retired in 2002 and Cartwright in 2005 to pursue their own interests. While the pair had clearly defined positions at Leeuwin Estate, any distinction between their roles became blurred when it came to winemaking. From the beginning, they shared an office and a close working relationship—winemaking at Leeuwin was clearly a team affair.

Cartwright had been at Houghton in the Swan Valley but was taking what he described as 'a short break' from winemaking in 1978 when he saw an advertisement in a magazine calling for expressions of interest in the position of winemaker at Leeuwin Estate. Denis Horgan has maintained that the approach for choosing the winemaker had been suggested by Mondavi, who believed that it was better to have a young winemaker, not locked into current thinking and dogma, who could set his own style and destiny and grow with the estate. Horgan has said many times that he didn't want a winemaker acknowledged for producing what were already recognised as great Australian wines because he wanted to have 'wines that are the top in the world, not the top in Australia'.

Cartwright was greeted at their West Perth offices by John Horgan. It was some time before he would meet Denis. He brought with him a bottle of Swan Valley riesling, of all things, that he had made from early picked Swan Valley grapes and considered a 'pretty good wine'. According to Cartwright, John

Horgan got a little angry, complaining, 'I have been looking all over Australia for the right winemaker for this job. Why has it taken you so long to come and see us? The job is yours.' Bob Cartwright started at Leeuwin Estate on 1 February 1978.

At the time, Cartwright could not have known what a life-changing event the appointment would be. Nor did he realise that his foray into a modest Swan Valley chardonnay a few years earlier would be a prophetic pointer to future recognition for his work with this variety. In fact, it is highly likely that it was Cartwright who, in 1975, using a 44-gallon drum, made Western Australia's first chardonnay. The wine was made at Valencia with Charlie Kelly using fruit from vines that had been brought in by the Department of Agriculture in the early 1970s, and planted at Gingin, largely for use as a virus indicator. These were Mendoza, prominent in California which subsequently came to be known as the Gingin clone.

There is an apocryphal story about Denis Horgan's search for a viticulturist which sheds some light on what has unfolded since. Horgan got to know leading Australian winemaker Brian Croser after businessman and major Petaluma shareholder Peter Fox died in a car accident. Horgan was asked to step in and help Croser's Petaluma out of serious financial problems associated with the Fox empire. Said Denis, 'They offered me half of it, and he and Len (Evans) were going to have a quarter each. I suggested that there'd be no way that would work, why don't we have a third each? Then I did the negotiations to get it out of the problem it was in, and put up most of the money to do it.'

It was Brian Croser who told Horgan about Brocksopp, whom he knew from working for Cowra Vineyards. Croser had seen Brocksopp follow his grapes into the winery to ensure that the winemaker treated them with care. Brocksopp claims that he was not overprotective or obsessive but was on a learning curve and just wanted to know more about winemaking. No matter, he had the commitment that Horgan was seeking and was hired.

John Brocksopp started at Leeuwin in May 1979.

The area under vine grew significantly over the years, but Brocksopp and Cartwright had the advantage of knowing the vineyard from the time it was small. For them, the secret of Leeuwin Chardonnay was tied up with two key plots of land—Block 20, which gave strength and finesse to the wine, and Block 22, which, while it had less aromatics, provided palate width and length.

From the beginning, Cartwright and Brocksopp experimented with winemaking and viticultural techniques. In a bold step, the Art Series Chardonnay was released four years after harvest, having been allowed longer oak maturation and bottle ageing than any other Australian white wine. Cartwright arrived at Leeuwin Estate to find three walls of a winery under construction and '100 or so acres of vines'. 'It was a good time to arrive because I was there when all the equipment arrived and it was my first chance at a complete winery build,' he said.

The first vintage was very small (about 20 tonnes) and to supplement it, Cartwright got some additional cabernet from Moss Wood's Bill Pannell. He admits it was an average first vintage and, as Mondavi was still there, he felt obliged to follow the winemaking procedures that he had been following in California.

'After the first vintage, I realised it was a mistake to be adopting all of those same methods because there were some fundamental differences between what he was doing in California and what we had to work with here in Margaret River,' Cartwright said. 'The big difference was that they were using fruit from mature vines so by following the Mondavi method, with the reds for instance, the tannins stood out too much because they were overworked. The same thing happened in 1979.'

Nearly forty years later, Cartwright remembered those first few vintages. 'There was Mondavi, John Horgan, Stan Heritage and me. We did it in a small basket press which is still out there at the winery. Denis wasn't around that much in those days, which wasn't surprising considering his growing business interests.'

Later in 1978, the winery was officially opened by the Premier Charles Court, although Cartwright missed it because he was doing a vintage with Mondavi in the Napa. John Brocksopp arrived at the end of that initial vintage in 1979. The 1979 vintage, which had reasonable volume, was 'pretty ordinary' according to Cartwright, with some cabernet, shiraz and riesling, plus a little bit of gewurztraminer. But in 1980 they realised they had something special with Block 20 chardonnay. With the branding and image of Leeuwin starting to evolve, 1980 became the first Art Series Chardonnay released and it was a pretty smart wine. That was followed by the first Leeuwin Estate Art Series Cabernet Sauvignon in 1982; and Leeuwin Estate Art Series Sauvignon Blanc in 1985.

Making Chardonnay at Leeuwin

Chardonnay had been one of the earlier plantings on the property and was surrounded by riesling and cabernet. Fortunately, it had been planted on a west-sloping site running roughly north which subsequently proved to be right in every way. Cartwright and Brocksopp realised quickly that while Mondavi had the ideas and stylistic concepts for making modern chardonnays, there were some fundamental differences. Some of their techniques were based on using mature vine chardonnay. Said Cartwright: 'The first thing I learnt was that Mondavi used a lot of oak and their chardonnay was all barrel fermented. The difference between that and what was traditionally done in Australia was significant. The potential of our site to produce great chardonnay was clear to us immediately from the 1980 vintage. And we quickly adopted some of Mondavi's innovative winemaking techniques. We were one of the first Australian chardonnay producers to ferment in barriques, mature on yeast lees, and carry out batonnage [lees stirring].

'And there were some differences. For instance, in California they started the fermentation in a tank and used a high foaming yeast which meant you could only put about half a barrel of juice in there. But the yeasts we used at Leeuwin didn't give us that problem and we could fill the barrels to about ninety per cent. As well as this we had cool areas in the winery which could be used to control the fermentation. We have always used cultured yeast and had clear juice with no solids. The reason was that we knew we had beautifully clean, pristine fruit. Back then, wild ferments were giving the people who used them all sorts of problems. We were after wines of extremely high quality and believed that they shouldn't include off-flavours or volatility.

'We also spent a few years trialling barrels to find the most suitable for our chardonnay. The first barrels were Limousin and Nevers of light to medium toast. However, in the first year, they just killed the fruit. At Mondavi, they loved Seguin Moreau oak and we secured some for the 1980 vintage. They were still from the forests of Nevers and Limousin and, as a result, the wine got deep into the oak and pulled out a lot of oak character. This was not what we were after, so it was rejected. Then the following year a guy came out from Seguin Moreau and we started to source tighter grained oak. For the next two or three years, we started to import direct.' To the question they asked about how tight a grain he wanted, Cartwright was typically direct: 'As tight as you can get it; fish-arse tight.'

It soon became evident that barrel fermentation and new oak were going to play a big part in Art Series Chardonnay and very quickly the amount of barrel fermentation and new oak changed. The 1980 Art Series used forty per cent barrel fermentation and for the following vintage it increased to 75 per cent. Cartwright explained: 'Initially we used mostly new oak. In fact, about 80 per cent barrels, with the rest in tank. We didn't know much about barrel fermentation but after a few vintages we realised that the wine in tank was so far below that in barrel. Then we started to use some once-used oak, but once again the new oak was better so we moved to 100 per cent new oak for the Art Series Chardonnay.'

Block 20 and Art Series Chardonnay

The Leeuwin Estate Art Series Chardonnay is a popular choice as the greatest example of this variety produced in Australia. Importantly, like the top Hunter semillons or Clare rieslings, these wines need time to show their best. While young Leeuwin chardonnays might appear tight, closed, austere and even oaky, with time they become opulent whites which have great concentration and power, pristine varietal character and, above all, impeccable balance, harmony and finesse.

The famous Block 20. Photo courtesy Leeuwin Estate

Those fortunate to participate in vertical tastings witness the remarkable capacity of these wines to age, something many Australian chardonnays still struggle to achieve. Perhaps the most amazing thing about the success of the Leeuwin Chardonnay is that its quality was outstanding from the first vintage. The 1981 topped a major international tasting of chardonnay by the English magazine *Decanter* and focused international attention on the winery and the Margaret River region. The 1986 was to repeat this success. The 1982 Leeuwin was lauded around

Australia and is still considered among the best ever produced. Many would believe the 1987 to be Australia's greatest chardonnay: a notion supported by its auction price. And the 1995 is just a whisker away. The fruit from Block 20 forms the backbone of Leeuwin's Art Series Chardonnay. As a result, it has been responsible for some of the greatest white wines ever made in Australia. According to Cartwright, the Block 20 vineyard was just about perfect. 'Someone jagged it because no one really knew in those days which was the best site. For instance, there were blocks of cabernet sauvignon that were totally in the wrong site.'

It became evident to Cartwright that Art Series Chardonnay need to be held back a few extra years to show at its best. This was atypical of Australian chardonnay, certainly in the 1980s, when most could not be cellared for any length of time. Indeed, the majority were starting to tire as Leeuwin was about to be released.

'We decided the Art Series Chardonnay needed to be held back for about five years because any earlier and they weren't ready for the market. Most people just wouldn't understand them. Once we held them back a little longer, it went crazy.'

In a paper written about Block 20, Brocksopp provided some insight into this important piece of dirt: *Block 20 is on the mid-to-low slopes of one of the rolling gravelly hills formed by the dissecting creek system of the vineyard. Aspect and exposure is to the north and west. The soils are moderately deep laterite gravels over ancient base rock and are generally acid pH of 5.4-5.8. These granite soils are some of the oldest and most leached in Australia. They also happen to be textbook quality for growing vines because of their general warmth and well-drained openness, which allows great root penetration and exploration. Compared to some of our other vineyard sites, the vines in Block 20 seem to grow in a perfectly balanced way. The sea breezes cool them, summer sun lights them gently and evenly both morning and afternoon as it passes across the direction of the rows. The soil appears to be just deep enough to allow leaf* growth up to the commencement of ripening, yet not so abundant as to confuse the vine into growing and ripening at the same time.

We humans just do what is necessary to maintain things by routinely controlling powdery mildew, weeds and unwanted shoots; training the foliage during the summer into a vertical hedge with a small amount of leaf removal where necessary near the bunches and then reaping the annual rewards in March. Yields are moderate, never more than 2.5 tonnes to the acre and the bunches are rather small with lots of 'hen and chicken', but it is always ripe with usually 8-9g/litre of natural acidity together with that delicate but extremely mouth-persistent varietal flavour pronounced. There will be rich pineapple and peach like flavours in the grapes that have to be preserved so the picking, loading, sorting and carting of the bunches is done gently. Leaves, damaged or green bunches, are sorted out. The motto is 'treat 'em like eggs'. The fruit flavours are mirrored in the resulting wine which originates with delicate balance but has *a capacity to age into something extraordinarily powerful and mouth-filling while still maintaining its finesse. Block 20 must certainly be one of the most valuable pieces of acreage in Australia.*

In an interview in the early 1980s with Simon Taylor Gill, of Leeuwin's UK importer Domaine Direct, Brocksopp said: 'Balance, rather than brute strength, makes for harmonious ageing. We're looking for delicacy combined with depth and presence of flavour. We particularly dislike any coarseness and oiliness in chardonnay varietal character. Block 20 is the basis and backbone of our wine, precisely because it delivers structure with refinement. Initially reticent in barrel, it takes 6-12 months of coaxing to bring back firstly the pineapple, then the pear, and sometimes the peach flavours of the grape. Then there is further time in wood, then bottle, to add to and confirm flavours from the vineyard. We seem to get more complexity from the vineyard than from the handling: barrel maturation never seems to overwhelm the vineyard contribution. Mature Art Series Chardonnay shows power and finesse and remarkable staying power and these are the hallmarks of Block 20 fruit.'

Two generations of Horgans—Denis, Tricia, Simone and Justin—running Leeuwin. Photo courtesy Leeuwin Estate

No single wine says more about excellence on a world stage than Art Series Chardonnay, which has been largely responsible for building Leeuwin's international reputation. Much of the success of the Leeuwin wines can be attributed to the quality of vineyard management and the close working relationship between winemakers and viticulturists. Initially it was the partnership between Bob Cartwright and

John Brocksopp. Theirs was one of the great winemaking partnerships in the world of wine, which, in the blink of an eye, changed the way Australians thought about and made chardonnay. More recently the winemaking and viticultural partnership of Paul Atwood and David Winstanley and subsequently Tim Lovett and Winstanley has built on Cartwright and Brocksopp's work and taken Leeuwin into a new era as an outstanding red wine producer, while deepening the quality of the other ranges in the portfolio. In fact, while the partnership of Cartwright and Brocksopp is rightly recognised as a watershed for Leeuwin, from Leeuwin's perspective, the partnership of Atwood, who joined in 1997 and became red-winemaker in 1999 and then senior winemaker in 2005 on Cartwright's retirement, and Winstanley, who joined in 1999 and became viticulturist in 2002 on Brocksopp's departure, was equally significant. It was on their watch that the red wines finally achieved the level of consistency and quality that the estate demanded. The work had been initiated by Cartwright and Brocksopp, who clearly recognised the various shortcomings in the cabernets and previous shiraz, but Atwood and Winstanley took up the challenge to take first the cabernet sauvignon and then the shiraz to a new level of excellence. In 2016 Tim Lovett became senior winemaker when Atwood left and with assistant winemaker Phil Hutchison is taking Leeuwin into its next phase. Now with the next generation of the Horgans in Denis and Tricia's daughter, Simone Furlong, and son, Justin, who had previously joined in management roles in 1990, becoming joint chief executives, Leeuwin continues its journey as one of Australia's premier family-owned wineries. Denis and Tricia have retired from daily operations but have retained director roles with Denis remaining chairman.

The World Plays Leeuwin's Stage

Outstanding wine, clever marketing and astute and fearless pricing have carved a place for Leeuwin Estate on the wine stage. But the one single event that may have done more to promote the Leeuwin brand internationally has been the annual Leeuwin Estate Concert. What started in 1985 as an audacious idea to bring the London Philharmonic Orchestra to the Australian bush, 280 kilometres south of Perth, has become one of the major events on the social business calendar in Western Australia. Over the years, some of the biggest names in global popular and classical entertainment have performed in this magical backdrop of Australian gums (competing with raucous local kookaburras) before an audience dressed in thongs and T-shirts to black tie and sequins. The seed for the concept may well have been planted on one of Denis Horgan's trips to Mondavi's Napa headquarters when he saw a winery concert featuring the great jazz pianist Oscar Peterson.

The annual Leeuwin Concert at dusk. Photo courtesy Leeuwin Estate

Tim Mondavi believes that from a marketing perspective this is what differentiated Denis from all the others in a very powerful way. 'It's not just the vineyards but also the ability to carry the message out. Denis had the stature and international connections to bring Margaret River to the forefront of a lot of people's minds. That is essential. There are a lot of wineries, so you must be able to get into people's minds and stick there. It's not just more of the same, it's something distinct and different.'

In 1985, the Director of the Festival of Perth, David Blenkinsopp, put out a feeler to Denis Horgan to gauge his willingness to underwrite a concert tour of Australia by the London Philharmonic

Orchestra. In 1985, the price of a couple of hundred thousand dollars was steep, but, typically, Horgan jumped at the idea, provided that the orchestra would agree to include a concert at Leeuwin Estate as part of their Australian tour. Blenkinsopp duly went off to London to organise it.

'To my surprise he came back and said they'd love to perform at Leeuwin as long as we underwrote the whole Australian tour. Tricia thought I was mad; in fact everybody I knew thought I was mad, but I said yes.' You would expect nothing less from Denis Horgan. Earlier, Horgan had approached the West Australian Symphony Orchestra to play at the estate but they had declined. Serious music and vineyards didn't mix, they said. He made similar requests to the local opera and ballet companies which were also rejected.

In a 2001 interview, Denis Horgan said: 'We didn't know that much about music and certainly nothing about being concert promoters. However, we thought the London Philharmonic Orchestra was a pretty good band to start our concerts with. They might be worth the risk and we needed to generate a profile for our wine business in a creative way. The concert was a sell-out. We had to turn away 500 people. It made front page news, and was described as "the most extraordinary concert ever held in Australia". Our wines were successfully launched nationally at functions held off the back of the concerts throughout Australia—it proved to be a highly successful promotion.'

After the first three concerts featured orchestras, Horgan decided to introduce household names as Ray Charles, Dionne Warwick, Sting, Dame Kiri Te Kanawa and James Galway, who have brought the 6,500-capacity audience to its feet each year, often against a backdrop of the fresh aromas of fermenting juice at the start of vintage.

A Test of Resolve

It is not possible to write the story of Leeuwin Estate without dealing with the corporate world that Denis Horgan created and rode with entrepreneurial daring until a series of events sent it spiralling which at one stage threatened the ownership of Leeuwin Estate itself. That he emerged from brutal boardroom battles, savage media analysis, a federal inquiry and a period when he had to call on friends to retain his beloved Leeuwin Estate, speaks volumes of his inner strength.

After building his business through the 1970s, Horgan, like many high-flying business people, was savaged by the share market slide of the 1980s, the plummeting gold price, and high debt levels. In the early 1980s Horgan was forced into relinquishing control of Metro Industries and went into a period of business limbo. He spent much of his time out of the public limelight at Leeuwin Estate, which at that stage was starting to attract considerable international recognition for the quality of its wines. Horgan emerged after the air was cleared and quickly built up his private company Barrack House largely because of its prime asset, Barack Mines Ltd. However, by the end of the 1980s and early 1990s, Horgan's dream of establishing a diversified mining house with a market capitalisation of more than $1 billion was gone. According to Horgan the primary reason for his economic problems was the collapse of a pit wall of the gold mine owned by Barrack Mines. 'Production was suspended and we could no longer meet our forward sales. Accordingly, our cash flow dried up and we defaulted under our banking securities.'

Business journalist Tim Treadgold in *Business Review Weekly* on 11 May 1990 summarised part of the reason for the Horgan decline. 'In the late 1980s, Horgan's Barrack House had become swamped in a sea of debt from which he was never able to recover. A series of asset sales designed to remove some of this debt were not able to solve the fundamental problem ... a problem that beset many corporates in the wake of the share market crash of 1987. The end of the financial dream came with his inevitable decision to sell his controlling interest in Barack Mines, the most valuable asset with his Barrack House group ... The demise of Horgan's Barrack House, put his Leeuwin Estate winery at risk of being sold off in the fire sale of his private assets held within

Barrack House to repay bank loans secured against shares in the public company.'

But on 5 July 1991, it was reported in *The West Australian* that a group of Australian and international investors had bought control of the company as part of a refinancing arrangement and a number of largely Perth business people joined the board. One of the conditions of the refinancing arrangement to satisfy the banks was that Leeuwin would have an independent board, something that Horgan believed in the circumstances was 'appropriate because these guys had put up their money'.

The estate itself remained under the direction of the Horgan family, with both Denis and Tricia maintaining a direct management role. The move effectively put Leeuwin outside Horgan's troubled Barrack House and meant that Horgan's jewel was insulated from being acquired to recoup some of the secured loan losses of the group.

In the *Australian Financial Review,* investigative reporter Mark Drummond wrote an extensive piece under the heading *Inside Horgan's amazing Leeuwin Escape* which described how Horgan retained his beloved winery as his corporate empire crumbled around him. It was an astonishing result that had as much to do with Horgan's devotion to the estate as it did with friends and associates pitching in to save one of their own. Drummond went on to describe how the security rights over Leeuwin Estate, previously held by the bank, were assumed by another company, while Leeuwin remained within the Horgan's company Rural Developments—control of which ultimately rested with the Horgan family. By the end of 1993, Horgan was able to refinance Leeuwin Estate and progressively pay back the shareholders.

In many ways, it was the right outcome. Horgan had created a winery which would become synonymous with the Margaret River region. Discipline and determination had driven its growth. As South Australian winemaker Brian Croser said, it would have been a travesty if he and Tricia had not been able to watch it continue to grow under the direction of their children.

Denis Horgan was also shrewd and observant. At a tasting with Robert Mondavi, his chief winemaker; Zelma Long, Napa's most famous winemaker; André Tchelistcheff; and key members of the American wine media, Horgan was asked to declare which he thought was the best wine. He simply chose the bottle that had the most taken from it.

Robert Mondavi's son Tim, in an interview with the authors, described Horgan as a visionary. 'If you look at the great people of the wine world, Baron Philippe de Rothschild clearly was one, my father was very much like him, and I think Denis is in that league ... a person who makes things happen.'

Chapter 19

Epilogue

So, that's the way it was. A remarkable story of courage, determination and circumstance, of colourful characters not afraid to take a chance. The late 1960s was a time of global change and optimism, and in many ways what took place in Margaret River was a vignette of the times. The wine industry was moving at increasing pace towards a new era, and Margaret River was about to join the race.

The line had been well and truly deep ripped into the soils of Margaret River, but while signs were positive and a cause for optimism, it would take just as much courage and fortitude to build on the momentum. When those pioneers set out, they did so with little thought of how it would end. It was tough physical work that in some cases took a greater mental and financial toll than they could have imagined. There were several cases of burnout. The work was relentless, absorbing and hugely demanding of time and mental and physical energy. Not only was there no appropriate infrastructure in the region, but for almost all involved, money was tight. However, in many ways, even bigger challenges lay ahead.

The Margaret River pioneers were not the only ones wondering what the future of the region might be. Some of the country's biggest and most important wine producers in the Eastern States were looking with interest at what was happening in the West. These were smart men, who had already initiated changes on their own patches to meet the shift in consumer tastes.

In 1968, Tom Cullity reported that within six months of the vineyard being planted, he had been visited by representatives of Australia's four largest wine companies, a director of wine research in France, and several Swan Valley winegrowers.

Current Wine Australia Chairman Brian Walsh toured the world in 1976 looking at properties owned by Gilbey's, for whom he worked. He tasted extensively in many of the world's finest wine regions. 'I remember the reds we tried in Margaret River, before we left Australia, were the best wines we saw on that trip.'

The interest from the East continued, most notably in 1973 when B. Seppelt & Sons made approaches to buy land for a winery. They guaranteed to buy the fruit from 400 acres (162 hectares) (at South Australian prices) as long as someone else planted the vines under their supervision. The deal would need to include a cellar door outlet (with single bottle sales) from which they could sell any of the company's products. Not surprisingly, the idea did not attract local attention.

The state government was convinced that the interest shown by Penfolds (in the person of Max Schubert), Yalumba (Wyndham Hill-Smith) and Orlando (Colin Gramp) had stimulated interest in viticulture in Western Australia, as each had reported favourably back to their head offices. While the interest in West Australian wineries was reasonably strong (Yalumba had previously operated a winery on the edge of the Swan Valley), none resulted in further investment at this point. Perhaps they were simply keeping a sharp eye on their potential competition in the future.

In the end, it would be left to the pioneers and others to follow the trail that had been blazed in Margaret River. There would be successes and there would be casualties.

And what of the pioneers? Harold Olmo retired in 1977 but continued to work as Emeritus Professor of Viticulture at the University of California, Davis, answering the phone at work early on a Monday morning to one of the authors when he was well into his nineties. John and Pat Gladstones continue to enjoy life in suburban Perth. John's autobiography is finished and awaiting publication; his body frailer but his mind clear and precise. Sir Charles Court is best remembered for his role in the development of the massive mining and energy resources in the north of the State as Minister for Industrial Development in the 1960s and later his eight years as Premier (1974–1982). Yet he also understood the economic potential of a rejuvenated wine industry and with the force of his personality broke it free of the bureaucratic and political shackles that had previously stifled growth. He was a largely unsung yet key figure in the development of Margaret River.

Having achieved all he set out to do at Vasse Felix, Tom Cullity sold the property to the Greggs in 1984, having retired from medicine the previous year. He decided to pursue his longtime love of French and completed a degree at the University of Western Australia. He may have left Vasse Felix but the spirit of Vasse continued to play a significant part in his life. He used his improved command of French to research the disappearance of Thomas Timothée Vasse, the sailor lost from the *Naturaliste* in 1801 in the surf near the river that bears his name. He published his work as a monograph in 1992. Louis de Freycinet had been the officer-in-charge of the cutter when Vasse was lost. Cullity discovered a rare first edition of de Freycinet's *Voyage autour du monde.* With characteristic energy, Cullity assembled a team which worked for a decade engaged in the first English translation of de Freycinet's important work. Tom Cullity lived to celebrate Vasse Felix's fortieth anniversary in 2007 but died a year later.

Bill Pannell bought a half share in Volnay's Domaine de la Pousse d'Or with an Australian group that included John Horgan in 1985. With these investors, he became a pioneer vigneron in Pemberton, planning, supervising and planting the sizeable Smithbrook vineyard from 1988. In 1993, he decided to leave the group and establish a family vineyard at nearby Picardy, where he was later joined by second son Daniel. The winery has gained a formidable reputation for the quality of its pinot noir and chardonnay.

David Hohnen retired from Cape Mentelle in 2003 and retains an interest in his family winery, McHenry Hohnen. However, much of his energy has gone into developing The Farm House, which markets Big Red pigs, raised on the Hohnens' farm, Arkady lamb and The Farm House beef. His lexicon doesn't include 'idle'.

Kevin Cullen lived to see the chief winemaker's role at Cullen pass to youngest daughter Vanya and Di to see

Vanya become the *Gourmet Traveller Wine* Winemaker of the Year in 2000, with their family winery cementing its position among Margaret River's finest.

Denis and Tricia Horgan are still involved in Leeuwin Estate but leave the hard work to the young members of the family—joint managing directors Simone and Justin. The winery continues to thrive.

What started as an idea, then germinated with curiosity and cultivated with single-minded resolve, has flourished. As Woodlands' David Watson said, 'No one knew at the time how good Gladstones' prediction would be.'

Perhaps Tom Cullity gets closest to describing why these pioneers took the risks and endured hardship and ridicule:

'I do know that you can't always win; that failure is an orphan, but success has a thousand fathers; and that you can't please everybody. There is no pleasure like climbing a ladder against a 2,000 gallon icy-cold stainless-steel tank of riesling at six o'clock on a cold May morning, with nobody else around for miles, sticking your head under the lid and taking a deep breath. That almost makes everything worthwhile.'

That's The Way It Was.

Ray Jordan

Ray Jordan is one of Australia's most experienced wine journalists. He has been writing about wine for nearly forty years. His first articles were published in the early issues of the national wine magazine *Winestate* in the late 1970s when he worked in Sydney as a correspondent for *The West Australian* newspaper. Ray is currently Wine Editor for Seven West Media, contributing two weekly columns to *The West Australian* and one to the *Sunday Times*. He also presents occasional segments on Channel Seven's *Today Tonight* and co-hosts a regular wine show on Curtin FM radio. Ray has judged at wine shows around Australia and is a member of the West Australian Governor's Wine Council. He previously co-authored with Peter Forrestal an earlier book on the Margaret River region and in 2016 released a Chinese language book, *Wine in the Blood: Australia's Family Wine Estates*. He has also written fifteen West Australian Wine Guides. Ray has been awarded the WA Wine Press Club Jack

Mann Medal for his contribution to the West Australian wine industry.

Peter Forrestal

Peter Forrestal has been a freelance wine and food writer for nearly thirty years. He has contributed to newspapers, magazines and books, locally, nationally and internationally. He was the 2009 WCA Wine Communicator of the Year. Peter was the founding editor of *Australian Gourmet Traveller Wine* on which he worked for five years from 1997 to 2002. He has been a contributor since. He has been wine columnist for *The Sunday Times, The West Australian, Perth Weekly* and *Homes and Living;* and food and wine editor of the *Western Review.* His thirty-three books include *The Global Encyclopedia of Wine* (HarperCollins), which was published in Australia, USA, Canada, and New Zealand; eleven editions of *Quaff* (Hardie Grant and New Holland); *Discover Australia: Wineries* (Random House); *Margaret River* with Ray Jordan (Fremantle Arts Centre Press); and *A*

Taste of the Margaret River (Ocean Glimpses).

Peter Forrestal has for many years been chairman of judges of *Gourmet Traveller Wine*'s Winemaker of the Year, Australia's Wine List of the Year, and China's Wine List of the Year. He has judged at international, national and regional wine shows. Over the past twenty years, Peter Forrestal has become familiar with all the wine regions of Australia. He has toured extensively overseas visiting vineyards and wineries in France, Spain, Italy, Greece, the United States, Canada and New Zealand. Prior to working as a full-time freelance wine and food writer, he had a successful career in English teaching and educational publishing.

Acknowledgments

The authors acknowledge, with gratitude, research grants from CAPEROC—the Capes Regional Organisation of Councils, a voluntary grouping of the Shire of Augusta – Margaret River and the City of Busselton—and the Margaret River Wine Association. These have made significant contributions to the book's development.

Margaret River producers, especially Vasse Felix, Cape Mentelle and Cullen, have been particularly helpful with accommodation in the region.

We are grateful to Caroline Wood, publisher of Margaret River Press, for her courage in taking on a manuscript such as this and producing a book in record time—to enable it to be part of the celebrations of the fiftieth anniversary of the Margaret River wine industry.

Thanks also to our editor, Jan Hallam. Jan has been a bloody marvel—efficient, precise, concise; applying her own version of invisible mending with ruthless efficiency;

merging the style and character of two authors into an harmonious narrative. The book has benefited immeasurably from her involvement.

Michael Wheatley has made a significant contribution, especially to the research for the book.

We have received tremendous support and help from the vignerons and their families as well as the people of Margaret River. While we are reluctant to single out any individuals, we do thank Ariane and Shelley Cullen for the reminiscences they have written especially for this book.

The following have given their time and expertise to help give us a clearer picture of the way it was:

Norm and Doreen Albury (Burekup General Store), Bruce Allen, Rina Bowden, Noel Brunning, Simon Burnell, Ian Cameron, Judy and Jim Cant, Pam Casellas, Peter and Val Clews, Claire Codrington, John Comerford, Paul Conti, Jon Cook, the Credaro family, Brian Croser, Anne Cullity, Denis Cullity, Garrett Cullity, Joe Cullity, Veronica Cullity, Jude Cullity, Margaret Cullity, Neil Cumpston, Margaret Dawson

(Busselton Historical Society), Tony Devitt, Michael Downie (AWRI Information Services), Anne-Marie Duce, John d'Espeissis, Doug Feutrill, Alice Garner (La Trobe University), John Gladstones, Karen and Rob Gough, Peter Granoff, David and Anne Gregg, Jane and Allan Guthrie, John Jens, Pablo Jimenez (Fulbright Commission), Sue Juniper, John Hancock, Jenny Hodge (Shields Library, UC Davis), Beck Hopkins, John Horgan, Jill Horwood, Bill and Marian Leiper, Ernie Lepidi, Rob Linn, Tim Madgwick (Tropicair, PNG), Angela Mann, Dorham Mann, Anthea Mann, Gary Mann, Joanne Marchioro (Department of State Development), Jan Matthews and John Alferink (Margaret River Historical Society), Gordon and Kathy Melsom, Terry Merchant, Michael Minchin, Cath Oates, Burke Owens, Peter Magarey, Giovanni Maiorana, Liz Mencel, Michael Mondavi, Tim Mondavi, Ross Pamment, Ian Parmenter, Dominique Portet, Ian Potter, Craig and Laurel Robertson, Royal National Capital Agricultural Society (Lisa Telling, Andrew Moore), Emily Sharland, Sarah Thomas, Gary Simpson and Erica Burgoyne

(Syndication Department, *The West Australian*), Ian Tolley, Stewart van Raalte, Jackie Vittino, Aengus Wagner, Brian Walsh, Glynn Ward and the Department of Agriculture, David Weightman, Virginia Willcock, Ben Wilson, Frank Wilson, Margaret Wilson, Mark and Jo Wilson, Amy Wislocki and Amanda Whiteland.

Libraries: the authors love libraries and librarians. The following have been particularly helpful with this book. Britt Foster (Librarian VE Petrucci Library, California State University, Fresno), Jessica Christie (WA Newspapers Library), Sandra Papenfus (Department of Primary Industry and Regional Development), Jenny Redman (Shire of Augusta Margaret River Library), J.S. Battye Library of Western Australian History, John Fornachon Memorial Library, Australian Wine Research Institute, Shire of Capel Library, State Records Office of Western Australia.

Lightning Source UK Ltd.
Milton Keynes UK
UKHW020628020622
403888UK00006B/724

9 780369 326003